POWER UP!

Other Kaplan Power Books:

Kaplan Grammar Power

Kaplan Word Power

Kaplan Writing Power

Kaplan Learning Power

Kaplan Resources for College and Career Success

The Buck Starts Here: The Beginner's Guide to Smart Financial Choices

Going Indie: Self-Employment, Freelance and Temping Opportunities

The "Good" Student Trap: Strategies to Launch Your Real Life in College

What to Study: 101 Fields in a Flash

Yale Daily News Guide to Internships

Yale Daily News Guide to Succeeding in College

Yale Daily News Working Knowledge

MATH POWER

SECOND EDITION

by Robert Stanton

Simon & Schuster

NEW YORK · LONDON · SINGAPORE · SYDNEY · TORONTO

Kaplan Publishing
Published by Simon & Schuster
1230 Avenue of the Americas
New York, NY 10020

For bulk sales to schools, colleges, and universities, please contact Order Department, Simon & Schuster, 100 Front Street, Riverside, NJ 08075. Phone: (800) 223-2336. Fax: (800) 943-9831.

Kaplan® is a registered trademark of Kaplan, Inc.

Project Editor: Jessica Shapiro
Cover Design: Cheung Tai
Interior Page Production: Michael Wolff, Vincent Jeffrey, Hugh Haggerty
Production Manager: Michael Shevlin
Editorial Coordinator: Dea Alessandro
Production Editor: Maude Spekes
Executive Editor: Del Franz
Special thanks to: Robert Reiss

Manufactured in the United States of America
Published simultaneously in Canada

March 2001
10 9 8 7 6 5 4

ISBN 0-7432-0520-0

TABLE OF CONTENTS

ABOUT THE AUTHOR

Robert Stanton has degrees in Slavic languages and literatures from Harvard and Yale. He taught his first SAT preparation course while at Yale, and since then he has helped thousands of high school and college students get ready to do their best on the math, verbal, and logic sections of such tests as the SAT, ACT, GRE, GMAT, and LSAT. Bob thinks standardized tests are fun, and he enjoys sharing his expertise and enthusiasm with his students. His other books include Kaplan's *SAT II: Mathematics Level IC, IIC*. Bob is a math head and proud of it—but he's also a muralist, gourmet cook, world traveler, backpacker, polyglot, and inveterate first-nighter at the Metropolitan Opera.

Getting Charged Up about Math

Whether math excites you so much you can't sleep at night or keeps you snoozing at your desk in the morning, whether you're thinking of a career as a CPA or just trying to balance your checkbook, this is the book for you. Think of it as a powerful tool, a helpful friend, a compassionate therapist; any way you slice it, you've finally got what you need to grasp the essentials of basic and intermediate algebra and geometry.

Math Power will help you master all the math concepts that a functioning member of society ought to know. And who knows, you may come away from this book actually enjoying the stuff. But even if not, the information here will help you make smart decisions about money, jobs, and many other subjects you just *ought to know*.

"WHY ME?"

First of all, you might be the type to ask yourself, "Do I *have* to learn math?"

If you're not headed into science, accounting, statistics, or some other career that requires math, then why do you need it? Here are two popular reasons:

- It's a subject you need in order to graduate from high school.
- You've got to be able to do the basics of math to pass a certain unnamed standardized test that will help you get into college.

> **Balancing Act**
>
> There's a lot of talk in the news and politics these days about balancing the national budget within a certain time frame, whether that's a good thing or not, and why. Learn the specifics behind this movement for balanced books. Does it mean that each day or each month or each year, the United States must spend exactly what it takes in? Or is it more complicated than that? (Hint: The answer is "YUP!") What's the difference between balancing the budget and erasing the national debt? Find out how this balancing act will affect you, your finances, your vote, and your future.

"I'M NOT CONVINCED!"

Those might be worthwhile reasons, but they may seem a little abstract. True as they may be, they just make learning math feel like a distasteful burden, which won't help you get through your trig final.

So here are three more reasons people might tell you in order to get you to stick your nose in that math textbook:

- From balancing your checkbook, to comparing mutual funds, to figuring out your proper tax bracket, to dividing your long-distance bill with your roommate, math will let you manage your personal finances like an adult.

- In the information-drenched culture we live in, it's important to be able to sort through the massive amounts of numbers, words, and sales pitches you're fed daily and make choices based on your own beliefs. With math power, you'll know how to understand and evaluate the statistics that impact your daily life, and act on your understanding.

- Thinking of starting your own business? Opening a record store? Publishing an online 'zine? Are you one of the millions of self-employed workers in the United States? Maybe you just want to know how much of your salary to put in the company's 401K plan each week. Whatever the circumstance, math will enable you to make good business decisions.

"I'VE HEARD THAT ONE BEFORE."

Okay, so these are the kinds of reasons you hear from parents and teachers; they especially start to preach when you really want to blow off studying and go have fun. While the above reasons are valid for studying and mastering math, they may not seem very important to you at the moment.

Nobody wants to be told, "It's for your own good. You'll understand someday." You came to this book because you want results. And anyway, do you really need algebra and geometry to be able to shop wisely, balance a checkbook, read a bar graph, make a voting decision, or even run a business? Well, you'd be surprised . . . but we'll get to that later.

For now, here are the absolute best reasons to learn math.

- It's a challenge. Besides the fact that you have to know it to get by in life, as we've illustrated above, it's not always the easiest thing to learn. The faster you can solidly master the skills in this book, the sooner you can concentrate on things that are more important to you, and the more confidence you'll have encountering math-heavy situations in your life.
- If you try it, you might like it. Math can be fun.

"ARE YOU KIDDING?"

Math . . . fun? Well, yeah, it can be. If you don't believe it, just think of it for now as a vegetable your parents make you eat before you can have dessert. It's good for you, and it will lead to tastier things.

The first step toward mathematical success is just to know one thing: Math's reliable; it's not going to turn against you, change outlandishly, and

You Need It

It's easy to get involved in power struggles with your parents, your teachers, your boss . . . even your own inner demons. You might resist learning math in order to get even with them all. Whether you're being coaxed, bribed, berated, or commanded, it doesn't change the fact that you *need* the math in this book. Don't let distractions get in the way of learning!

ultimately confuse you. Math has been around a long time; it's just about the oldest and most continuously studied branch of knowledge in human history. Like language, it's an essential form of communication. So just hunker down at your desk and decide right now: "I'm going to get into this."

You may be learning math only because it's required for a job or because it's on a test. Maybe you feel you have no choice. Still, you might as well try to enjoy it. And we know you're going to need it, sooner than you'll think.

You'll thank us later for helping you amp up your math power. We swear it.

Pure Poetry

Almost any field of study can become interesting, engaging—even fun—if you give it a chance. Math has engaged the minds of great thinkers since ancient times. It has lots of practical applications, but in fact, the more you get into it, the closer it relates to the study of *philosophy*. Even poets have been enraptured by the power and beauty of math. Go figure!

"I'LL NEVER GET IT. I'M NOT GOOD AT MATH."

One often hears a person declare with a perverse sense of pride, "I've never been good at math." Perhaps because of the way math is often taught, it is acceptable today to proclaim mathematical ignorance, to announce to the world that there's something you can't do and that you don't believe you'll ever be able to do. In fact, many of those who seem to take pride in their quantitative ineptitude are secretly embarrassed about it. And this embarrassment just contributes to the vicious cycle. "I don't get it. What are they talking about? Oh, who cares? It's not important."

The best way to succeed at math once and for all—the way to finally "get it"—is just to decide to focus yourself, dive in, and take the plunge. Math is not inherently boring or difficult. If you have the brains to read and to count, you have the brains to do math.

Here's one powerful way to think of math: Math is its own language. Just like the language of words, grammar, and punctuation, the language of math is precise. It helps to know as much of the vocabulary and methods as possible to make informed decisions *and* sound really smart at the same time.

Most of the time, what's really wrong is the way math is taught. You get it in tiny pieces. You never get a chance to step back and get the wide view. It's the inability to see the proverbial forest for its lush and mathematical trees.

Our aim in this book is to give you the holistic view of math—to give you the aerial view of the forest. Of course we'll climb some individual trees, too—fractions, percents, quadratic equations, the Pythagorean Theorem, and more—but you will understand individual concepts better because you'll be able to see how they relate to the larger picture.

HOW TO USE THIS BOOK

When you first learned math, you learned it cumulatively. You learned the basics first and then built upon them bit by bit. But by now you've seen it all, and there's no reason that you have to review or relearn math in the same, tedious, step-by-step fashion.

This book is designed *not* to be read straight through from beginning to end, like a novel. It is designed to allow you to enter just about anywhere and to move backwards or forwards. Jump around however you choose. Math is one big, internally consistent universe, and all the topics are interrelated.

Numbers: How Many Are Enough?

Mathematics was born when people first started counting. It began with numbers. Later it came to be about more—shapes and logic, for example—but not at first. Your own mathematical evolution probably began with plain old numbers, too.

⌇⌇DO THE MATH⌇⌇

Which is greater, the number of rational numbers or the number of irrational numbers? (See the solution near the end of this chapter.)

IN THE BEGINNING . . .

First there were the numbers you learned from watching *Sesame Street*, or from counting your fingers and toes: 1, 2, 3, 4, 5, and so on. When you first started to quantify the things in the world around you, these numbers sufficed. Most of the things you dealt with—people, gumdrops, cookies—came in these amounts. Some math books call these the *counting numbers*. Others call them the *natural numbers*. (This sounds a little more impressive, don't you think?)

At first, the natural numbers seemed like a self-sufficient society. They were complete unto themselves, and for awhile you never even imagined there were other types of numbers. You could add any two natural numbers, or you could multiply any two natural numbers, and the result was always a natural number. You learned your addition and multiplication tables and never had to worry about anything "unnatural."

A set of numbers is said to be *closed* under an operation if performing that operation on members of the set always produces a result that is also a member of that set. The set of natural numbers is closed under addition and multiplication. But with subtraction, you found that the natural numbers weren't enough.

KEEPING YOUR INTEGER INTEGRITY

Even when you were little, you were able to see that "2 take away 1" would equal 1. But what's the result of "2 take away 2" or "2 take away 3"? To cover the results of subtracting any two natural numbers, including such cases as "2 – 2" and "2 – 3," you needed to expand your number system a bit and admit 0 and the negative whole numbers. This expanded set of whole numbers is called the *integers*.

—○∿∿○ **SPARK** ○∿∿○—

Integers have become so popular with mathematicians that you hardly ever hear them refer to natural numbers any more. The preferred term today to describe the set {1, 2, 3, 4, 5, . . . } is *positive integers*.

Warning! This is the stage at which some people begin to lose touch with math. What are these negative numbers anyway? Aren't they just figments of some mathematician's imagination? Do they really exist? Do they have any application to real-life experience?

In fact, they do. For example, they are useful in distinguishing debts from assets and in representing very cold temperatures. Perhaps some of us prefer to remain blissfully ignorant about negative numbers because of their traditional associations with such depressing phenomena as debts or cold. Maybe we could cheer ourselves up and overcome this block by thinking about happier applications, like subpar golf scores, weight loss, or cash rebates. Negative numbers are really both logical and practical.

ADDING AND SUBTRACTING POSITIVES AND NEGATIVES

You've known how to add, subtract, multiply, and divide pairs of positive integers since elementary school. One thing you may still be a little tentative about is applying these basic operations to integers that are not all positive.

This book assumes that you know how to add and subtract positives. Here are the rules for adding and subtracting positives and negatives.

To Add a Pair of Negatives: First add the number parts, and then put a minus sign in front of the result. Negative plus negative will always be negative.

Question: $-23 + (-41) = ?$

Solution: Add 23 and 41 to get 64, and then put a minus sign in front: $-23 + (-41) = -64$

To Add a Positive and a Negative: First ignore the signs and find the positive difference between the number parts. Then attach the sign of the original number with the larger number part. The sum is positive if the positive number "outweighs" the negative, and the sum is negative if the negative number "outweighs" the positive.

Question: $23 + (-34) = ?$

Solution: First ignore the minus sign and find the positive difference between 23 and 34—that's 11. Then attach the sign of the number with the larger number part—in this case it's the minus sign from -34. So, $23 + (-34) = -11$.

To Subtract Signed Numbers: Turn subtraction into addition and proceed as above.

Question: $-17 - (-24) = ?$

Solution: Subtracting a negative is the same as adding a positive, so $-17 - (-24) = -17 + 24$. Now it's a matter of adding a negative and a positive. The positive difference between 17 and 24 is 7, and the positive 24 outweighs the negative 17, so the answer is positive:

$$-17 - (-24) = -17 + 24 = 7$$

To Add or Subtract a String of Positives and Negatives: First turn everything into addition. Then combine the positives and negatives to reduce the string to the sum of a single positive number and a single negative number.

Question: $3 + (-4) - (-5) - 6 + (-7) = ?$

Solution: First turn the subtractions into additions:

$$3 + (-4) - (-5) - 6 + (-7) = 3 + (-4) + 5 + (-6) + (-7)$$

Then combine all the positives into one positive and all the negatives into one negative to reduce the string to the sum of a single positive and a single negative:

$$3 + (-4) + 5 + (-6) + (-7) = (3 + 5) + [(-4) + (-6) + (-7)]$$
$$= 8 + (-17)$$
$$= -9$$

MULTIPLYING POSITIVES AND NEGATIVES

This book assumes you know how to multiply positive integers. It's only slightly more complicated to multiply a positive and a negative. The computational part of the task is the same as when both numbers are positive; the only complication is figuring out whether to attach a minus sign to the result. Here's the general rule.

To Multiply a Positive and a Negative: When multiplying two signed numbers, if the signs are different—one positive and one negative—the product is negative. If the signs are the same—both positive or both negative—the product is positive.

The rules for multiplying signed numbers are not arbitrary. They make sense. Suppose, for example, you're on a weight-loss plan that takes off 2 pounds each week. Five weeks from now you will weigh 10 pounds less than you do now, and you can represent this fact arithmetically this way:

$$5 \times (-2) = -10$$

Three weeks *ago* you weighed 6 pounds *more* than you do now, and you can represent this fact arithmetically this way:

$$(-3) \times (-2) = +6$$

The rules for multiplying signed numbers can be generalized, as follows.

To Multiply a String of Positives and Negatives: When multiplying any number of signed numbers, attach a minus sign to the result if there is an odd number of negatives.

Question: $(-2) \times (-3) \times (-5) = ?$

Solution: First multiply the number parts: $2 \times 3 \times 5 = 30$. Then go back and note that there were *three* negatives. That's an odd number of negatives, so the product is negative (the answer is -30).

DIVIDING POSITIVES AND NEGATIVES

The rule for dividing is pretty much the same as for multiplying. The computational part is the same as when the numbers are positive. You just have to figure out what sign to attach.

To Divide a Positive and a Negative: When dividing signed numbers, the result is negative if the original numbers have different signs, and the result is positive if they have the same sign.

Question: $(-12) \div (-3) = ?$

Solutions: First divide the number parts: $12 \div 3 = 4$. Then go back and note that the original numbers had the same sign (both negative), so the result is positive:

$$(-12) \div (-3) = +4$$

> ◦∿∿◦ **CONNECTION** ◦∿∿◦
> To improve your math power, connect with the "divisibility" material in chapter 2.

UNDERSTANDING RATIONAL NUMBERS

You hit another big bump in the "I understand math" road when you start dividing integers. You find that the integers are insufficient. You can add, multiply, or subtract any two integers and the result is always an integer. But what about division? Sometimes when you divide integers you get integer results. These are cases of "divisibility."

$$12 \div 3 = 4$$
$$(-10) \div (-5) = 2$$

But if you just pick a couple of integers at random, you are more likely to come up with a case where division produces a noninteger result:

$$12 \div 5 = \frac{12}{5}$$

$$(-10) \div (-6) = \frac{5}{3}$$

These numbers may be nonintegers, but they're still special in their own way. They are members of a bigger, yet still exclusive group. A number that can be expressed as the ratio of two integers is called a *rational number*. All integers are rational numbers because they can be written as ratios of themselves to 1:

$$12 = \frac{12}{1}$$

$$-10 = \frac{-10}{1}$$

$$0 = \frac{0}{1}$$

Likewise, all fractions, all finite decimals, and all repeating decimals can be written as ratios of integers:

$$2\frac{2}{3} = \frac{8}{3}$$

$$-0.13 = \frac{-13}{100}$$

$$0.23232323\ldots = \frac{23}{99}$$

So what does this mean in real terms? Rational numbers are a broad enough set to accommodate the results of addition, multiplication, subtraction, and—with one exception—division of its own members. Of course, there's always an exception. In this case, that exception is division by zero.

MAKING SENSE OUT OF NOTHING

You may remember from math class once upon a time that "division by zero is undefined." What in the world does that mean? Can't somebody just define it? Wouldn't it be logical enough just to say that 6 divided by 0 is 0?

In fact, that wouldn't be logical at all. Convenient, maybe, but not logical. It wouldn't make sense with the definition of division, which is the "inverse of multiplication." When we ask, "What is 6 divided by 2?" we are asking, "What number times 2 equals 6?" The answer is 3 because 3 times 2 equals 6. So, when we ask "What is 6 divided by 0?" we are asking, "What number times 0 equals 6?" There is no such number.

Even 0 divided by 0 is undefined! When we ask, "What is 0 divided by 0?" we are asking, "What number times 0 equals 0?" There are infinitely many such numbers: *any* number times 0 equals 0. Think of it as an irresolvable conflict of rules. One rule says that 0 divided by anything equals 0: 0 divided by 2 equals 0; 0 divided by −3 equals 0. Another rule says that any number divided by itself equals 1: 2 divided by 2 equals 1; −3 divided by −3 equals 1. So then, to divide 0 by 0, which rule do you follow? There is no way to decide between the rules, so we say that 0 divided by 0 is undefined.

Question: Which is greater, the number of positive integers or the number of rational numbers?

Solution: Because all positive integers are rational numbers, the positive integers are a subset of the rational numbers. However, even though there are lots and lots of rational numbers that are not positive integers, it can be shown that the two sets have the same number of members.

Watch closely. It is possible to list all the rationals systematically. Start with the one whose digits add up to 1 (that's 0/1), then the one whose digits add up to 2 (that's 1/1) and its opposite (−1/1), then the ones whose digits add up to 3 (1/2 and 2/1) and their opposites (−1/2 and −2/1), and so on. (Leave out ratios like 2/2 and 2/4, which are equal to ratios previously listed.) Here's the beginning of the systematic list:

$$\frac{0}{1}, \frac{+1}{1}, \frac{-1}{1}, \frac{+1}{2}, \frac{-1}{2}, \frac{+2}{1}, \frac{-2}{1}, \frac{+1}{3}, \frac{-1}{3}, \frac{+3}{1}, \frac{-3}{1}, \frac{+1}{4}, \frac{-1}{4}, \frac{+2}{3}, \frac{-2}{3}, \frac{+3}{2}, \frac{-3}{2},$$

$$\frac{+4}{1}, \frac{-4}{1}, \frac{+1}{5}, \frac{-1}{5}, \frac{+5}{1}, \frac{-5}{1}, \frac{+1}{6}, \frac{-1}{6}, \frac{+6}{1}, \frac{-6}{1}, \frac{+2}{5}, \frac{-2}{5}, \frac{+5}{2}, \frac{-5}{2}, \frac{+3}{4},$$

$$\frac{-3}{4}, \frac{+4}{3}, \frac{-4}{3} \cdots$$

Obviously the list can never be completed, but you can imagine how it continues, and that eventually any rational number you can think of will appear. Now, once you have a systematic list, you can match each item on the list with a positive integer. You would pair 1 with $\frac{0}{1}$, then 2 with $\frac{+1}{1}$, then 3 with $\frac{-1}{1}$, and so on. There's a positive integer for every rational number—this is what's called a *one-to-one correspondence*—and therefore, paradoxically, there are just as many rational numbers as there are positive integers.

This is not to say that *all* infinite sets are the same size. In fact, there are infinitely many orders of infinity (expand your brain with that one!). But the rational numbers are a set having the smallest degree of infinity; they are said to be *countably infinite*. A set is countably infinite if its members can be paired off with the positive integers. Countably infinite sets are within the realm of imagination.

So now, having expanded the number system to include positives and negatives, whole numbers and fractions, you thought you had enough numbers to work with. Wrong. Square roots came along.

UNDERSTANDING REAL NUMBERS

Alas, even the set of rational numbers turns out to be too exclusive to cover the results of taking the square roots of its own members. Pick a positive integer and find its positive square root. If the integer you pick happens to be a perfect square, then the result is an integer:

$$\sqrt{1} = 1$$

$$\sqrt{9} = 3$$

$$\sqrt{121} = 11$$

But if the integer you pick is *not* a perfect square, then you end up with a non-repeating decimal:

$$\sqrt{2} \approx 1.4142135624$$

$$\sqrt{10} \approx 3.1622776602$$

$$\sqrt{122} \approx 11.045361017$$

These are *irrational numbers*. They have precise values. They can be compared to any rational numbers. They just can't be written precisely in fraction or decimal form. There is no rational number—*no ratio of integers*—that when squared gives you 2, or 10, or 122.

Memorize These Square Roots: Two irrational square roots that come up with great frequency, especially in geometry, are $\sqrt{2}$ and $\sqrt{3}$. If you have a calculator handy, you can always produce an approximation for these square roots, but try to have a fair approximation memorized. It's usually enough to remember that $\sqrt{2}$ is about 1.4 and $\sqrt{3}$ is about 1.7.

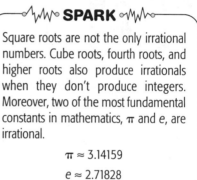

⌁⋀⋁⋀⋁∘ SPARK ∘⋀⋁⋀⋁⌁

Square roots are not the only irrational numbers. Cube roots, fourth roots, and higher roots also produce irrationals when they don't produce integers. Moreover, two of the most fundamental constants in mathematics, π and e, are irrational.

$$\pi \approx 3.14159$$

$$e \approx 2.71828$$

When you expand the numbers system to include not just rational numbers, but irrational numbers as well, you get what's called the *real numbers*. You can think of these as all the numbers that have a place on the number line:

$$\xleftarrow{} \underset{-4}{\;} \; \underset{-3}{\;} \; \underset{-2}{\;} \; \underset{-1}{\;} \; \underset{0}{\;} \; \underset{1}{\;} \; \underset{2}{\;} \; \underset{3}{\;} \; \underset{4}{\;} \xrightarrow{}$$

For any given real number, you can always come up with a number that's greater (that is, further to the right on the number line) and a number that's less (that is, further to the left on the number line). For any two given real numbers, you can always come up with a number between them.

Notice that irrational numbers are just as "real" as rational numbers. It doesn't matter that $\sqrt{2}$ cannot be expressed precisely as a fraction or decimal. It still has its own unique position on the number line. It's between 1.41 and 1.42. Or, to be more precise, it's between 1.4142 and 1.4143. Or, to be even more precise, it's between 1.414213562 and 1.414213563. We can be as precise as we want to be—or have the calculating capacity to be. The point is that you can compare $\sqrt{2}$ to any other real number and say that it's greater than or less than the other number.

Now you're ready for chapter 1's Do the Math solution.

DO THE MATH

Which is greater, the number of rational numbers or the number of irrational numbers?

Solution: There are infinitely many rational numbers, and there are infinitely many irrational numbers. That does not mean, however, that the two sets have the same numbers of members. In fact, it has been shown (by real math heads) that the number of irrational numbers is of a higher order of infinity than the number of rational numbers.

You've seen that the number of rational numbers is countably infinite—they can be paired off with the positive integers.

The irrational numbers, however, are *uncountably infinite*—they cannot be paired off with the positive integers. The proof involves demonstrating that any attempt to list the irrational numbers systematically will necessarily leave something out.

What this means, then, is that there are vastly many more irrational numbers than rational numbers. The irrationals and the rationals combined make up the real numbers. But because the number of irrationals is so incalculably many times greater than the number of rationals, you can actually say that virtually all the real numbers are irrational.

DON'T FORGET THOSE COMPLEX NUMBERS

Even the set of real numbers is not big enough to include the results of taking the square roots of its own members. Here we go again, expanding your numbering horizons! What do you get if you try to take the square root of –4? There is no real number you can square to produce –4. To accommodate the square roots of negative numbers, mathematicians invented the concepts of *imaginary numbers* and *complex numbers*. These are numbers that turn up a lot in algebra.

For now, you shouldn't worry about such theoretical things; it's enough to know that imaginary and complex numbers have something to do with the square roots of negative numbers. Concern yourself only with real numbers at this early stage.

CONNECTION

To improve your math power, connect with the "imaginary and complex numbers" material in chapter 12.

POWER SURGE

Take the set of all the real numbers between 0 and 1. Suppose you could somehow select one of those numbers truly at random. What is the probability that the number you select is rational? The probability is zero! *Zero probability* means impossible. Does that make sense? It does if you can grasp the concept of differing orders of infinity. Think of the rational numbers as infinitesimal, intangible specks lost in an unfathomably dense continuum of irrational numbers. There are innumerably many times more irrationals than rationals, and it's mathematically impossible to select a rational number at random! Hmmm . . . .

If real numbers are defined as numbers that have positions on the number line, then you might suspect that there are numbers that do not have positions on the number line. Indeed there are. Hmmm (again) . . . .

🔌 *Plug In*

Now that we've taken you on the Magical Mystery Tour of Numbers, see how much math power you've managed to scoop up and retain. Try your hand at these review questions. The answers are in the "Plug-In Solutions" section at the back of the book.

1. $-42 + (-40) =$ _____

2. $-25 - 25 =$ _____

3. $(-1) \times (-2) \times (-3) \times (-4) =$ _____

4. $\dfrac{48}{-6} =$ _____

5. Which is greater, the number of rational numbers between 0 and 1 or the number of rational numbers between 0 and 2?

CHAPTER TWO

The Positive Integers: The Whole Truth

In chapter 1, you began to build math power by grasping the properties of some of the numbers systems in basic mathematics. Now that you know how things begin to fit together, let's get back to the source and look at the oldest and most basic set of numbers: *positive integers*. In this chapter, you'll pick up the basic terminology and operations necessary to work with *positive integers*; you'll also find out some wild facts about how these numbers organize themselves into patterns in nature.

> **DO THE MATH**
>
> What is the smallest positive integer that will leave a remainder of 1 when divided by 2, a remainder of 2 when divided by 3, a remainder of 3 when divided by 4, a remainder of 4 when divided by 5, a remainder of 5 when divided by 6, a remainder of 6 when divided by 7, a remainder of 7 when divided by 8, a remainder of 8 when divided by 9, and a remainder of 9 when divided by 10? (See the solution near the end of this chapter.)

Here's what's in it for you when you study this chapter: factors, prime numbers, prime factorization, relative primes, multiples, remainders, perfect numbers, and—for something completely different—Fibonacci numbers.

FACTOR THIS!

Since ancient times, the positive integers (also known as the natural numbers or the counting numbers) have commanded special attention. There are many things in real life that come only in positive integer amounts—most notably people! The study of integers is an ages-old branch of math that is today called "number theory," and it begins with observing the *factorability of integers.*

To *factor* an integer means to re-express it as the product of integers. Here, for example, are ten ways to factor 84:

$$84 = 1 \times 84$$
$$= 2 \times 42$$
$$= 3 \times 28$$
$$= 4 \times 21$$
$$= 6 \times 14$$
$$= 7 \times 12$$
$$= 2 \times 3 \times 14$$
$$= 2 \times 6 \times 7$$
$$= 3 \times 4 \times 7$$
$$= 2 \times 2 \times 3 \times 7$$

Any of the individual integers on the right will divide into 84 with no remainder. The numbers on the right are called the *factors* of 84, and they are: 1, 2, 3, 4, 6, 7, 12, 14, 21, 28, 42, and 84.

To Determine Factors: To check whether one integer is a factor of another, you can use your calculator. If when you divide you get an integer, then you have a factor. But if you get a readout with something other than zeros after the decimal point, then you do *not* have a factor.

Question: What is the greatest integer that will divide into both 84 and 96 with no remainder?

Solution: Look at the above list of factors of 84. Starting with the greatest, try dividing them into 96 until you find one that fits. If you punch "96 ÷ 84 =" into your calculator, you'll get something like "1.1428571429." That's not an integer, and so 84 is not a factor of 96. Next try punching in "96 ÷ 42 =" and you get something like "2.2857142857"—not an integer. Keep trying until you find one that works. "96 ÷ 28," "96 ÷ 21," "90 ÷ 14"—not integers. But when you punch "96 ÷ 12 =" into your calculator, you get "8," which is an integer, so 12 is a factor of 96. You tried all the factors of 84 greater than 12, so 12 must be the greatest integer that divides into both 84 and 96 with no remainder.

In answering this question, you found what is called the *greatest common factor* of 84 and 96. In this case, you already had the factors of 84 to start with. The more general method for finding the greatest common factor (GCF) of two integers is to look for overlaps in their *prime factorizations*, the factorizations that consist entirely of prime numbers. (Remember prime numbers?)

IN THEIR PRIME

A *prime number* is a positive integer that has exactly two factors—no more, no less. Every positive integer has a factor of 1, so all positive integers have at least one factor. Besides that, every positive integer has itself as a factor, so in fact, except for 1, all positive integers have at least *two* factors. Because 1 has only one factor, it is not a prime number. The smallest prime number is 2, which has exactly two factors—1 and 2. The next smallest prime number is 3, whose only factors are 1 and 3. The next integer—4—is not a prime number because it has three factors—1, 2, and 4.

To Use the Sieve of Eratosthenes: Prime numbers have fascinated math heads for a long, long time. One mathematician in classical Greece came up with an efficient way of listing all the prime numbers—well, up to a point. His name was Eratosthenes, and his method is called the "Sieve of Eratosthenes."

	2	3	4	5	6	7	8	9	10
11	12	13	14	15	16	17	18	19	20
21	22	23	24	25	26	27	28	29	30
31	32	33	34	35	36	37	38	39	40
41	42	43	44	45	46	47	48	49	50
51	52	53	54	55	56	57	58	59	60
61	62	63	64	65	66	67	68	69	70
71	72	73	74	75	76	77	78	79	80
81	82	83	84	85	86	87	88	89	90
91	92	93	94	95	96	97	98	99	100

Question: What are all the prime numbers up to 100?

Solution: Use the Sieve of Eratosthenes. First, we'll write down all the integers from 2 to 100 (see our list of integers). The first number in the list is 2. Take our list and do the following steps:

1. Circle the 2 and cross out every second number after it.

2. The next number in the list is 3. Circle it and cross out every third number after it. (Some of these numbers have already been crossed out; there's no need to cross them out a second time unless you enjoy that sort of thing. But you still count them as you look for every third number.)

3. The next number (that's not crossed out) is 5. Circle it and cross out every fifth number after it, and do likewise with 7.

4. How far do you have to go? Only up to the square root of the biggest number. The square root of 100 is 10. You've already crossed out the multiples of all the prime numbers up to 10, so you're finished. Circle all the numbers not crossed out. These are the prime numbers up to 100. The Sieve of Eratosthenes is really quite an efficient tool!

WHEN IS A NUMBER PRIME?

There's no simple test to determine whether a given integer is prime. You just have to keep trying to prove that it's *not* prime by looking systematically for factors.

To Test for Primeness: When testing for primeness, you can stop when you get to the square root of the number you're checking.

KAPLAN

Question: Is 851 a prime number?

Solution: Try dividing 851 by every prime number, starting with 2. If you find a prime number that divides into 851 with no remainder, then you'll know that 851 is not prime. But if you get up to the square root of 851 without finding a factor, then you'll know that 851 is prime.

The square root of 851 is about 29.2, so you can stop and say 851 is prime if you get up to 29 without finding a factor. You can see at a glance that 851 is not divisible by 2—you know that an even number will always end with an even digit. Do you know how to tell quickly that 851 is not a multiple of 3? Add up its digits. 8 + 5 + 1 = 14. The sum, 14, is not a multiple of 3, and therefore 851 is not a multiple of 3.

To Find Integer Multiples of 2 and 4: An integer is divisible by 2 (even) if the last digit is even. An integer that is not even is odd. An integer is divisible by 4 if the last two digits form a multiple of 4. The last digit of 562 is 2, which is even, so 562 is a multiple of 2. The last two digits form 62, which is not divisible by 4, so 562 is not a multiple of 4. The integer 512, however is divisible by 4 because the last two digits form 12, which is a multiple of 4.

To Find Integer Multiples of 3 and 9: An integer is divisible by 3 if the sum of its digits is divisible by 3. An integer is divisible by 9 if the sum of its digits is divisible by 9. The sum of the digits in 957 is 21, which is divisible by 3 but not by 9, so 957 is divisible by 3 but not by 9.

To Find Integer Multiples of 5 and 10: An integer is divisible by 5 if the last digit is 5 or 0. An integer is divisible by 10 if the last digit is 0. The last digit of 665 is 5, so 665 is a multiple 5 but not a multiple of 10.

Of course, you can always take the easy way out and test for divisibility with a calculator. If, when you divide, you get a result with no decimal, or with nothing but zeros after the decimal, you have found a factor. Try it. Divide 851 by 5, 7, 11, 13, and so on. Find any factors? No? Then keep on dividing. Divide it by 17 and 19. Still no factors, right? But look what happens when you divide 851 by 23. You get 37, an integer. Just when you're about to declare 851 prime, you find that it's factorable:

$$851 = 23 \times 37$$

PRIMENESS IS NOT SKIN DEEP

You'd think that mathematicians would have figured out an easier way to test for primeness by now, but they haven't. That's one of the traits of prime numbers that make them fascinating (or annoying, depending on how you look at it). They don't come in any sort of regular pattern. They don't have any superficial characteristic traits.

Recognizing prime numbers is difficult because you have to try to factor to do it. Factoring is always a lot harder than multiplying. To multiply numbers is just a matter of routine. To factor huge numbers is much more complicated. If multiplying is like riding a bike down a hill with the wind at your back, then factoring is akin to riding up a hill, after a long day, with a refrigerator strapped to your back. Okay, maybe not that bad, but you get the idea.

CALLING ALL PRIME NUMBERS

So how many prime numbers are there? It was Euclid, another ancient Greek math head, who figured out the answer to this question.

Question: Are there infinitely many prime numbers?

Solution: Euclid's answer was yes. Here's his reasoning: Suppose the answer was no. In other words, suppose there was a finite number of prime numbers. In that case, you could theoretically list them all, and then multiply them all.

$2 \times 3 \times 5 \times 7 \times 11 \times 13 \times 17 \times 19 \times 21 \times 23 \times 29 \times 31 \times 37 \times 41 \times 43 \times 47 \times 53 \times 59 \times 61 \times 67 \times 71 \times 73 \times 79 \ldots$

⌐⌐w⌐**CONNECTION**⌐w⌐⌐

To improve your math power, connect with the "countably infinite" material in chapter 1!

The result would be a huge number that is divisible by 2, 3, 5, 7, and every other prime number. Now, take that huge product—let's call it N—and add 1. The result, $N + 1$, would be a number that is 1 greater than a multiple of 2, so it could not itself be divisible by 2.

Try it: Take a few multiples of 2 and add 1. You never get another multiple of 2, do you?

Likewise, $N + 1$ would be 1 greater than a multiple of 3, so it could not itself be divisible by 3. By the same reasoning, $N + 1$ could not be divisible by any of the numbers in your list. But every integer greater than 1 is divisible by at least one prime number, which in some cases is the number itself. This was supposed to be a list of all *prime* numbers. If $N + 1$ is not divisible by any of the numbers on the list, then it must be divisible by some other prime number. This contradicts the assumption that you had already listed all the *prime* numbers, so in fact there are infinitely many prime numbers, and there is no "greatest prime number." Our conclusion: The set of prime numbers is *countably* infinite.

⌐ⱮⱮ° POWER SURGE °ⱮⱮⱴ

Even after centuries of study, math heads are still unable to prove some facts about prime numbers that seem to be true. A proposition that is still unproved is called a *conjecture*.

One famous conjecture about prime numbers concerns *twin primes*, which are prime numbers exactly 2 apart. There are eight pairs of twin primes less than 100: 3 and 5; 5 and 7; 11 and 13; 17 and 19; 29 and 31; 41 and 43; 59 and 61; 71 and 73. There are seven pairs of twin primes between 100 and 200. There are four pairs in the 200s and only two pairs in the 300s. Twin primes become fewer and farther between as the numbers get bigger. But do they ever come to an end? Is there a greatest pair of twin primes? The "Twin Primes Conjecture" says that the number of twin primes is infinite. This has not yet been proved or disproved.

Another famous conjecture about prime numbers is "Goldbach's Conjecture," which says that every even integer greater than 2 can be expressed as the sum of two primes. For example 42 can be expressed as 19 + 23, and 428 can be expressed as 331 + 97. No one has ever found a contradiction for this conjecture, but no one has yet proved it either.

To Find the Prime Factorization: Every positive integer that is not prime can be expressed as the product of primes. To get this *prime factorization* of a positive integer, keep breaking it down into factors until all the factors are prime.

Question: What is the prime factorization of 84?

Solution: Start by breaking 84 down into any positive factors that you see—$84 = 4 \times 21$—and continue breaking each factor down until all you have is prime factors: $84 = 4 \times 21 = 2 \times 2 \times 3 \times 7$.

Question: What is the prime factorization of 96?

Solution: Start by breaking 96 down into any positive factors that you see—$96 = 8 \times 12$—and continue breaking each factor down until all you have is prime factors:

$$96 = 8 \times 12 = 2 \times 2 \times 2 \times 2 \times 2 \times 3.$$

Once you have the two prime factorizations, it's easy to find the greatest common factor.

To Find the Greatest Common Factor: The *greatest common factor* (GCF) is equal to the overlap in the prime factorizations. Look for the overlap between $84 = 2 \times 2 \times 3 \times 7$ and $96 = 2 \times 2 \times 2 \times 2 \times 2 \times 3$:

$$
\begin{aligned}
84 &= \qquad\quad \left(2\right) \times \left(2\right) \times \left(3\right) \times 7 \\
94 &= 2 \times 2 \times \left(2\right) \times \left(2\right) \times \left(3\right)
\end{aligned}
$$

They have two 2s and a 3 in common. $2 \times 2 \times 3 = 12$, so the greatest common factor is 12.

Sometimes you'll find two prime factorizations that have no overlap, in which case the greatest common factor is 1.

Question: What is the greatest common factor of 84 and 85?

Solution: First break both 84 and 85 into prime factorizations: $84 = 2 \times 2 \times 3 \times 7$ and $85 = 5 \times 17$. The two have no prime factors in common, so their greatest common factor is 1.

Integers with no common factors greater than 1 are called *relative primes*. (By the way, you might have known immediately that the greatest common factor of 84 and 85 is 1, because consecutive integers are always relative primes.)

MULTIPLE PERSONALITIES

The *multiples* of 84 are the numbers you get when you multiply 84 by a positive integer. Except for the number 84 itself, the factors are all smaller than 84 and the multiples are all greater than 84. Every positive integer has a finite number of factors, but an infinite number of multiples. The multiples of 84 are: 84, 168, 252, 336, 420, 504, 588, . . .

A *common multiple* is a number which is a multiple of two or more integers. You can always get a common multiple of two integers by multiplying them, but, unless the two numbers are relative primes, the product will not be the least common multiple. For example, to find a common multiple for 12 and 15, you could just multiply: $12 \times 15 = 180$.

To Find the Least Common Multiple: One way to find the least common multiple (LCM) of two integers is to check out the multiples of the larger integer until you find one that's also a multiple of the smaller.

Question: What is the smallest positive number that is a multiple of both 12 and 15?

Solution: Check out the multiples of 15: 15 is not divisible by 12; 30 is not; nor is 45. But the next multiple of 15, 60, is divisible by 12, so the LCM of 12 and 15 is 60.

Another way to find the least common multiple of two integers, especially useful when the integers are relatively large, is to use the prime factorizations. Just like when you were looking for the greatest common factor, you look for the overlap. But this time you eliminate the overlap from one of the factorizations and then combine what's left.

Question: What is the least common multiple of 84 and 96?

Solution: Look for the overlap between $84 = 2 \times 2 \times 3 \times 7$ and $96 = 2 \times 2 \times 2 \times 2 \times 2 \times 3$:

$$84 = \qquad\qquad \boxed{2} \times \boxed{2} \times \boxed{3} \times 7$$
$$94 = 2 \times 2 \times 2 \times \boxed{2} \times \boxed{2} \times \boxed{3}$$

They have two 2s and a 3 in common, so you eliminate two 2s and a 3 from one factorization:

$$2\!\!\!/\times 2\!\!\!/\times 3\!\!\!/\times 7$$
$$2\times 2\times 2\times 2\times 2\times 3$$

And then you combine what's left. $2 \times 2 \times 2 \times 2 \times 2 \times 3 \times 7 = 672$. The least common multiple of 84 and 96 is 672.

SERVING UP LEFTOVERS

The *remainder* is the integer amount that's left over after division. For example, if you divide 48 by 5, you get 9 with a remainder of 3. The remainder is 3 because 48 is 3 more than a multiple of 5. Notice that remainders are integers. If you punch "48 ÷ 5 = " into your calculator, you'll get an answer of "9.6." Don't take that to mean that the remainder is ".6." You can use your calculator to find a remainder, but you have to take an extra step. Here's how.

To Find a Remainder: To use your calculator to find a remainder, after dividing, subtract the whole number part of the result, and then multiply the leftover decimal by the original divisor. So in the above example (48 ÷ 5 = 9.6), take .6 and multiply it by 5, and you get 3, which is the remainder.

Question: What is the remainder when 473 is divided by 17?

Solution: Punch "473 ÷ 17 =" into your calculator, and you'll get something like "27.823529412." Subtract the whole number part (27) and multiply the decimal part by 17: .823529412 × 17 = 14.000000004. That's extremely close to the integer 14, so the remainder is 14.

More mind bending than using a division problem to find a remainder is using a remainder to figure out something about the original division problem. Here's an example.

Question: What is the smallest integer greater than 3 that will leave a remainder of 3 when divided by either 7 or 8?

Solution: If the remainder is 3 when an integer is divided by 7, then that integer is 3 more than a multiple of 7. The remainder is the same when that integer is divided by 8, so the integer you're looking for is also 3 more than a multiple of 8. In other words, it's 3 more than a common multiple of 7 and 8. The LCM of 7 and 8 is 56, so the integer you're looking for is 3 more than that, or 59.

(Notice that the question specifically asks for an integer "greater than 3." If it had asked for just the smallest positive integer that leaves a remainder of 3 when divided by 7 or 8, the answer would be 3. Each of the numbers 7 and 8 goes into 3 zero times with a remainder of 3.)

Here's the same sort of problem, but with more numbers.

Question: What is the smallest integer greater than 1 that will leave a remainder of 1 when divided by 2, 3, 4, 5, 6, 7, 8, 9, or 10?

Solution: The number you're looking for is 1 greater than the LCM of 2, 3, 4, 5, 6, 7, 8, 9, and 10. To find that LCM, look at the prime factorizations:

$2 = 2$	$7 = 7$
$3 = 3$	$8 = 2 \times 2 \times 2$
$4 = 2 \times 2$	$9 = 3 \times 3$
$5 = 5$	$10 = 2 \times 5$
$6 = 2 \times 3$	

To get the LCM of these nine integers, put together a prime factorization that will just cover all nine of the above factorizations. You need three 2s, two 3s, a 5, and a 7. $LCM = 2 \times 2 \times 2 \times 3 \times 3 \times 5 \times 7 = 2{,}520$.

The number you're looking for is 1 greater than that, or 2,521.

Now you're ready to tackle this chapter's Do the Math question, which is really just a slight variation of the above.

DO THE MATH

What is the smallest positive integer that will leave a remainder of 1 when divided by 2, a remainder of 2 when divided by 3, a remainder of 3 when divided by 4, a remainder of 4 when divided by 5, a remainder of 5 when divided by 6, a remainder of 6 when divided by 7, a remainder of 7 when divided by 8, a remainder of 8 when divided by 9, and a remainder of 9 when divided by 10?

Solution: This is a tricky problem because you're tempted to think, "I'm looking for an integer that's 1 greater than a multiple of 2, 2 greater than a multiple of 3, 3 greater than a multiple of 4, etc." It's easier instead to look for an integer that's 1 less than a multiple of 2, 1 less than a multiple of 3, 1 less than a multiple of 4, etc. In other words, the number you're looking for is 1 less than the LCM of 2, 3, 4, 5, 6, 7, 8, 9, and 10. We just found that LCM to be 2,520, and so the answer to this question is 1 less than that, or 2,519.

PRACTICALLY PERFECT

Prime numbers are not the only positive integers whose factorizations have special characteristics. Another type that has attracted attention since ancient times is the perfect number. A *perfect number* is a positive integer that is equal to the sum of its proper factors—that is, all of its factors except for itself. The smallest perfect number is 6. The proper factors of 6 are 1, 2, and 3, and the sum of 1, 2, and 3 is 6. The next perfect number is 28, whose proper factors are 1, 2, 4, 7, and 14. The next two perfect numbers are 496 and 8,128.

—⌇⌇⌇ **SPARK** ⌇⌇⌇—

The first four perfect numbers were known to the ancients. Only comparatively recently have bigger ones been found (yes, math heads have been keeping up the search!). All the perfect numbers known so far are even, but no one knows for sure whether there are any odd perfect numbers, and no one knows whether there are infinitely many perfect numbers.

Very few positive integers are perfect—most are either *abundant* or *deficient*. In an abundant number, the sum of the proper factors is greater than the number itself, and in a deficient number the sum of the proper factors is less than the number itself. The proper factors of 24, for example, are 1, 2, 3, 4, 6, 8, and 12. The sum of those factors is 36, which is greater than 24, so 24 is an abundant number.

Run that by you again? The proper factors of 25 are 1 and 5. Their sum is 6, which is less than 25, so 25 is a deficient number.

HOW TO SUCCEED IN RABBIT FARMING

In 1202, a mathematician from Pisa, Italy, nicknamed Fibonacci was moonlighting as a rabbit farmer. In order to help him figure out what to expect in terms of workload and production rate, he posed the following problem about the rate of rabbit reproduction:

Suppose that rabbits are too young in their first month of life to reproduce, but that beginning with their second month they generate a new pair of rabbits every month. Now suppose you start with one pair of newborn rabbits. How many rabbits will you have at the end of each month?

Well, here's the process. Follow along on our handy rabbit breeding chart!

- If you start with a newborn pair, after a month you'll still have just the one pair.
- By the end of the next month, however, that pair will have generated a new pair. That's 2 pairs, one mature and one newborn. (The black pairs are the newborns in the diagram.)
- In the next month the mature pair generates another new pair:
- That's 3 pairs. Now there are 2 pairs ready to reproduce, and so by the end of the next month there will be 2 more pairs.
- Now you're up to 5 pairs of rabbits. The next month, there are 2 pairs too young to reproduce, but there are 3 pairs that do. That's 8 pairs now.
- A month later, you can see the number of rabbit pairs soon begins to increase rapidly. Not only that, the numbers don't seem to occur in an easily readable pattern.

The sequence of integers representing the number of rabbit pairs at the end of each month turns out to have so many impressive properties, it was named the *Fibonacci sequence:* 1, 1, 2, 3, 5, 8, 13, 21, 34, 55, 89, 144, etc. After other math heads got together and took a look at what Fibonacci had discovered, they found that his sequence showed up in a lot of unexpected places. To see what we mean, keep reading.

After the first two 1s, each term in the sequence is generated by adding the last two terms. So the next term in the sequence after 144 will be 89 + 144 = 233, and the term after that will be 144 + 233 = 377: 1, 1, 2, 3, 5, 8, 13, 21, 34, 55, 89, 144, 233, 377, 610 . . . .

FUN WITH FIBONACCI

Here are a few of the fascinating characteristics of the Fibonacci sequence.

- The third number in the sequence is 2, and every third number after that is a multiple of 2. The fourth number in the sequence is 3, and every fourth number after that is a multiple of 3. The fifth number is 5, and every fifth number after that is a multiple of 5. The sixth number is 8, and every sixth number after that is a multiple of 8. To generalize: If the *n*th number in the sequence is *a*, then every *n*th number after that is a multiple of *a*.

- Take any number in the Fibonacci sequence and square it. The result will always be 1 more than the product of the previous number and the following number in the sequence. For example, compare the square of 89, which is 7,921, to the product of the preceding 55 and succeeding 144, which is $55 \times 144 = 7{,}920$.

- Take any number in the Fibonacci sequence and the third number after that, add them, and the sum will be exactly twice the second number between them in the sequence. For example, take 144 and the third number after that in the sequence, which is 610. Add them and you get $144 + 610 = 754$. Divide that by 2 and you get 377, which is the second number between 144 and 610 in the sequence.

- Take any number in the Fibonacci sequence and the fourth number after that, add them, and the sum will always be exactly 3 times the number halfway between them in the sequence. For example, take 34 and the fourth number after that in the sequence, which is 233. Add them and you get $34 + 233 = 267$. Divide that by 3 and you get $267 \div 3 = 89$, which is the number halfway between 34 and 233 in the sequence.

- Add up all the numbers in the Fibonacci sequence up to any point, and the sum will be 1 less than the second number yet to come. For example, the sum of all the numbers in the sequence up to and including 89 is 232, which is 1 less than the second number yet to come, 233.

Can you find any other interesting properties with the Fibonacci sequence? We could tell you lots more, or you could look them up for yourself, but it's more fun to investigate and discover properties on your own. Strain your brain, give your calculator a workout, and burn up the scratch paper!

THE CULT OF FIBONACCI

Fibonacci numbers pop up everywhere. Notice in the earlier rabbit diagram, that the number of newborn pairs and the number of mature pairs each month are both Fibonacci numbers. The Fibonacci sequence also

⌇⌇ SPARK ⌇⌇

If you've ever thought math wasn't "natural," think again. The individual integers in the Fibonacci sequence are called Fibonacci numbers, and these numbers turn up with remarkable frequency in nature. The number of petals or petal-like parts of many flowers are Fibonacci numbers. Daisies, for example, tend to have 21, 34, 55, or 89 petals. The numbers of spirals in pine cones, pineapples, and sunflower seedheads also tend to be Fibonacci numbers.

relates to a shape thought since ancient times to be of especially harmonious and aesthetically satisfying proportions. And this just scratches the surface. Fibonacci numbers have acquired an almost cult status. They are the subject of periodicals, societies, and even Web pages.

> ⌇⌇⌇° **CONNECTION** °⌇⌇⌇⌇
> To improve your math power, connect with the "Golden Rectangle" material in chapter 15!

🔌 *Plug In*

Are you tempted to join an exotic Fibonacci society and devote your life to studying numbering sequences? Yeah, right. Well, even though you might not be giving away your CD collection and moving to some math commune in California yet, understanding the properties of some of the numbers systems in basic mathematics will build a solid foundation for increasing your math power. Try these review questions, and check out the answers in the Plug-In Solutions section at the back of the book.

1. What is the greatest prime number less than 700? _____

2. What is the greatest common factor of 105 and 255? _____

3. What is the least common multiple of 45 and 63? _____

4. What is the smallest integer greater than 12 that leaves a remainder of 12 when divided by either 13 or 14? _____

5. Is 56 a perfect, deficient, or abundant number? _____

Superpowered Math: Perfect Digital Variants

So you're hooked on number systems? You want to "superpower" your math skills? Then take time out of your busy schedule to ponder the mysteries of the number 371, a very special positive integer. If you take the three digits—3, 7, and 1—and cube them, the sum of those cubes equals the number 371 itself: $3^3 + 7^3 + 1^3 = 371$.

Another example is 407, because: $4^3 + 0^3 + 7^3 = 407$. These are called *perfect digital variants*. Can you find any other examples?

For rainy day chuckles, observe what happens if you find the sum of the cubes of the digits of an integer, and then find the sum of the cubes of the digits of the result, and then find the sum of the cubes of the digits of the result, and so on. You'll always end up eventually with a perfect digital variant . . . or you'll find yourself in a loop. Start with 98, for example:

- Add the cubes of 9 and 8: $9^3 + 8^3 = 1,241$.
- Now add the cubes of the digits of the result, and continue to do so:

  $1^3 + 2^3 + 4^3 + 1^3 = 74$

  $7^3 + 4^3 = 407$

  $4^3 + 0^3 + 7^3 = 407$
- Once you hit 407, you stay at 407, because 407 is a perfect digital variant.

For another example, start with 5,431:

   $5^3 + 4^3 + 3^3 + 1^3 = 217$

   $2^3 + 1^3 + 7^3 = 352$

   $3^3 + 5^3 + 2^3 = 160$

   $1^3 + 6^3 + 0^3 = 217$

   $2^3 + 1^3 + 7^3 = 352$

Once you hit 217 again, you're in a loop: 217 yields 352, which yields 160, which yields 217 again, which yields 352 again, and so on. Can you find other such loops?

Fractions: Pieces Of the Pie

In the preceding chapter, we learned about the myriad functions and properties of positive integers, or "regular old numbers" for non–math heads. Now let's take a look at the ways we delineate smaller units within the whole: fractions and decimals. In this chapter we'll show you how to do the basic operations with these units of measure. After that, in chapter 4, we'll show you how to work with percents.

> **⌁⋀⋁⋀∘DO THE MATH∘⋀⋁⋀⋁∘**
>
> Re-express the repeating decimal $.1\overline{405}$ as a fraction in lowest terms. (See the solution near the end of this chapter.)

BITS AND PIECES

A *common fraction* is a number written in the form $\frac{A}{B}$ in which the top number (A) is called the *numerator* and the bottom number (B) is called the *denominator*. The denominator tells you into how many pieces the whole is divided, and the numerator tells you how many of those pieces you're considering. For example, to obtain $\frac{3}{5}$ of a pie, you'd divide the pie into five equal pieces ("fifths of the pie") and take three of them.

You can multiply or divide both the top and bottom of a fraction by the same number (except for zero) without changing the fraction's value, changing only its appearance. For example, $\frac{1}{2}, \frac{3}{6},$ $\frac{9}{18},$ and $\frac{50}{100}$ are all *equivalent fractions*. That means they look different, but they're all worth the same amount.

oɅʌʌo **CONNECTION** oʌʌʌo

To improve your math power, connect with the "relative primes" material in chapter 2!

To Simplify a Fraction: When you *simplify* a fraction, or reduce it to *lowest terms*, divide out all factors that the numerator and denominator have in common.

Question: Reduce $\frac{24}{42}$ to lowest terms.

Solution: Since the numerator and denominators are both multiples of 2, you can divide them both by 2: $\frac{24}{42} = \frac{24 \div 2}{42 \div 2} = \frac{12}{21}$

You're not finished yet, though, because the new numerator and denominator are both multiples of 3: $\frac{12}{21} = \frac{12 \div 3}{21 \div 3} = \frac{4}{7}$.

Okay, you're finished—the numerator and denominator are now relative primes.

$\frac{24}{42}, \frac{12}{21},$ and $\frac{4}{7}$ are equivalent fractions, but only the last is expressed in lowest terms or *simplest* form. What does $\frac{4}{7}$ mean to you? Do you have a sense of how much $\frac{4}{7}$ is? If you're accustomed to working with fractions, $\frac{4}{7}$ is more than just two stacked numbers with a line between them.

Take a closer look. We know, for example, that this fraction is a quantity of easily understood size. We also know it's positive, so it's greater than 0. And, finally, we can see it has a numerator that's less than the denominator, so it's less than 1.

To be more precise, $\frac{4}{7}$ is a bit more than $\frac{1}{2}$. You know that because the numerator is more than half of the denominator. To go back to the old metaphor again, if you cut a pie into seven equal pieces and eat four of them, there will be only three pieces left—you'll have eaten more than half of the pie (oink!).

∿∘POWER SURGE∘∿

In everyday, colloquial lingo, the word *fraction* connotes a *small* part of something. Hence: "a fraction closer" or "at a fraction of the cost."

But if you take these phrases literally—in math terms—they're really meaningless. To a math head, a fraction does not have to be a small number, or a number between 0 and 1. A fraction can also be huge, like $\frac{2\text{ trillion}}{1}$; or zero, like $\frac{0}{1}$; or negative, like $\frac{-2}{3}$.

Of course, mathematicians are equally guilty of taking words from everyday language and assigning them new definitions. The "natural" numbers we talked about earlier aren't the only numbers in nature, and the "imaginary" numbers didn't just appear in some egghead's imagination. Be sensitive to the subtle differences between the technical and non-technical uses of the same word.

THE PLUSES AND MINUSES OF FRACTIONS

Addition and subtraction of common fractions is easy *if* the fractions have the same denominator.

Question: Rhonda has already read $\frac{2}{5}$ of a book. If she reads another $\frac{1}{5}$ of the book, what fraction of the book will she have read?

Solution: $\frac{1}{5}$ plus $\frac{2}{5}$ is $\frac{3}{5}$. Altogether, she will have read $\frac{3}{5}$ of the book.

To Add or Subtract Fractions (Same Denominator): To add or subtract fractions with the same denominator, you just add or subtract the numerators, keeping the same denominator.

Question: $\frac{2}{5} + \frac{1}{5} = ?$

Solution: Add the numerators $(2 + 1 = 3)$ and keep the same denominator:

$$\frac{2}{5} + \frac{1}{5} = \frac{2+1}{5} = \frac{3}{5}$$

You cannot add or subtract fractions without this so-called *common denominator*.

To Add or Subtract Fractions (Different Denominators): If the fractions you want to add or subtract do not already have the same denominator, you need to "unsimplify" one or both

◦◦◦◦**CONNECTION**◦◦◦◦

To improve your math power, connect with the "least common multiple" material in chapter 2!

of them until they do. You may want to aim for the *lowest common denominator*—that is, the least common multiple of the two denominators. But any common denominator will work.

You can always use the product of the denominators for a common denominator, though that will not always be the lowest one. Using the lowest keeps all the numbers as small and manageable as possible, and often prevents the need to reduce the result.

Question: $\frac{1}{6} + \frac{1}{4} = ?$

Solution: You need a common denominator. Look for an integer that is a multiple of both 6 and 4. Their product, 24, is one possibility, but the best choice is the least common multiple, which is 12. Express both fractions in terms of twelfths:

$$\frac{1}{6} = \frac{1 \times 2}{6 \times 2} = \frac{2}{12}$$

$$\frac{1}{4} = \frac{1 \times 3}{4 \times 3} = \frac{3}{12}$$

Now you can add them:

$$\frac{2}{12} + \frac{3}{12} = \frac{2+3}{12} = \frac{5}{12}$$

THEY'RE MULTIPLYING!

Multiplying fractions is often easier than adding them, because you don't need a common denominator to multiply.

To Multiply Fractions: To multiply fractions, multiply the numerators and multiply the denominators.

Question: $\frac{5}{7} \times \frac{3}{4} = ?$

Solution: Multiply the numerators (the numbers on top, 5 and 3) and multiply the denominators (the bottom ones, 7 and 4):

$$\frac{5}{7} \times \frac{3}{4} = \frac{5 \times 3}{7 \times 4} = \frac{15}{28}$$

In this problem, the result is in simplest form. Often, however, the result can be simplified. Try this next one.

Question: $\frac{3}{4} \times \frac{2}{3} = ?$

Solution: Multiply the numerators and multiply the denominators:

$$\frac{3}{4} \times \frac{2}{3} = \frac{3 \times 2}{4 \times 3} = \frac{6}{12}$$

The result $\frac{6}{12}$ can be simplified:

$$\frac{6}{12} = \frac{6 \div 6}{12 \div 6} = \frac{1}{2}$$

To Simplify Fraction Multiplication: You can sometimes avoid big numbers and a lot of simplification by canceling common factors *before* you multiply. Look for factors common to the numerator of one fraction and the denominator of the other.

Question: $\frac{12}{35} \times \frac{14}{27} = ?$

Solution: You could just go ahead and multiply the numerators and multiply the denominators. A calculator will come in handy here:

$$\frac{12}{35} \times \frac{14}{27} = \frac{12 \times 14}{35 \times 27} = \frac{168}{945}$$

The product is indeed $\frac{168}{945}$, but that can be simplified. You could look for factors common to 168 and 945, but it's easier to cancel out common factors before you multiply. This may look a little strange at first, but you'll learn to love this little shortcut in time—we're sure of it.

The numerator of $\frac{12}{35}$ and the denominator of $\frac{14}{27}$ are both multiples of 3, so you can cancel a factor of 3 from each:

$$\frac{12}{35} \times \frac{14}{27} = \frac{12 \div 3}{35} \times \frac{14}{27 \div 3} = \frac{4}{35} \times \frac{14}{9} = ?$$

Similarly, the denominator of the first fraction and the numerator of the second fraction are both multiples of 7, so you can cancel a factor of 7 from each:

$$\frac{4}{35} \times \frac{14}{9} = \frac{4}{35 \div 7} \times \frac{14 \div 7}{9} = \frac{4}{5} \times \frac{2}{9} = ?$$

Now, after canceling, the multiplication is easier, and you don't have to simplify the result:

$$\frac{4}{5} \times \frac{2}{9} = \frac{8}{45}$$

Also, it may seem obvious, but it's always good to be sure the fractions you're multiplying are in their simplest form before you start.

DIVIDE AND CONQUER

Dividing fractions is almost as easy as multiplying them; there's just one extra—and, may we add, quick and easy—step. Think of it like fractional gymnastics: just *flip the second fraction*. Once you've inverted the fraction *after* the division sign, you multiply according to the procedure just described above.

To Divide Fractions: To divide fractions, invert the second one and multiply.

Question: $\frac{1}{2} \div \frac{5}{3} = ?$

Solution: When you invert $\frac{5}{3}$ you get $\frac{3}{5}$.

Multiply: $\frac{1}{2} \div \frac{5}{3} = \frac{1}{2} \times \frac{3}{5} = \frac{3}{10}$

What does it mean to divide by a fraction? For example, what does it mean to divide by $\frac{1}{2}$?

Question: $10 \div \frac{1}{2} = ?$

Solution: When you invert $\frac{1}{2}$, you get $\frac{2}{1}$, or 2.

Invert and multiply: $10 \div \frac{1}{2} = 10 \times 2 = 20$

Does that make sense? Wouldn't you think that 10 divided by one-half would be 5? Not if you take *divided by* in its strict mathematical sense. Division can be thought of as the *inverse* of multiplication. To divide 10 by $\frac{1}{2}$ means to answer the question, "What number multiplied by $\frac{1}{2}$ would give you 10?" Or, put another way, "How many $\frac{1}{2}$'s would you have to add together to get 10?"

IMPROPER FRACTIONS AND MIXED NUMBERS

A fraction is an integer over an integer. It doesn't matter if the integer on top is less than, equal to, or greater than the integer on the bottom, if it's an integer over an integer, it's a fraction. Unfortunately, this fact can be confusing, since the term *improper fraction* is used to describe a fraction with a numerator greater than the denominator. Here are some improper fractions:

$$\frac{3}{2} \qquad \frac{100}{3} \qquad \frac{999}{998}$$

A *mixed number* is a number with an integer part and a fraction part that is less than 1. Here are some mixed numbers:

$$1\frac{1}{2} \qquad 33\frac{1}{3} \qquad 1\frac{1}{998}$$

> ⌁⌁⌁ **SPARK** ⌁⌁⌁
>
> The word *improper* suggests something wrong—even lascivious—about such a fraction. In fact sometimes, particularly when multiplying or dividing, the so-called improper form is preferable to the alternative "mixed" form.

You should know how to go back and forth between the two forms.

To Convert Mixed Numbers to Improper Fractions: To convert a mixed number to an improper fraction, multiply the whole number part by the denominator of the fraction, then add the numerator. The result is the new numerator (over the same denominator).

Question: Express $7\frac{1}{3}$ as an improper fraction.

Solution: First multiply 7 by 3, then add 1, to get the new numerator, 22. Put that over the same denominator, 3, to get $\frac{22}{3}$.

To Convert Improper Fractions to Mixed Numbers: To convert an improper fraction to a mixed number, divide the denominator into the numerator to get a whole number quotient with a remainder. The quotient becomes the whole number part of the mixed number, and the remainder becomes the new numerator—with the same denominator.

Question: Express $\frac{108}{5}$ as a mixed number.

Solution: First divide 5 into 108, which yields 21 with a remainder of 3. Therefore, $\frac{108}{5} = 21\frac{3}{5}$.

IT'S RECIPROCAL

The technical definition of *reciprocals* is two numbers whose product is 1. For example, $\frac{2}{5}$ and $\frac{5}{2}$ are reciprocals because: $\frac{2}{5} \times \frac{5}{2} = 1$.

Finding the reciprocal of a common fraction is way too easy (but we'll show you anyway).

To Find Reciprocals of Fractions: To find the reciprocal of a fraction, flip it—that is, switch the numerator and the denominator.

Question: What is the reciprocal of $\frac{3}{7}$?

Solution: Flip it. The reciprocal is $\frac{7}{3}$.

To find the reciprocal of another type of number, first re-express it as a common fraction.

Question: What is the reciprocal of $3\frac{6}{7}$?

Solution: First turn the mixed number into a common fraction. Multiply 7 times 3 and add 6 to get the numerator: $7 \times 3 + 6 = 27$. Put that 27 over the same denominator 7 and you have $\frac{27}{7}$. Now you can flip. The reciprocal is $\frac{7}{27}$.

DARE TO COMPARE

When you have a pair of positive integers, you can differentiate pretty easily the larger of the two from the smaller. It's obvious that 33,452,678 is greater than 3,512,854, because one has more digits than the other. It's obvious that 5,812 is greater than 5,798. Although they have the same number of digits, and although the thousands' digits are the same (5), the first integer has a greater hundreds' digit.

Comparing fractions is more complicated. It's simplest when you have a pair of positive fractions with a common denominator. In that case, the one with the larger numerator is the larger fraction. Clearly $\frac{5}{7}$ is greater than $\frac{4}{7}$.

To Compare Fractions: One way to compare fractions that do not have a common denominator is to re-express them so that they do.

Question: Which is greater, $\frac{3}{4}$ or $\frac{5}{7}$?

Solution: Re-express both fractions with a common denominator of 28:

$$\frac{3}{4} = \frac{21}{28} \text{ and } \frac{5}{7} = \frac{20}{28}$$

$\frac{21}{28}$ is greater than $\frac{20}{28}$, so $\frac{3}{4}$ is greater than $\frac{5}{7}$.

But if you're really clever (which you are), you might compare fractions by other methods. For example, if two positive fractions have a common numerator, there's no need to re-express them. The one with the *smaller* denominator will be the *larger* fraction.

Question: Which is greater, $\frac{11}{29}$ or $\frac{11}{31}$?

Solution: The fractions have the same numerator. The first fraction, $\frac{11}{29}$, has the smaller denominator, so it is greater than the other fraction.

In general, successful problem solvers don't just blindly apply *algorithms* (see accompanying sidebar). You've got to be prepared to use several possible methods and be flexible in applying those methods. Look at this example:

─◦/\/\/◦ **SPARK** ◦/\/\/◦─

No, an algorithm isn't a new beat on a hip-hop record. It's a way of figuring things out; more literally, it's "a process or rules for calculating something" (*Oxford American Dictionary*). Now you can impress your friends and family by throwing your snazzy, new math vocabulary into casual conversations.

Question: Which is greater, $\frac{7}{18}$ or $\frac{14}{37}$?

Solution: If you insist on using the lowest-common-denominator method to figure this out, you'll find yourself working with fractions whose denominators are 666. That number would be no fun to work with—not because you'd be conjuring up demonic forces, but because all the numbers involved would be bigger and more cumbersome than you'd want to deal with!

The clever math head will notice the relationship between the numerators of these two fractions—one is simply twice the other. It's going to be pretty easy to re-express the fractions with a common numerator. You don't often have reason to find a common numerator, but it makes sense here. Just double the top and bottom of $\frac{7}{18}$ and you get $\frac{14}{36}$. That's easy to compare with $\frac{14}{37}$. The one with the smaller denominator is greater. $\frac{14}{36}$ is greater than $\frac{14}{37}$, and so $\frac{7}{18}$ is greater than $\frac{14}{37}$.

Another way to compare fractions is to convert them both to decimals. Keep reading, and we'll show you how.

THE DISH ON DECIMALS

Decimals are just another kind of fraction—a fraction whose (implied) denominator is 10, 100, 1,000, or some other so-called power of 10. Decimal fractions are very handy because they're much easier to add, subtract, and compare than common fractions are. They're also easier to use with a calculator!

Question: Which is greater, .947109 or .94715?

Solution: Starting at the decimal point and moving to the right, compare the numbers digit by digit. The first, second, third, and fourth digits are the same. The numbers do not differ until the fifth digit after the decimal point. That digit is 0 in the first number and 5 in the second, so the second number is greater. The first number may have more digits, but when it comes to decimals, *more* is not always *greater*. A 6-digit positive integer will certainly be greater than a 5-digit positive integer, but a 6-digit positive decimal may or may not be greater than a 5-digit positive decimal.

Because decimals are more useful than fractions in some situations, you should know how to turn a fraction into a decimal.

To Convert Fractions to Decimals: To convert a fraction to a decimal, divide the bottom into the top.

Question: Re-express $\frac{5}{8}$ as a decimal:

Solution: Divide 8 into 5, yielding .625.

On the other hand, there are times you want to do just the opposite—that is, turn a decimal into a fraction. For instance, if you are using a calculator to tally the survey results taken from a group of people, you may work in decimals at first, then switch to fractions to report your findings most clearly.

To Convert Decimals to Fractions: To convert a decimal to a fraction, set the decimal over 1 and multiply the numerator and denominator by 10 raised to the number of digits *to the right of the decimal point.*

Question: Re-express .625 as a common fraction in lowest terms.

Solution: Multiply $\frac{.625}{1}$ by $\frac{10^3}{10^3}$, or $\frac{1,000}{1,000}$.

Then simplify: $\frac{625}{1,000} = \frac{5 \times 125}{8 \times 125} = \frac{5}{8}$.

FAMILIAR FRACTION-DECIMAL EQUIVALENTS

You should not have to resort to the above algorithms every time you want to convert a fraction to a decimal or vice versa. Ideally, you should file the decimal equivalents for many fractions somewhere in an accessible part of your brain. You should know these equivalents, at least:

$\frac{1}{20} = .05$	$\frac{7}{20} = .35$	$\frac{2}{3} = .666666...$
$\frac{1}{10} = .1$	$\frac{3}{8} = .375$	$\frac{7}{10} = .7$
$\frac{1}{8} = .125$	$\frac{2}{5} = .4$	$\frac{3}{4} = .75$
$\frac{3}{20} = .15$	$\frac{9}{20} = .45$	$\frac{4}{5} = .8$
$\frac{1}{6} = .166666...$	$\frac{1}{2} = .5$	$\frac{5}{6} = .8333333...$
$\frac{1}{5} = .2$	$\frac{11}{20} = .55$	$\frac{17}{20} = .85$
$\frac{1}{4} = .25$	$\frac{3}{5} = .6$	$\frac{7}{8} = .875$
$\frac{3}{10} = .3$	$\frac{5}{8} = .625$	$\frac{9}{10} = .9$
$\frac{1}{3} = .333333...$	$\frac{13}{20} = .65$	$\frac{19}{20} = .95$

REPEATING DECIMALS

Working in decimal notation does introduce one complication—the endlessly repeating decimal. Sometimes when you turn a fraction into a decimal by dividing the bottom into the top, you get a decimal that goes on forever like a scratched record. But as long as you're dividing an integer by an integer, the endless decimal will be a *repeating decimal*, that is, a decimal with a sequence of digits that repeats indefinitely.

Sometimes it's a single digit that repeats forever, as in the following example.

Question: What is the decimal equivalent for $\frac{26}{45}$?

Solution: To convert a fraction to a decimal, divide the bottom into the top. Here you divide 45 into 26, and when you do so, you get:

$$
\begin{array}{r}
0.5777777777777 \\
45\overline{)26.0000000000000...}
\end{array}
$$

Sometimes it's a sequence of many digits.

Question: What is the decimal equivalent for $\frac{45}{26}$?

Solution: This time you divide 26 into 45, and when you do so, you get:

$$\begin{array}{r} 1.73076923076923... \\ \overline{26)45.0000000000000...} \end{array}$$

Repeating decimals are written in abbreviated form by placing a bar over the sequence of digits that repeats:

$$1.7\overline{307692}$$

To Find a Digit in Repeating Decimals: To find a particular digit in a repeating decimal, note the number of digits in the cluster that repeats. If there are 2 digits in that cluster, then every 2nd digit is the same. If there are 3 digits, then every 3rd digit is the same. And so on.

Question: What is the 50th digit after the decimal point in the decimal equivalent of $\frac{1}{27}$?

Solution: The decimal equivalent of $\frac{1}{27}$ is .037037037. . . , which is best written $.\overline{037}$. There are 3 digits in the repeating cluster, so every 3rd digit is the same: 7. To find the 50th digit, look for the multiple of 3 just less than 50—that's 48. The 48th digit is 7, and with the 49th digit, the pattern repeats with 0. The 50th digit is 3.

To Convert Repeating Decimals to Fractions (Part 1): Converting a repeating decimal to a fraction is a little complicated—but *Math Power* to the rescue! If the bar starts over the digit right after the decimal point, then take the whole sequence of digits under the bar and put it over 9 or 99 or 999 or whatever—you want the number of 9s on the bottom to be equal to the number of digits in the number on top. Got it? We'll show you.

Question: Express $.\overline{45}$ as a fraction in simplest form.

Solution: Take what appears under the bar—45—and put it in the numerator. For the denominator, take 99—two digits on top, so two 9s on bottom:

$$\overline{.45} = \frac{45}{99}$$

This fraction can be reduced. Divide the top and bottom by 9 and you get:

$$\frac{45}{99} = \frac{45 \div 9}{99 \div 9} = \frac{5}{11}$$

To Convert Repeating Decimals to Fractions (Part 2): If the bar starts somewhere after the first digit, then you must first multiply the decimal by 10 over 10, or by 100 over 100, or by 1,000 over 1,000.

Now you're ready to check out this chapter's Do the Math solution:

DO THE MATH

Re-express the repeating decimal $.1\overline{405}$ as a fraction in lowest terms.

Solution: First multiply by 10 over 10:

$$.1\overline{405} = \frac{10 \times .1\overline{405}}{10} = \frac{1.\overline{405}}{10}$$

Now convert $.\overline{405}$ as above:

$$.\overline{405} = \frac{405}{999} = \frac{15}{37}$$

So:

$$\frac{1.\overline{405}}{10} = \frac{1 + \frac{15}{37}}{10} = \frac{\frac{37}{37} + \frac{15}{37}}{10} = \frac{\frac{52}{37}}{10} = \frac{52}{370} = \frac{26}{185}$$

Plug In

Is your math power glass half empty or half full? Which part of this chapter did you fully grasp? Show off your great knowledge of fractions and decimals by tackling these review questions. The answers are in the "Plug-In Solutions" section at the back of the book.

1. $3\frac{3}{5} \div \frac{9}{10} = ?$ _____

2. Which is greater, $\frac{9}{25}$ or $\frac{18}{51}$? _____

3. Express the sum of $\frac{1}{50}$ and $\frac{1}{1000}$ as a decimal. _____

4. What is the 300th digit after the decimal point in the decimal equivalent of $\frac{3}{70}$? _____

5. Re-express the repeating decimal .123333333. . . as a fraction in lowest terms. _____

CHAPTER FOUR

Percents: A System with *Hundreds* of Uses

In the last chapter, we covered fractions and decimals as different ways to express parts of whole numbers. We discussed common mathematical operations with both, and checked out some of the problems that can come up when we try to convert one to the other. Now let's look at how percents figure in to the equation. Think of percents as tools of communication; they're a way to give people an idea of what you mean when you're talking about numbers.

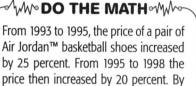

⌁〰️DO THE MATH〰️⌁

From 1993 to 1995, the price of a pair of Air Jordan™ basketball shoes increased by 25 percent. From 1995 to 1998 the price then increased by 20 percent. By what percent would the 1998 price of the shoes have to be *decreased* in order to restore it to the 1993 price? (See the solution near the end of this chapter.)

THE POWER OF 100

As logical and as useful as fractions are, they're often difficult to compare or combine. It takes a little thought and manipulation to answer such questions as:

- One candidate got $\frac{3}{8}$ of the votes and another candidate got $\frac{7}{20}$ of the votes. Who got more votes?

- One-fifth of the students got A's, and $\frac{1}{4}$ of the students got B's.

    What fraction of the students got something other than an A or a B?

It's the different denominators that make these questions a little troublesome. Wouldn't it be a lot easier if every fraction had the same denominator? Then, to add or subtract fractions, all you'd have to do is add or subtract the numerators. To compare the fractions, all you'd have to do is compare the numerators.

As a matter of fact, there exists just such a system. Percents are nothing more than fractions, all with the same denominator: 100. See how much easier it is to answer the above questions when the fractions are converted to percents:

- One candidate got $37\frac{1}{2}$ percent of the votes and another candidate got 35 percent of the votes. Who got more votes?

- Twenty percent of the students got A's, and 25 percent of the students got B's. What percent of the students got something other than an A or a B?

To Decipher Percents: A number followed by the word *percent* or the symbol % means that many out of 100. Literally, *per* means *out of* and *cent* means *hundred.*

So, when you hear that one candidate received $37\frac{1}{2}$ percent of the votes, you know that she got $37\frac{1}{2}$ out of every 100 votes cast.

That doesn't mean there were 100 votes cast in all. In fact, since the total was 37 and *one-half* percent, there could not have been 100 votes cast in all, unless it was possible to split one's vote—half for one candidate and half for another. A percent is like a fraction in that it gives you a sense of relative size, but not necessarily actual size. A candidate who got $37\frac{1}{2}$ percent of the votes might have gotten 3 votes out of 8 votes cast, or 3 million out of 8 million cast.

⟋W⟍**POWER SURGE**⟋W⟍

Grammatically speaking, is a percent singular or plural? Curiously enough, it can be either. It depends on what it's a percent of:

Twenty percent of the apples **are** gone.

Twenty percent of the applesauce **is** gone.

The same is true of fractions:

Two-fifths of the voters **are** undecided.

Two-fifths of the electorate **is** undecided.

TIME TO CONVERT

To convert a percent into a decimal, remove the word *percent* or the % symbol and move the decimal point two places to the left. (What you're actually doing is *dividing* by 100 percent.)

To Convert Percents to Fractions: To convert a percent into a fraction, remove the word *percent* or the % symbol and put the number over 100. (You can again think of this as *dividing* by 100 percent.) Then, if you can, reduce.

Question: Express 32% as a fraction in lowest terms.

Solution: Drop the percent symbol, put 32 over 100, and reduce:

$$32\% = \frac{32}{100} = \frac{8}{25}$$

To Convert Decimals to Percents: To convert a decimal to a percent, move the decimal point two places to the right and attach either the % symbol or the word percent. (You can think of this as *multiplying* by 100 percent.)

Question: Express .035 as a percent.

Solution: Move the decimal point two places to the right and .035 becomes 3.5. Attach the word *percent* (or its symbol) and you can say that .035 equals 3.5 percent (or 3.5%).

To Convert Fractions to Percents: To convert a fraction to a percent, first turn the fraction into a decimal (by dividing the bottom into the top), and then move the decimal point two places to the right.

> o/w\vo**CONNECTION** o/w\vo
>
> To improve your math power, connect with the "converting a fraction to a decimal" material in chapter 3!

Question: Express $\frac{13}{25}$ as a percent.

Solution: When you divide 25 into 13, you get .52. Move the decimal two places to the right and you get 52 percent.

To Remember How to Convert: Here's some alliteration which we know will help you *love* what we've just gone over:

To **D**rop a percent, **D**ivide by 100 percent.

To **M**ake a percent, **M**ultiply by 100 percent.

THE ALL-PURPOSE PERCENT FORMULA

The destiny of a percent is to be multiplied by the whole. Most percent problems can be solved by plugging into one simple formula:

$$\text{Percent} \times \text{Whole} = \text{Part}$$

This formula defines a relationship between three quantities. If you know two of them, you can find the third. Whether you need to find the part, the whole, or the percent, just use the same formula, as the following three examples illustrate. Remember that division will be used as the *inverse* of multiplication.

Question: What is 12% of 25?

Solution: Part = $.12 \times 25 = 3$

Question: 45 is 3% of what number?

Solution: $45 = .03 \times \text{Whole}$; so Whole = $45 \div .03 = 1500$

Question: 36 is what percent of 9?

Solution: $36 = \text{Percent} \times 9$; so Percent = $36 \div 9 = 4 = 400\%$

In the last example, note that the *part* is greater than the *whole*—we're stretching the meanings of part and whole a bit—and that's why the answer to the question is greater than 100%. To say that 36 is 400% of 9 is to say that 36 is 4 times 9. Remember, percents are not always less than or equal to 100.

Are you still a little foggy on this? It takes some time to master.

You may ask, if the part can be bigger than the whole, how do you know which quantity is the part and which quantity is the whole? You can tell by taking note of two little words: *of* and *is*. (Sometimes it's *of* and *are*.) The whole is generally associated with the word *of*, and the part is generally associated with the verb *is/are*. Look at the same three examples again and see how *of* and *is* identify the wholes and the parts:

Question: What is 12% of 25?

Solution: The 25 is associated with the word *of*, so it's the whole. The unknown *what* is associated with the word *is*, so it's the part that you're looking for.

Question: 45 is 3% of what number?

Solution: The unknown *what number* is associated with the word *of*, so it's the whole that you're looking for. The 45 is associated with the word *is*, so it's the part.

Question: 36 is what percent of 9?

Solution: The 9 is associated with the word *of*, so it's the whole. The 36 is associated with the word *is*, so it's the part.

USELESS CALCULATING CRITTERS

Our all-purpose percent formula—Percent × Whole = Part—does not explicitly address the fact that percents per se are *useless* when it comes to calculation. Before you can do anything with a percent, you have to turn it into a more usable number—that is, a fraction or a decimal. To find 16% of 25, for example, you know that *of* means *multiply*, but before you can multiply, you must first convert 16% to a fraction or a decimal.

Question: What is 16 percent of 25?

Solution: The unknown *what* is associated with the word *is*, so it's the part you're looking for. Part equals percent times whole. But before you can multiply 16 percent by 25, you must convert 16 percent to a fraction or a decimal. The decimal is easy—it's .16. So:

$$\text{Part} = .16 \times 25 = 4$$

◦◠◦ **POWER SURGE** ◦◠◦

How does *A* percent of *B* compare to *B* percent of *A*? They're equal. Compare, for example, 20 percent of 50 to 50 percent of 20:

$$20\% \text{ of } 50 = .20 \times 50 = 10$$
$$50\% \text{ of } 20 = .50 \times 20 = 10$$

You can use this fact sometimes to make mental math calculations. When you're asked to find 16 percent of 25, you can do it in your head if you think of it as 25 percent of 16.

THE UPS AND DOWNS OF PERCENTS

Percents do indeed get complicated when you start using them to describe changes. Funny things happen when you're working with *percent increase* and *percent decrease*. What makes a percent change problem potentially tricky is that there are *two* wholes—the *old* whole and the *new* whole. The part is the difference between the old whole and the new whole. If the new whole is bigger than the old whole, then the difference is used to find the percent *increase*. If the new whole is less than the old whole, then the difference is used to find the percent *decrease*. Got it? Don't worry if this feels like a chore. This handy guide (and everything else in this book) will always be here for easy reference.

But this raises one last question: Which whole are you supposed to use in the all-purpose percent formula—Percent × Whole = Part? Answer: You *always* use the *old* whole.

Question: If the price of a hamburger is increased from $1.00 to $1.25, what is the percent increase?

Solution: The amount of increase is $0.25. Use the all-purpose percent for-mula to figure out what percent that is of the *old* whole, $1.00. The part is the amount of change (0.25), and the whole is the *old* whole (1.00).

$$\text{Part} = \text{Percent} \times \text{Whole}$$

$$0.25 = \text{Percent} \times 1.00$$

$$\text{Percent} = \frac{0.25}{1.00} = .25 = 25\%$$

The most important thing to remember is to use the *old* whole as the base. Look at how the answer to the following question is different even though it uses the same numbers as the last question:

Question: If the price of a hamburger is decreased from $1.25 to $1.00, what is the percent decrease?

Solution: The amount of decrease is $0.25. Use the all-purpose percent formula to figure out what percent that is of the old whole, which this time is $1.25. The part is the amount of change (0.25), and the whole is the old whole (1.25).

$$\text{Part} = \text{Percent} \times \text{Whole}$$

$$0.25 = \text{Percent} \times 1.25$$

$$\text{Percent} = \frac{0.25}{1.25} = .20 = 20\%$$

To Calculate Percent Change: If you like formulas, here's the formula for percent change:

$$\text{Percent Change} = \frac{\text{Amount of change}}{\text{Old whole}} \times 100\%$$

Don't take the term *old whole* too literally. The old whole is whatever whole is being used as the basis of comparison. It's possible for the wording of a question to make the chronologically later quantity what we are calling the *old whole.*

Question: One month ago, the price of plums was 20 percent less than it is now. If plums now cost 90 cents a dozen, how much did they cost one month ago?

Solution: Because of the way the question is worded—*price . . . was 20 per-cent less than it is now*—take the current price as the old whole and last month's price as the new whole. Last month's price is described as the result of a percent decrease applied to this month's price:

$$\text{Percent decrease} = \frac{\text{Amount of decrease}}{\text{Old whole}} \times 100\%$$

$$20\% = \frac{\text{Amount of change}}{90 \text{ cents}} \times 100\%$$

$$\text{Amount of decrease} = \frac{20\%}{100\%} \times 90 \text{ cents}$$

$$= .2 \times 90 \text{ cents} = 18 \text{ cents}$$

Last month's price was 18 cents less than this month's, so it was 72 cents.

To Find the Old Whole: Given the percent change and the old whole, it is relatively easy to figure out the new whole. It's more challenging when you're given the percent change and the new whole and asked to figure out the *old* whole.

Question: The price of a dozen eggs has increased by 20 percent in the last month. If the price is now 90 cents, what was it a month ago?

Solution: This looks a lot like the last question, but the answer's different because different prices are used as the so-called old whole. This time it's the old whole you're solving for. The best way to handle this is to think of this month's price as 100% plus another 20% of last month's price. In other words the new whole is 120% of the old whole, which is the same as 1.2 times the old whole:

$$\text{New whole} = 120\% \text{ of old whole}$$

$$90 \text{ cents} = 1.2 \times (\text{old whole})$$

$$\text{Old whole} = \frac{90 \text{ cents}}{1.2} = 75 \text{ cents}$$

MORE FUN WITH PERCENTAGE UPS AND DOWNS

You really have to be careful when you encounter a scenario of multi-step percent change. It may seem to defy logic, as in the next question. Every time there's a percent increase or decrease, the whole changes—the new whole from one step becomes the old whole for the next step. That's significant, because you cannot add or subtract percents of different wholes. Here's a question whose answer may surprise you.

Question: The original price P of an item is increased 10 percent, resulting in price Q. Price Q is then increased by 20 percent, resulting in final price R. The final price R is what percent greater than the original price P?

Solution: Don't just add 10% and 20% to get an answer of 30%. It's not that simple. Say the original price P is $100. A 10% increase will yield a new whole of $110. Now that new whole becomes the next *old whole*. To find the final price, take 20% of $110—that's $22—and increase it by that much. The final price is $132, which is 32 percent more than the original price of $100.

Now you're ready to look at the Do the Math solution from chapter 4.

DO THE MATH

From 1993 to 1995, the price of a pair of Air Jordan basketball shoes increased by 25 percent. From 1995 to 1998 the price then increased by 20 percent. By what percent would the 1998 price of the shoes have to be *decreased* in order to restore it to the 1993 price?

Solution: Suppose the original 1993 price was $100. A 25% increase will bring that up to $125. Now, to increase that by 20%, find 20% of $125 and add that on:

$$\text{1998 price} = (\text{1995 price}) + (20\% \text{ of 1995 price})$$
$$= \$125 + (20\% \text{ of } \$125)$$
$$= \$125 + \$25$$
$$= \$150$$

That's $50 more than the 1993 price. So the net effect of a 25 percent increase followed by a 20 percent increase is a 50 percent increase. But 50 percent is *not* the answer to this question. It asks not what percent greater is the 1998 price than the 1993 price. It asks, by what percent must the 1998 price be *decreased* to get back to the 1993 price for the shoes. In other words, what is

 55

the percent decrease from \$150 to \$100? The amount of decrease is \$50, and you need to think of that as a percent of the \$150, the 1998 price:

$$\text{Part} = \text{Percent} \times \text{Whole}$$

$$50 = \text{Percent} \times 150$$

$$\text{Percent} = \frac{50}{150} = .33333\ldots = 33\frac{1}{3}\%$$

🖫 *Plug In*

Personally, we find percents to be perfect for a math head like you! Now that you are fully indoctrinated into the Wonderful World of 100, put 100% of your math persona into these review questions. The answers are in the "Plug-In Solutions" section at the back of the book.

1. What is 8.4 percent of 125? _____

2. 450 is what percent of 3? _____

3. The price of a newspaper goes up from 5 cents to 15 cents. What is the percent increase in price? _____

4. After a 5% increase, the population was 59,346. What was the population before the increase? _____

5. The population of a certain country increases 50 percent every 50 years. If the population in 1950 was 810,000, in what year was the population 160,000? _____

CHAPTER FIVE

Mean, Median, and Mode: Just Your Average Chapter

In the first four chapters of this book, you learned basic operations with different sets of numbers, from adding and subtracting positive integers to the conversions of fractions, decimals, and percents. If you're not a dedicated math head, that can seem a bit abstract, so in the next few chapters we'll help you explore concepts that have to do with using numbers to represent very real situations and problems.

> ∿**DO THE MATH**∿
>
> The median value of a set of nine positive integers is 6. If the only mode is 25, what is the least possible value of the mean? (See the solution near the end of this chapter.)

THREE KINDS OF AVERAGE

You might have trouble coming up with an answer for the above Do the Math question if you don't know the definitions of *mean, median,* and *mode*. Each of the three is a way to *summarize a set of numbers with a single number*. They are three different types of average.

Average is one of those math words that is somewhat ambiguous. You won't often hear a math head use the word *average* without some sort of throat clearing and clarification. You're more likely to hear about the *mean* (or, to be even more precise, the *arithmetic mean*). The *median* is a different way to describe a set of numbers.

The *mode* doesn't really come up all that often, but it seems that whenever a math book gets into the mean and the median, it brings in the mode as well. Okay—they all begin with M, and math heads will try for logical sets whenever they can find them—but, seriously, it can get confusing, and we'll try to clear the fog for you.

BY ALL MEANS

Most of the time you hear the word *average*, what's meant is the arithmetic *mean*, which is defined as the sum of a set of numbers divided by the number of numbers in the set. If we call the numbers in the set *terms*, then we can write an all-purpose mean formula.

To Find the Mean: All-purpose means can be cranked out by using the terms in your calculation as follows:

$$\text{Mean} = \frac{\text{Sum of the terms}}{\text{Number of terms}}$$

An example of finding the mean that is familiar (and sometimes painful) to most students is the grade point average (GPA):

Question: If an A is worth 4 grade points, a B is worth 3 grade points, and a C is worth 2 grade points, what is your GPA if you have 5 A's, 4 B's, and 1 C?

Solution: You're looking for the mean of these 10 terms:

4, 4, 4, 4, 4, 3, 3, 3, 3, 2

To apply the all-purpose mean formula, you add them up and divide by 10:

$$\text{Average} = \frac{\text{Sum of the terms}}{\text{Number of terms}}$$

$$= \frac{4 + 4 + 4 + 4 + 4 + 3 + 3 + 3 + 3 + 2}{10}$$

$$= \frac{34}{10} = 3.4$$

A special characteristic of the mean is that the sum of the deviations is 0. A term's *deviation* is that term minus the mean. Terms greater than the mean have positive deviations; terms less than the mean have negative deviations. Take the above set of ten grades with a GPA of 3.4. These are the terms/deviations: 4/.6, 4/.6, 4/.6, 4/.6, 4/.6, 3/–.4, 3/–.4, 3/–.4, 3/–.4, and 2/–1.4.

The five positive deviations add up to 3.0, and the five negative deviations add up to –3.0. They exactly cancel each other. The sum of all the deviations is 0.

A VERY WEIGHTY MEAN

In our GPA example, there were 10 terms, but there were only three distinct numbers among those terms. To find their mean, you first had to find their sum, but to find their sum you didn't have to add them up one by one. You may have used multiplication to help you. The sum of five 4's is the product of 5 and 4, and the sum of four 3's is the product of 4 and 3.

What you actually figured out was a *weighted mean*. The only terms were 2, 3, and 4, but the mean turned out to be well above 3. That's because there were a lot more 4's than 2's—the 4's carried greater weight.

The concept of the weighted mean helps when you want to combine means.

Question: Manny's mean bowling score for the month of January was 150. His mean bowling score for the month of February was 162. What was his mean score for the two-month period?

Solution: Faked you out! You can't tell. It depends on the *relative* number of games bowled each month.

The mean will be 156—exactly halfway between 150 and 162—only if Manny bowled the same number of games each month. If, in fact, he bowled more games in January, then his overall mean will be somewhat closer to the January mean of 150. If, on the other hand, he bowled more games in February, then his overall mean will be somewhat closer to the February mean of 162. You need more information—specifically, something about the relative number of games bowled each month—to answer the question. About the only thing you can say is that Manny's two-month mean will be somewhere between 150 and 162.

Question: Manny's mean bowling score for the month of January was 150. His mean bowling score for the month of February was 162. If he bowled exactly twice as many games in February as in January, what was his mean score for the two-month period?

Solution: Now you have the information you need. You still don't know just how many games he bowled each month, but you do know how to weight the two monthly means. The larger mean gets twice the weight, so you can essentially think of it as finding the mean of one score of 150 and two scores of 162.

$$\text{Mean} = \frac{(\text{January mean}) + 2(\text{February mean})}{3}$$

$$= \frac{150 + 2(162)}{3} = \frac{474}{3} = 158$$

Just as we predicted, the mean turned out to be closer to 162 than to 150.

Actually, an alternative way to find this weighted mean would have been to use the special characteristic noted above—that all the deviations add up to 0. Whatever the mean of 150, 162, and 162 is, the deviation of 150 from that mean will be negative, and the deviation of each 162 will be positive. That's one negative deviation and two equal positive ones. For the one negative to exactly cancel the two equal positives, the magnitude (absolute value) of the negative will need to be exactly twice that of each positive. Thus, the mean is twice as far from 150 as it is from 162, or, in other words, it's two-thirds of the way from 150 to 162. That's 158. Decent bowling, Manny!

SOME SPACEY NUMBER STUFF

Another situation that offers an alternative method for finding the mean is when the terms are evenly spaced—that is, the difference from one term to the next (when they're in order of size) is always the same.

To Find the Mean of Evenly Spaced Numbers: The mean of evenly spaced numbers is simply the mean of the smallest and largest numbers.

Question: What is the mean of all the positive 2-digit multiples of 7?

KAPLAN

Solution: The multiples of 7 are evenly spaced—the difference from one to the next is always 7—and so all you need to do is identify the smallest and the largest and then find the mean of those. The smallest positive two-digit multiple of 7 is 14, and the largest is 98. The mean is:

$$\text{Mean} = \frac{14 + 98}{2} = \frac{112}{2} = 56$$

If you were to write down all the positive two-digit multiples of 7, the mean of 56 is right smack in the middle: 14, 21, 28, 35, 42, 49, 56, 63, 70, 77, 84, 91, 98.

Another Way to Find the Mean of Evenly Spaced Numbers: The mean of evenly spaced numbers is the middle number. If there is an even amount of numbers, the mean is halfway between the two middle numbers.

Question: Find the mean of this set of numbers: 269, 273, 277, 281, 285, 289.

Solution: The numbers are evenly spaced—the difference from one to the next is always 4—and there are so few numbers, you can figure out the mean just by looking at them. There are six numbers, so the mean will be halfway between the third and the fourth. That's halfway between 277 and 281, which is 279.

USING YOUR OLD MEAN

The all-purpose mean formula is a statement that relates three quantities: the *mean*, the *sum*, and the *number of terms*. The most familiar application of the formula is to find the mean when you're given the sum and the number of terms. But you can use the formula to find any of the three quantities whenever you're given the other two. For example, if you know the mean and the number of terms, you can find the sum.

Question: What is the sum of all the positive integers from 1 through 100, inclusive?

Solution: The positive integers are evenly spaced—the difference from one to the next is always 1—so their mean is simply the mean of the smallest and largest, 1 and 100. Those two numbers add up to 101, and that divided by 2 is 50.5, so the mean of all of these integers is 50.5. And because there are 100 of them, the sum is 50.5 times 100:

Sum of the terms = (Mean) × 3 (Number of terms)

$$= 50.5 \times 100$$

$$= 5,050$$

To Use the Mean to Find a Missing Term: Use the all-purpose mean formula to find a missing term when you know the mean and all the other terms. Once again, the key is to go by way of the sum.

Question: The mean age of five teammates is 32.2. If two of the teammates are 25 years old, a third is 27, and a fourth is 38, how old is the fifth?

Solution: If the five ages have a mean of 32.2, then the sum of the five ages is 5 times 32.2, or 161. The four ages given add up to 25 + 25 + 27 + 38 = 115. The fifth age must therefore be 161 − 115 = 46.

MASTERING THE MEDIAN

There are times when the mean can be misleading. Take this example:

Question: The annual salaries of the five members of the Fleagle Company's board of directors are: $10,000, $20,000, $30,000, $40,000, $900,000. What is the mean annual salary of the five board members?

Solution: Add the salaries and divide by 5. They add up to $1,000,000, which divided by 5 yields $200,000.

If someone told you that the mean annual salary of five board members is $200,000, you would probably tend to think that each of the five people makes something in the neighborhood of $200,000. In fact, four of the five board members make significantly less than that.

The mean is misleading because the distribution of the numbers is highly skewed—one of the numbers is much larger than any of the others. (You wish *you* made that much!) In a case like this, the *median* is more informative than the mean.

To Find the Median: The median is defined as the middle number when the numbers are put in order of size.

Question: The annual salaries of the five members of Cool Company's board are: $10,000, $20,000, $30,000, $40,000, $900,000. What is the median annual salary of the five board members?

Solution: The numbers are already put in order of size. The one in the middle is $30,000, so that's the median.

To Find the Median of an Even Number of Numbers: If there's an even number of numbers, then the median is defined as the mean of the two middle numbers.

Question: The ages of the school's "Adventures in Eating" Cafeteria Committee members are 35, 37, 46, 59, 60, and 63. What is the median of the ages?

Solution: There's an even number of numbers, so there's no one number in the middle. The two middle numbers are 46 and 59. The median will be the *mean* of those two numbers, which is $\frac{46 + 59}{2}$ = 52.5. Bon appétit!

IN THE MODE

Our third type of average is the easiest one to figure out, but it is unfortunately the least useful. The *mode* of a set of numbers is simply the number that appears most often. If there is a tie for the most frequent number, then there is more than one mode. If no number appears more than once, there is no mode. The mode is most useful when the relative size of the numbers under consideration is irrelevant. Here's an example.

Question: When 10 people were asked to name their favorite one-digit integer, two answered "1," one answered "2," three answered "3," and four answered "7." What is the mode of the answers?

Solution: The mode is 7. More people answered "7" than any other number.

The fact that all the other numbers mentioned were somewhat less than 7 is irrelevant. The most popular answer was "7." Who cares what the mean or median of the answers would be? This is a rare instance where the mode is more informative than the mean or the median.

Now that you're clear on the definitions of mean, median, and mode, you're ready to take another look at Do the Math solution from chapter 5.

DO THE MATH!

The median value of a set of nine positive integers is 6. If the only mode is 25, what is the least possible value of the mean?

Solution: To get the least possible mean, you want to come up with the nine smallest positive integers that fit the given conditions—that is, that have a median of 6 and a single mode of 25. Think of the problem as one of filling nine slots. The middle slot gets the median, 6. If the mode is 25, you need to fill at least two slots with 25's. To keep the mean as small as possible, you'll make the two 25's the biggest of the nine integers:

$$\underline{\quad}\ \ \underline{\quad}\ \ \underline{\quad}\ \ \underline{\quad}\ \ \underline{6}\ \ \underline{\quad}\ \ \underline{\quad}\ \ \underline{25}\ \ \underline{25}$$

Now fill in the remaining slots with the smallest integers you can. Note that, if 25 is the only mode, no other integer can appear more than once. So you can't fill in the first four slots with 1's. You have to fill them in with a 1, 2, 3, and 4:

$$\underline{1}\ \ \underline{2}\ \ \underline{3}\ \ \underline{4}\ \ \underline{6}\ \ \underline{\quad}\ \ \underline{\quad}\ \ \underline{25}\ \ \underline{25}$$

The last remaining slots have to get integers greater than 6. They must also be distinct—only 25 can appear more than once—and you want them to be as small as they can be. The smallest integers that fit are 7 and 8:

$$\underline{1} \quad \underline{2} \quad \underline{3} \quad \underline{4} \quad \underline{6} \quad \underline{7} \quad \underline{8} \quad \underline{25} \quad \underline{25}$$

This is the set of integers that will give you the smallest possible mean under the conditions described. Add the nine numbers and divide by 9. They add up to 81, which divided by 9 yields the correct answer of 9.

Plug In

Whether you're just an average math student—or way, way above the mean, median, or mode of achievement for all math heads—you'll find the following review questions an exciting plunge into the above average world of averages. See how many you can ace. The answers are in the "Plug-In Solutions" section at the back of the book.

1. In Flower Arranging 101, Lily earned an 82 on the first test, another 82 on the second test, a 76 on the third test, and a 92 on the fourth test. What score does she need to get on the fifth test to end up with a five-test mean score 86? _____

2. In the Aardvark Grooming class, there are 12 boys and 18 girls. If the class mean score on a test is 90, and the boys' mean score is 87, what is the girls' mean score? _____

3. The mean of a set of 32 numbers is 66. If the numbers 95 and 97 are removed, what is the mean of the remaining set? _____

4. What is the sum of all the multiples of 3 between 400 and 500?

   _____

5. If the median of a set of numbers is not one of the numbers in the set, what do you know about the set of numbers? _____

CHAPTER SIX

Ratios: Two-to-One Readers Prefer This Chapter

All we're going to tell you about this chapter is that you can breathe a sigh of relief: Ratios, proportions and rates are three concepts which have a lot going for them. They are useful, clear and easy to understand. What more could you ask from a mathematical concept!

> **DO THE MATH**
>
> If you jog halfway from A to B at a steady rate of 2 miles per hour, how fast would you have to run the rest of the way in order to average 4 miles per hour for the entire trip? (See the solution near the end of this chapter.)

GET YOUR RED HOT RATIOS HERE!

A *ratio* is a representation of the relative size of two quantities by means of division. The "ratio of A to B" can be written either with a colon—A:B—or with a fraction bar — $\frac{A}{B}$ The fraction version is more useful because ratios do behave a lot like fractions. For example, you can reduce a ratio to lowest terms just like a fraction.

Question: Joe is 16 years old, and Mary is 12 years old. What is the ratio of Joe's age to Mary's age?

Solution: The ratio is 16:12, which can also be written as $\frac{16}{12}$. That ratio can be reduced. Divide both terms by 4:

$$\frac{16}{12} = \frac{16 \div 4}{12 \div 4} = \frac{4}{3}$$

The ratio of their ages is 4 to 3.

In a ratio, how do you know which number to put on the top and which number to put on the bottom? Watch for the words *of* and *to*. The number that goes on top is generally the quantity that comes after the word *of*, and the number that goes on the bottom is generally the quantity that comes after the word *to*.

To Decipher Ratios: Here's our handy Ratio Formula: Ratio = $\frac{of}{to}$.

The ratio of Joe's age to Mary's age is $\frac{\text{Joe's age}}{\text{Mary's age}}$.

WHAT RATIOS REALLY TELL YOU

Ratios typically describe parts of a whole. The whole is the entire set, such as all the workers in a factory. The part is a certain section of the whole, such as the female workers in the factory. The ratio of male workers to female workers can be called a *part-to-part ratio*. It compares one part of the whole to another part of the whole.

It's important to understand what ratios tell you and what they do not tell you.

Question: If you are told that the ratio of male workers to female workers in a certain factory is 3:2, which of the following questions can you answer?

1. Are there more male workers or female workers in the factory?

2. What fraction of the workers in the factory are male?

3. What is the total number of workers in the factory?

Solution: You can answer question 1—if there are 3 male workers for every 2 female workers, then there are clearly more males than females. You can also answer question 2—if there are 3 male workers for every 2 female workers, then you can say that there are 3 males in every 5 workers. Thus $\frac{3}{5}$ of the workers are male.

You can't answer question 3, however. A ratio is a description of *relative* size—not actual size. There might be 5 workers, in which case there would be 3 males and 2 females. But there might instead be 500 workers, in which case 300 are male and 200 are female.

One thing you *do* know about the total number of workers is that, if the ratios are exact, the total number of workers has to be a multiple of 5. If the total were not a multiple of 5, the numbers of males and females would turn out to be nonintegers. (What?) For example, if the total number of workers were 12, then the number of males would be $\frac{3}{5}$ of 12, or 7.2, and the number of females would be $\frac{3}{5}$ of 12, or 4.8. That's impossible. People come only in integer amounts. (But if you meet someone who exists as a fraction, please be sure and let us know!)

It's a different story when you're dealing with quantities that do not have to be integers. For example, if you're told that the ratio of oil to vinegar in a certain recipe is 3:2, you still can't say anything about what kind of number the amount of oil and vinegar will add up to.

When we say that $\frac{3}{5}$ of the workers are male, we are saying in essence that the ratio of the number of males to the total number of workers is 3 to 5. Thus, a fraction can be called a *part-to-whole ratio*.

The following question is very similar to the previous one, but there's one crucial difference.

Question: If you are told that the ratio of Democrats to Republicans in a certain room is 3:2, which of the following questions can you answer?

1. Are there more Democrats or Republicans in the room?

2. What fraction of the people in the room are Democrats?

3. What is the total number of people in the room?

Solution: This time you can answer only question 1—clearly there are more Democrats. Question 3 is unanswerable for the same reason it was last time.

But why can't you answer question 2? What's the difference between the male-female situation and this Democrat-Republican situation? The difference is that all people are either male or female, but all people are not necessarily Democrats or Republicans. There are other parties, and there are Americans who belong to no party.

The difference is that in the male-female situation, the parts add up to the whole, while in the Democrat-Republican situation, the parts do not necessarily add up to the whole. Ratios demand you use your powers of logic to think beyond the simple mathematics aspects of a given problem.

To Convert Part-to-Part Ratios: When the parts add up to the whole, you can turn a part-to-part ratio into a part-to-whole ratio.

Question: The ratio of domestic widget sales to foreign widget sales is 3:5. What fraction of the total widget sales are domestic sales?

Solution: In this case, the whole—total widget sales—is equal to the sum of the parts—domestic and foreign—so you can turn the given part-to-part ratio into a part-to-whole ratio. The parts are 3 and 5, so the whole is 3 + 5 = 8. The domestic-to-total ratio, then, is 3:8.

Question: The ratio of red marbles to blue marbles in a certain bag is 3:5. What fraction of the marbles in the bag are blue?

Solution: This time you can't turn the part-to-part ratio—red marbles to blue marbles—into a part-to-whole ratio—red marbles to total marbles—because you do not know whether there are marbles of any other color in the bag. Red and blue don't necessarily add up to all the marbles. There might be some green ones, or yellow ones, or black ones—or who knows? This question can't be answered.

⟨♦️POWER SURGE♦️⟩

Here's a case where ratios are actually music to your ears! Pluck a stretched string and you'll produce a musical sound of a certain pitch. Pluck a shorter string of the same material and thickness and you'll produce a higher pitch. When the ratios between the lengths of the two strings can be expressed with small integers, the pitch interval produced will be a relatively consonant one. Strings of equal lengths—that is, with lengths in a 1-to-1 ratio—sound in "unison," the most consonant interval. Strings whose lengths are in a 2-to-1 ratio make what's called an "octave" (such as C to C'), the second most consonant interval. Strings whose lengths are in a 3-to-2 ratio make what's called a "perfect fifth" (e.g., C to G).

Here are the ratios corresponding to the most consonant intervals, listed in order of decreasing consonance:

unison (C to C)	1:1		major third (C to E)	5:4
octave (C to C')	2:1		minor third (C to Eb)	6:5
perfect fifth (C to G)	3:2		minor sixth (C to Ab)	8:5
perfect fourth (C to F)	4:3		major second (C to D)	9:8
major sixth (C to A)	5:3			

The bigger the numbers in the ratio, the more dissonant the interval. These are the ideal ratios of the so-called "just" scale. Most modern musical instruments use a slight variant called the "even-tempered" scale, which allows them to be played in any key. So now you can "note" how ratios play a very "sound" role in music.

ON TO PROPORTIONS

When you have equal ratios, you have a *proportion*. Because each ratio contains two numbers, a proportion has *four* numbers. When you know three of the numbers in a proportion, you can figure out the fourth because the product of the top number in the first ratio and the bottom number in the second ratio is equal to the product of the bottom number in the first ratio and the top number in the second ratio.

To Solve a Proportion: To solve a proportion, set the two ratios equal and cross-multiply.

Question: The male-female ratio of a legislative committee is equal to the male-female ratio of the entire legislature. There are 34 men and

51 women in the legislature. If there are 4 men on the committee, how many women are on the committee?

Solution: Set the two male-female ratios equal:

$$\frac{\text{males in the legislature}}{\text{females in the legislature}} = \frac{\text{males on the committee}}{\text{females on the committee}}$$

$$\frac{34}{51} = \frac{4}{\text{females on the committee}}$$

Now cross-multiply:

$$34 \times (\text{females on the committee}) = 51 \times 4$$

$$\text{females on the committee} = \frac{51 \times 4}{34} = \frac{204}{34} = 6$$

So, we've divided 34 into 204 and got the result. Remember the line that separates the integers of a fractional or rational relationship, such as the one above, is a line that signifies division of the bottom into the top.

HOW DO YOU RATE?

A *rate* is a special type of ratio. Instead of relating a part to a part, or a part to the whole, a rate relates one kind of quantity to a completely different kind. To be more precise, a rate relates quantities with different units. This lets you put two different units of measure under one convenient stylistic roof.

Rates usually involve the word *per*, as in *miles per hour*, *cost per item*, and so on. Since the word *per* means "for one" or "for each," rates are generally expressed as ratios reduced to a denominator of 1. For example, if you travel at a steady speed and cover 100 miles in 2 hours, then you can say that you are traveling at a rate of $\frac{100}{2} = 50$ miles per hour.

In reality, you can't ever really travel at a steady speed for a couple of hours. There's always some slowing down and speeding up, stopping for bathroom breaks, and passing the slow cars on the right. But if you can still cover 100 miles in 2 hours, you can say that your *average rate* is 50 miles per hour. Rates are frequently described as average rates because they are not always constant.

To say that your average rate is 50 miles per hour says nothing about your rate of speed at any particular moment during the trip. What it does say is that the total distance traveled divided by the total time it took to travel that distance is equal to 50 miles per hour.

To Calculate Rates: Here are a couple of formulas that show you exactly what we're talking about:

$$\text{Average Rate of } A \text{ per } B = \frac{\text{Total } A}{\text{Total } B}$$

$$\text{Average Rate of Speed} = \frac{\text{Total distance}}{\text{Total time}}$$

Question: In the first week of the season, Williams got 5 hits in 10 at bats. In the second week she got 3 hits in 15 at bats. What was her average rate of hits per at bat for the two weeks?

Solution: Her total number of hits is $5 + 3 = 8$, and her total number of at bats is $10 + 15 = 25$. Her average batting rate, then is:

$$\frac{\text{Total hits}}{\text{Total at bats}} = \frac{8}{25} = .320$$

The thing to remember about an average rate is that it isn't equal to the average of the rates! Williams averaged .500 hits per at bat in week 1, and .200 hits per at bat in week 2. If you had tried to answer the question by just averaging those rates, you would have gotten a wrong answer of .350. That method inflates her batting average because it gives as much weight to week 1—when she was hot but had fewer at bats—as to week 2—when she was cool but had more at bats.

Help Harry hurry, and make up for lost time. Read on . . .

Question: Harry is driving 120 miles from Town A to Town B. If he averages 40 miles per hour for the first half of the distance and 60 miles per hour for the second half of the distance, what is his average rate of speed for the whole trip?

Solution: Don't just average the two speeds. To get the average rate of speed, you need divide the total distance of 120 miles by the total time. He drives the first 60 miles at 40 miles per hour, which will take $1\frac{1}{2}$ hours. Then he drives the next 60 miles at 60 miles per-hour, which will take 1 hour. The total time, then, is $2\frac{1}{2}$ hours. Now you can find Harry's average speed:

$$\text{Average Rate of Speed} = \frac{\text{Total distance}}{\text{Total time}} = \frac{120 \text{ miles}}{2.5 \text{ hours}} = 48 \text{ mph}$$

Because Harry spends more time driving at the slower speed—it takes more time to travel 60 miles at 40 mph than it does to travel the same distance at 60 miles per hour—it makes sense that the average speed is somewhat closer to the slower 40 than it is to the faster 60.

Now you're ready to look at chapter 6's Do the Math solution.

DO THE MATH

If you jog halfway from A to B at a steady rate of 2 miles per hour, how fast would you have to run the rest of the way in order to average 4 miles per hour for the entire trip?

Solution: The complication in this question is that no distance is specified. The easiest way to get around that black hole is to pick a number for the total distance. You should pick a number that's easy to work with, like a multiple of 4. Say the total distance is 12 miles. Each half-distance would then be 6 miles. If you jog 6 miles at 2 miles per hour, it will take $6 \div 2 = 3$ hours. To average 4 miles per hour over 12 miles, you have to traverse the whole distance in $12 \div 4 = 3$ hours. But 3 hours have already elapsed and you're only halfway there. You can't do it. Even if you could run the second half at the speed of light, your average rate of speed for the whole trip will be less than 4 miles per hour.

So the answer to the question is that it is impossible! If you thought you could just average separate rates to get an average rate, you would have thought that the answer was 6 miles per hour. But halfway at 2 miles per hour plus halfway at 6 miles per hour does not average out to all the way at 4 miles per hour. In fact, if you were to go 6 miles at 2 miles per hour, followed by 6 miles at 6 miles per hour, the total time would be $3 + 1 = 4$ hours, and your average speed would be $\frac{12}{4} = 3$ miles per hour.

Plug In

You have been invited into the Ratios, Proportions, and Rates Club. The annual dues are $7.50, payable by Visa™, American Express™, Mastercard™, or Discover™. We meet every Friday night at 6:30 at the local Donut Hut (the back dining room has lots of tables we can push together for a really big crowd). You will be sent a complete orientation kit, stating the rules and regulations of the Club. But first—sorry we didn't bring this up earlier—we have some review questions we'd like you to answer before we officially can invite you into the Club. The answers are in the "Plug-In Solutions" section at the back of the book. Good luck—and may the Lucky Ratio be with you!

1. If the ratio of Americans to non-Americans in a group is 4 to 1, what fraction of the people in the group are non-Americans? _____

2. There are fewer than 100 people in the waiting room of Dr. Coldhands. If the ratio of males to females in the waiting room is 5 to 4, and if the ratio of those 21 and older to those under 21 is 4 to 3, how many people are in the room? _____

3. On a certain map, $\frac{1}{4}$ inch represents 1 mile. How many miles are represented by $1\frac{5}{8}$ inches? _____

4. If Skippy's Dodge Duster travels $\frac{1}{100}$ of a kilometer each second, how many kilometers does it travel in 1 hour? _____

5. In the first half of the season, Jones averaged more hits per at bat than Lopez. In the second half of the season, Jones again averaged more hits per at bat than Lopez. For the season as a whole, however, Lopez averaged more hits per at bat than Jones. How can this be?

CHAPTER SEVEN

Permutations and Probability: You'll Probably Read This Chapter

In this chapter we're going to give you some easy formulas to help you deal with some real and basic situations with *permutations* and *probability*. For example, to know how many different combinations of clothing you could wear based on your current wardrobe, check out the example below. Permutations and probability may

~w~**DO THE MATH**~w~

A bag contains 10 balls, each labeled with a different integer from 1 to 10. If 2 balls are drawn from the bag at random, what is the probability that the sum of the integers on the balls drawn will be greater than 6? (See the solution near the end of this chapter.)

sound complex, but they're actually commonsense math knowledge—we bet you'll pick them up quicker than you think!

COUNTING THE POSSIBILITIES

Suppose you have five pairs of pants and seven shirts.

For each pair of pants you have a choice of seven shirts. So you could go one week wearing the same pair of pants and a different shirt each day. Then you could go the next week wearing a second pair of pants and a different shirt each day. Altogether you could go five weeks without ever wearing the same outfit twice—as long as you wash your clothes each week, of course!

Five pairs of pants and seven shirts gives you 5 × 7 = 35 possible outfits. This is the *Fundamental Counting Principle* in action.

The Fundamental Counting Principle: If there are *m* ways one event can happen and *n* ways a second event can happen, then there are *m* × *n* ways for the two events to happen.

Question: A prix fixe menu gives you four choices for the first course, five choices for the second course, and three choices for dessert. How many different three-course meals can you put together?

Solution: Four choices followed by five choices followed by three choices gives you a total of 4 × 5 × 3 = 60 different three-course meals.

PERMUTATIONS—THE BASIC THEME

Suppose you have a row of five chairs and five people to seat in those chairs. Fill the chairs one at a time. You have a choice of five people for the first chair, but once you've seated someone there, that leaves you with a choice of just *four* people for the second chair. Then you have three choices for the third chair, two choices for the fourth chair, and just one choice for the fifth chair. That's a total of $5 \times 4 \times 3 \times 2 \times 1 = 120$. There are 120 ways to arrange five objects in a row—that's 120 permutations.

A *permutation* is an arrangement of objects in a definite order. The number of possible arrangements is called the "number of permutations." To find the number of permutations for any number of objects, find the product of all the positive integers up to and including that number.

Question: A singer wants to perform 12 songs in a recital. In how many different orders can she present the songs?

Solution: The number of permutations of 12 songs is the product of all the positive integers up to and including 12, which is $12 \times 11 \times 10 \times 9 \times 8 \times 7 \times 6 \times 5 \times 4 \times 3 \times 2 \times 1 = 479,001,600$.

The product of all the positive integers up to N is called "N factorial," and it's written with an exclamation point: $N!$ The number of permutations of 12 objects, then, can be written simply as "12!" With this factorial notation you can express the basic permutations formula quite succinctly: The number of permutations of n distinct objects is $n!$

> **MATH LAUGH**
>
> There is a vicious rumor going around that math heads don't have a sense of humor. Let this joke (from a math head) dispel that notion once and for all!
>
> Q. I'm a mathematician who solves an assembly line of permutations. What am I called?
>
> A. A Factorial Worker.

So the basic theme of permutations is the factorial. Now you're ready for some variations.

PERMUTATIONS—VARIATIONS ON THE THEME

Variation #1. Sometimes you will want to arrange objects not in a row, but in a circle. In such a circular permutation, some arrangements are indistinguishable because they are just rotations of the same order. Here are five indistinguishable circular arrangements of the letters A, B, C, D, and E:

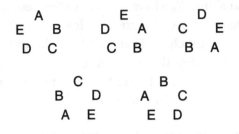

If you were to use the regular permutations formula with five objects, you'd conclude there are "5!" possible arrangements. But every one of those arrangements is indistinguishable from four other rotated versions of the same arrangement. The regular permutations formula yields a result that is five times the correct result. The number of *circular* permutations of five objects is not 5!, but 4!, 24.

To Count Circular Permutations: To find the number of circular permutations of any number of objects, find the product of all the positive integers up to but not including the number itself. The number of circular permutations of n distinct objects is $(n - 1)!$

Question: In how many different orders can 8 people sit in a circle?

Solution: To find the number of circular permutations of 8 objects, plug n = 8 into the formula:

number of circular permutations = $(n - 1)! = (8 - 1)! = 7! =$ 5,040

Variation #2. This variation covers situations when the objects are *not all distinguishable*. Suppose, for example, you wanted to count the number of ways you could rearrange the letters of the word CANADA. The word has six letters, but some of the letters are indistinguishable. If you were to use the regular permutations formula with six objects, you'd conclude there are 6! = 720 possible arrangements. But that would be the answer if you could tell the A's apart. If the A's had identifying subscripts, you could call these rearrangements:

$$C \ A_1 \ N \ A_2 \ D \ A_3$$
$$C \ A_1 \ N \ A_3 \ D \ A_2$$
$$C \ A_2 \ N \ A_1 \ D \ A_3$$
$$C \ A_2 \ N \ A_3 \ D \ A_1$$
$$C \ A_3 \ N \ A_1 \ D \ A_2$$
$$C \ A_3 \ N \ A_2 \ D \ A_1$$

But without the identifying subscripts, these six arrangements really count as only one. The regular permutations formula yields a result that is six times the true result. The true number is $\frac{6!}{6}$, which is $\frac{720}{6} = 120$. When you have any number of indistinguishable objects, find the factorial of the total number of objects, and divide the result by the factorial of the number of indistinguishable objects.

To Count Permutations with Indistinguishables: The number of permutations of n objects, a of which are indistinguishable, is $\frac{n!}{a!}$

Question: How many five-digit positive integers can you construct using the digits 1, 1, 2, 3, and 4?

Solution: You have five objects, two of which are indistinguishable, so use the appropriate formula and plug in $n = 5$ and $a = 2$:

$$\text{number of permutations} = \frac{n!}{a!} = \frac{5!}{2!} = 60$$

Variation #3. Permutations get trickier when you have *more objects than slots to fill.* Suppose, for example, you had to choose, from a committee of 10 people, one person to be president, one person to be vice president, and one person to be secretary. How many ways are there to fill those positions? You have 10 people, but $10! = 3,628,800$ is way too large. That would be the answer if you had ten slots to fill—you have only three.

You might think $3! = 6$ would be the answer, but that's way too small. You don't have just three choices for one officer, two for the next, and one for the last. You have, in fact, 10 choices for president, and then 9 choices for vice president, and then 8 choices for secretary, and therefore $10 \times 9 \times 8 = 720$ ways to fill the three positions.

To find the number of permutations of any number of objects taken a smaller number at a time, you start multiplying consecutive integers starting with the larger number, but you stop when the number of factors is equal to the smaller number. This sounds complicated when put into words. The formula is easier. The number of permutations of *n* objects taken *r* at a time is:

$$\frac{n!}{(n-r)!}$$

Variation #4. On the further adventures of "Fun with Permutations," you reach another variation when you're not filling distinct slots, but just *taking subgroups*. Suppose all you wanted to do was select a three-member subcommittee from the committee of 10. Are there 720 different ways to do that, too? No, there are not so many ways, because this time the order doesn't matter. When filling three distinct positions, these count as six possibilities:

1. Chris, president   Leslie, vice president   Robin, secretary
2. Chris, president   Robin, vice president   Leslie, secretary
3. Leslie, president   Chris, vice president   Robin, secretary
4. Leslie, president   Robin, vice president   Chris, secretary
5. Robin, president   Chris, vice president   Leslie, secretary
6. Robin, president   Leslie, vice president   Chris, secretary

When making a subcommittee, however, all of the following are indistinguishable versions of just one possibility:

Chris, Leslie, Robin

Chris, Robin, Leslie

Leslie, Chris, Robin

Leslie, Robin, Chris

Robin, Chris, Leslie

Robin, Leslie, Chris

When you're making subcommittees—as opposed to filling positions—what you're counting is not permutations but combinations. A *combination* is a subgroup of a larger group, with no regard to order. As you can see, in the case of a three-member subcommittee from a committee of ten, the permutations formula for a number of objects taken a smaller number at a time yields a result that will be six times too big. When order is irrelevant, you have to divide the number of permutations by the factorial of the number of objects you're putting in the subgroup.

To Count Combinations: The number of combinations of n objects taken r at a time is $\dfrac{n!}{(n-r)!r!}$

Question: Mario wants to make a soup with exactly 5 different vegetables and 3 different herbs. If he has 12 vegetables and 6 herbs to choose from, how many different soups can he make?

Solution: Order doesn't matter here. It all becomes soup. So this is a combinations question. First figure out the number of combinations of 12 vegetables taken 5 at a time:

$$\frac{n!}{(n-r)!r!} = \frac{12!}{(12-5)!5!} = 792$$

Then figure out the number of combinations of 6 herbs taken 3 at a time:

$$\frac{n!}{(n-r)!r!} = \frac{6!}{(6-3)!3!} = 20$$

For each of the 792 vegetable combinations there are 20 herb combinations, so the total number of possible soups will be the product of 792 and 20, or 15,840.

PROBABILITY—THE BASIC THEME

Once you know how to count the possibilities, you're ready to calculate probabilities. *Probability* is a numerical representation of the likelihood of an event or combination of events. Probabilities range from 0 to 1. When the probability of an event is 0, that means the event is impossible. When the probability is 1, that means the event is certain to happen. A very small probability, such as "one in a million," $\frac{1}{1,000,000}$, means the event is highly unlikely. A probability greater than $\frac{1}{2}$ means the event is more likely than not.

To calculate the probability of an event, you need to know two things. The first is how many different ways the event you're concerned with can happen. Each of those ways is called a *favorable outcome*. The second thing you need to know is the total number of possible outcomes, favorable or otherwise.

Suppose you have twelve slips of paper in a hat. On each slip of paper is written the name of a different contestant. Three of the contestants are members of the Wong family. A slip of paper is selected at random. In considering the probability that the selected slip of paper will be a Wong, there are three favorable outcomes and twelve total possible outcomes. To get the probability, you divide the favorable by the total: 3 divided by 12 is $\frac{1}{4}$ or 0.25. The probability that the slip of paper will be a Wong is $\frac{1}{4}$ or 0.25. (You could also say the probability is 25%.)

To Calculate Probability: Here's the handy formula:

$$\text{Probability} = \frac{\text{Number of favorable outcomes}}{\text{Total number of possible outcomes}}$$

Question: If you draw a card at random from a regular 52-card deck, what is the probability that it will be a face card?

Solution: The number of favorable outcomes is the number of face cards. That's four kings, four queens, and four jacks, for a total of 12 face cards. The total number of possibilities is 52—the number of cards in the deck. The probability of drawing a face card is 12 out of 52, or $\frac{12}{52}$, which reduces to $\frac{3}{13}$.

PROBABILITY—VARIATIONS ON THE THEME

When you know the probability that some event will happen, it's just one easy step to figure out the probability that the event will not happen. It is certain that either the event will happen or it won't, so the two probabilities add up to 1. If the probability of winning a certain contest is $\frac{1}{24}$, then the probability of not winning is $\frac{23}{24}$. If there's a 30 percent chance of rain, then there's a 70 percent chance it will not rain.

To Calculate "Not" Probabilities: If the probability that a certain event will occur is a, the probability that it will *not* occur is $1 - a$.

When you know the separate probabilities of two independent events, you can easily find the probability that *both* events will occur—you multiply.

To Find Concurrent Probabilities: If the probability that one event will occur is a, and the independent probability that another event will occur is b, the probability that both events will occur is ab.

Question: There's a 70 percent probability that it will rain today in New York. There's also a 70 percent probability that it will rain today in Tokyo. What is the percent probability that it will rain today in both New York and Tokyo?

Solution: Assuming that whether it will rain in New York today has nothing to do with whether it will rain in Tokyo—in other words, that the probabilities are independent—the probability that both wet events will occur is the product of the separate probabilities. To multiply percents, you first have to convert them to something mathematically more useful, like decimals:

$$70\% \times 70\% = 0.70 \times 0.70 = 0.49 = 49\%$$

When there's a 49 percent probability that it will rain in both New York and Tokyo, you can say that it's more likely—there's a 51 percent probability—that it will *not* rain in both cities. That's *not* the same thing as saying that it's 51 percent likely that it will rain in *neither* city. It's 51 percent likely that it will rain in either New York only or in Tokyo only . . . or in neither. To find the probability that it will rain in neither city, you need to start with the separate probabilities that it will not rain.

Question: There's a 70 percent probability that it will rain today in New York. There's also a 70 percent probability that it will rain today in Tokyo. What is the percent probability that it will rain today in neither New York nor Tokyo?

Solution: If there's a 70 percent probability that it will rain today in one city, then there's a 30 percent probability that it will *not* rain. Two 30 percent probabilities combine to make a much smaller joint probability:

$$30\% \times 30\% = 0.30 \times 0.30 = 0.09 = 9\%$$

Now you're ready to look at the Do the Math solution.

DO THE MATH

A bag contains 10 balls, each labeled with a different integer from 1 to 10. If 2 balls are drawn from the bag at random, what is the probability that the sum of the integers on the balls drawn will be greater than 6?

Solution: To find the probability, you need to know the number of favorable outcomes and the total number of possible outcomes. The latter is the number of combinations of 10 items taken 2 at a time:

$$\text{number of combinations} = \frac{10!}{(10-2)!2!} = \frac{10 \times 9}{2} = 45$$

To find the number of favorable outcomes, it's easiest to find the number of unfavorable outcomes—that is, where the numbers add up to 6 or less—by listing and counting them. These are the only unfavorable outcomes:

1 and 2	1 and 5
1 and 3	2 and 3
1 and 4	2 and 4

That's 6 unfavorable outcomes. All the other $45 - 6 = 39$ outcomes are favorable, and the probability you're looking for is $\frac{39}{45} = \frac{13}{15}$.

Plug In

What's the probability that you are now contemplating becoming a serious math head after reading this chapter? Have you considered the many distinctly different ways you could rearrange your life in order to devote more time to the study of mathematics? Perhaps you could take that TV correspondence course in "Radio Repairs and Permutations." Before you scoff, test yourself on these review questions—you may be brimming with math power! The answers are in the "Plug-In Solutions" section at the back of the book.

1. How many distinct ways are there to arrange the letters in the word OHIO? _____

2. How many ways are there to seat six people in a circle? _____

3. How many ways are there to seat five people in a row of six chairs?

    _____

4. If you toss a fair coin five times in succession and it comes up heads every time, what's more likely on the sixth toss: heads or tails?

    _____

5. A bag contains 10 balls, each labeled with a different integer from 1 to 10. If 2 balls are drawn from the bag at random, what's more likely to be the sum of the numbers on the balls drawn: 10 or 13? _____

Exponents and Roots: Get the Power and Get Radical

So, you think you've got this math stuff? Ready to impress your friends, parents, and potential dates by reducing fractions in a single bound? Can you break down the prime factorization of 3,293 like it was *no big deal*?

〜〜〜●**DO THE MATH**●〜〜〜

Which is greater, $\sqrt{999^5 \times 999^2}$ or $\sqrt[3]{(999^5)^2}$? (See the solution near the end of this chapter.)

Well, get ready to test your limits again, because in the next few chapters, we're going to pump up the volume a notch and take you one step further, into the realm of the unreal, the complex, the exponential—the algebraic even.

That's right. Just when you thought it was safe to turn to the next chapter: We're starting to get into algebra. But don't start palpitating just yet, we're going to take it slow at first; this chapter just scratches the surface with *exponents* and *radicals*. By the end of chapter 9 you'll be juggling variables like a pro.

SUBSCRIPTS AND SUPERSCRIPTS

Math gets more complicated when subscripts and superscripts start to creep in. But, as you've probably noticed in your math travels, what happens when you attach a little *sub*script number is very different from the effect of attaching a *super*script number.

Oh, yeah. Just so you don't forget, *sub-scripts* are the little numbers that go *below* the variable you're working with, and *superscripts* go *above*.

CONNECTION

To improve your math power, connect with the "permutations of CANADA" material in chapter 7.

Subscript numbers don't do anything mathematically; they just work like little yellow sticky notes, letting you tell the difference between two items that look alike. It's like a math head game show, and they have to keep track of what's behind "Door #1, Door #2, and Door #3." In the last chapter, for instance, we used subscripts when we wanted to distinguish the A's in the word CANADA:

$$C \, A_1 \, N \, A_2 \, D \, A_3$$

Superscripts are something completely different. Attaching a little superscript number can amp up the power considerably.

INTRODUCING . . . THE EXPONENTS!

These little numbers are called *exponents*, and when you attach an exponent to something, you're indicating the product of that many of those things. So, when you attach an exponent of 6 to 3, it represents the product of 6 factors of 3:

$$3^6 = 3 \times 3 \times 3 \times 3 \times 3 \times 3$$

You say 3^6 as "3 raised to an exponent of 6," or most simply, "3 to the 6th." The expression 3^6 is called a power. 3 is the base and 6 is the exponent. In general, b^n is a power, b is the base, and n is the exponent. When the exponent is 2, you could say "to the 2nd," but it's much more common to say "squared." And when the exponent is 3, it's more common to say "cubed."

Less is More

You have to be extra careful when you mix minus signs and exponents. Here's why. Take a look at this easy-to-confuse expression:

$$-5^2$$

At first, it looks like the square of negative 5, or negative 5 times itself, which would be +25. In fact, it's just the opposite—it's the negative of the square of 5, which is –25. The exponent should be understood to apply only to the 5, not to the minus sign. What this means—in English—is that you're supposed to do the multiplication first, then add the minus sign.

Got it? If the writer had wanted you to apply the minus sign before the exponent, she would have written the expression like so:

$$(-5)^2 = (-5) \times (-5) = 25$$

But without the parentheses, you apply the exponent first:

$$-5^2 = -(5 \times 5) = -25$$

FOLLOW THE RULES

There are a whole ton of rules about when to add, subtract, multiply, and divide exponents, but like most of us, you probably find them hard to keep straight.

As we get into the wonderful (yeah, right) world of algebra, you'll want to be solid enough with exponents to whip them off without breaking a sweat. And if you aren't sure you remember a rule correctly, we'll show you how to reconstruct it in your mind.

It's Basically the Same

Suppose you wanted to multiply 3^6 and 3^4. If you have all the time in the world, you could do it this way:

$$3^6 \text{ times } 3^4 = 3 \times 3 \times 3 \times 3 \times 3 \times 3 \text{ times } 3 \times 3 \times 3 \times 3$$
$$= 3 \times 3 \times 3 \times 3 \times 3 \times 3 \times 3 \times 3 \times 3 \times 3$$

That's the product of ten 3's, which can of course be written 3^{10}. But check this out! The new exponent, 10, is the *sum* of the original exponents 6 and 4; and that takes a lot less time to figure out than all that multiplying.

So the general rule is as follows.

To Multiply Powers with the Same Base: Add the exponents and keep the same base.

Question: Express the product of 5^{25} and 5^4 as a power of 5.

Solution: Add the exponents and keep the same base:

$$5^{25} \times 5^4 = 5^{25+4} = 5^{29}$$

Divide and Conquer

So far so good? Good. Now suppose you wanted to *divide* powers with the same base, like dividing 3^6 by 3^4. You could do it this way:

$$3^6 \text{ divided by } 3^4 = \frac{3 \times 3 \times 3 \times 3 \times 3 \times 3}{3 \times 3 \times 3 \times 3}$$

Cancel the four factors of 3 that the numerator and denominator have in common, which would leave you with 3×3, which can be written 3^2. Notice that the new exponent, 2, is the positive *difference* between the original exponents 6 and 4.

To Divide Powers with the Same Base: *Subtract* the exponents and keep the same base.

Question: What is 7^{21} divided by 7^7 expressed as a power with a base of 7?

Solution: Subtract the exponents and keep the same base:

$$7^{21} \div 7^7 = 7^{21-7} = 7^{14}$$

Power Raised to an Exponent

Still with us? Excellent! Now suppose you wanted to take 3^6 and raise it to the exponent 4 (raising a power to an exponent). You could do it this way:

$$(3^6)^4 = 3 \times 3 \times 3 \times 3 \times 3 \times 3 \text{ times } 3 \times 3 \times 3 \times 3 \times 3 \times 3 \text{ times } 3 \times 3 \times 3 \times$$
$$3 \times 3 \times 3 \text{ times } 3 \times 3 \times 3 \times 3 \times 3 \times 3$$

$$= 3 \times 3 \times 3 \times 3 \times 3 \times 3 \times 3 \times 3 \times 3 \times 3 \times 3 \times 3 \times 3 \times 3 \times 3 \times 3 \times 3 \times 3 \times$$
$$3 \times 3 \times 3 \times 3 \times 3 \times 3$$

That's the product of twenty-four 3's, which can of course be written 3^{24}. But that was a pretty exhausting process, and it looks a little silly, too. Notice that the new exponent, 24, is the *product* of the original exponents 6 and 4. Can you tell we've got a new rule coming up?

To Raise a Power to an Exponent: *Multiply* the exponents.

Question: Express 16^3 as a power of 2.

Solution: Re-express 16 as 2^4:

$$16^3 = (2^4)^3$$

Now it's a power raised to an exponent, so multiply the exponents:

$$(2^4)^3 = 2^{4 \times 3} = 2^{12}$$

This stuff is pretty easy, right?

Power, Power, Power to Spare

And finally, since you're doing so well, let's say you wanted to multiply powers with the same exponent, like 3^6 and 4^6. You could do it this way:

$$3^6 \times 4^6 = 3 \times 3 \times 3 \times 3 \times 3 \times 3 \times 4 \times 4 \times 4 \times 4 \times 4 \times 4$$
$$= (3 \times 4) \times (3 \times 4) \times (3 \times 4) \times (3 \times 4) \times (3 \times 4) \times (3 \times 4)$$

That's the same as the product of six 12's:

$$12^6 = (3 \times 4) \times (3 \times 4) \times (3 \times 4) \times (3 \times 4) \times (3 \times 4) \times (3 \times 4)$$
$$= 12 \times 12 \times 12 \times 12 \times 12 \times 12 = 12^6$$

Notice that the *base*, 12, is the product of the original bases 4 and 3. So the general rule is . . .

To Multiply Powers with the Same Exponent: Multiply the bases and attach the same exponent.

Question: Express the product of 4^5 and 9^5 as a power of 6.

Solution: Because 4^5 and 9^5 have the same exponent, their product is the product of 4 and 9 with that same exponent:

$$4^5 \times 9^5 = (4 \times 9)^5 = 36^5$$

Now, re-express the 36 as 6^2:

$$36^5 = (6^2)^5 = 6^{2 \times 5} = 6^{10}$$

GOOD FOR NOTHING

From the basic rules of exponents we just covered, you can work out the meanings of zero, negative, and fractional exponents. First look at the *zero exponent*. What is the meaning of 3^0? You might think, "Who cares," or "That's easy—3^0 equals 0." Sorry, but it's not that simple; keep reading.

Let's say you have to divide 3^6 by 3^6. According to the rule for dividing powers, you'd subtract the exponents:

$$3^6 \div 3^6 = 3^{6-6} = 3^0$$

To Work with the Zero Exponent: Any nonzero number raised to an exponent of 0 equals 1.

As you already know, if you divide a number by itself, you get 1. So 3^0, or almost any number—except zero—raised to an exponent of 0 equals 1. 0^0 is *undefined*.

⚡ POWER SURGE ⚡

Why should 0^0 be undefined? It's a classic impasse. One general rule says that 0 raised to any exponent is 0:

$$0^1 = 0, \text{ and } 0^2 = 0, \text{ and } 0^3 = 0$$

Another general rule says that any number raised to an exponent of 0 is 1:

$$1^0 = 1, \text{ and } 2^0 = 1, \text{ and } 3^0 = 1$$

So, which rule applies in the case of 0^0? There's no good reason to think that one of these rules takes precedence over the other. Instead, math heads just scratch their heads and wonder, and say that 0^0, just like $\frac{0}{0}$, is *undefined*.

TAKING A NEGATIVE ATTITUDE

Suppose you wanted to divide 3^4 by 3^6. You could do it the long way:

$$3^4 \text{ divided by } 3^6 = \frac{3 \times 3 \times 3 \times 3}{3 \times 3 \times 3 \times 3 \times 3 \times 3}$$

After getting rid of the four factors of 3 that the numerator and denominator have in common, you'd have:

$$\frac{1}{3 \times 3}$$

Which can also be written as $\frac{1}{3^2}$. If you subtract the original exponents, you get $4 - 6 = -2$. So it makes sense to say that $3^{-2} = \frac{1}{3^2}$, and to say that, where defined, a number raised to a *negative exponent* means the reciprocal of the corresponding positive exponent.

To Raise a Number to a Negative Exponent: A number raised to a negative exponent is equal to the reciprocal of the number raised to the opposite, or positive, exponent.

ⵗⴸⵗ **SPARK** ⵗⴸⵗ

A lot of us have an image of the quintessential math head: a guy with a pocket-protector full of pens, tape on his eyeglasses, and hair that should have been washed a couple of days ago. In fact, since the 16th century and before, there have been hundreds of discoveries, formulas, and theories that have been made by powerful, heroic *women*. Often they had to overcome nearly unbeatable societal (not to mention mathematical) odds just to do their work! If you want to find out about the history of women who've amped up their math power, check out the Website devoted just to them: http://www.agnesscott.edu/lriddle/women.htm

Question: $100^0 \div 10^{-2} = ?$

Solution: As you already know, any nonzero number raised to an exponent of 0 equals 1, so $100^0 = 1$. And a negative exponent means the reciprocal of a positive exponent, so $10^{-2} = \frac{1}{10^2} = \frac{1}{100}$. Now all you've got to do is divide by a fraction, which we're sure you're a whiz at by now:

$$100^0 \div 100^{-2} = 1 \div \frac{1}{100} = 1 \times \frac{100}{1} = 100$$

All that math just to get to a hundred—don't you wish math heads would find something better to do with their time!

A PIECE OF THE POWER

Now let's look at fractional exponents. Think about what $3^{\frac{1}{2}}$ might mean. If you were to raise that power to an exponent of 2, you would multiply the exponents:

$$\left(3^{\frac{1}{2}}\right)^2 = 3^{\frac{1}{2} \times 2} = 3^1 = 3$$

So $3^{\frac{1}{2}}$ is a number that squared equals 3—in other words, $3^{\frac{1}{2}}$ is equal to $\sqrt{3}$. Similarly $3^{\frac{1}{3}}$ is equal to $\sqrt[3]{3}$, and $3^{\frac{1}{4}}$ is equal to $\sqrt[4]{3}$.

To Work with a Fractional Exponent (Part 1): A number raised to an exponent of 1 over n is equal to the nth root of that number.

Now let's dig a little deeper. Consider what $3^{\frac{3}{2}}$ might mean. If you were to raise that power to an exponent of 2, you would multiply the exponents:

$$\left(3^{\frac{3}{2}}\right)^2 = 3^{\frac{3}{2} \times 2} = 3^3$$

So you can think of $3^{\frac{3}{2}}$ as either the square root of 3 cubed or the cube of the square root of 3—they're the same.

To Work with Fractional Exponents (Part 2): A number raised to an exponent of *a* over *b* is equal to the *bth* root of that number raised to an exponent of *a*.

FORMULAS FOR SUCCESS: EXPRESSING THE RULES OF EXPONENTS ALGEBRAICALLY

As you can see from what we've just been doing, the rules for working with exponents can take you longer to express in words than it took to do the math in the first place. Here's the short version, the same rules, in the same order we just learned them, but this time expressed *algebraically*.

To Work with Exponents: Our advice to you: Memorize these formulas!

Rule: Multiplying powers with the same base
Formula: $x^a \times x^b = x^{a+b}$

Rule: Dividing powers with the same base

Formula: $x^a \div x^b = x^{a-b}$

Rule: Raising a power to an exponent

Formula: $(x^a)^b = x^{ab}$

Rule: Multiplying powers with the same exponent

Formula: $(x^a)(y^a) = (xy)^a$

Rule: The zero exponent

Formula: $x^0 = 1 \ (x \neq 0)$

Rule: Negative exponents

Formula: $x^{-1} = \dfrac{1}{x} \ (x \neq 0)$

Formula: $x^{-a} = \dfrac{1}{x^a} \ (x \neq 0)$

Rule: Fractional exponents:

Formula: $x^{\frac{a}{b}} = \sqrt[b]{x^a} = \left(\sqrt[b]{x}\right)^a \ (x \geq 0)$

Still a little foggy? You can make the connection by rereading the section that corresponds to one of the rules above, then flipping back to the formula, until it makes sense. Trust us, a little extra sweat now will give your math know-how a powerful glow very soon.

LEARNING TO GET RADICAL!

No, we're not going to teach you to skateboard a half-pipe upside down. But this section does involve its own kind of backflip. Right now, we're going to cover the *reverse* of the exponent otherwise known as the *radical*—that symbol that looks like a cross between a checkmark and a long-division sign: $\sqrt{}$. The big number under the radical is the number you want the root of, and the little number inside the crook of the radical tells you which root you want. For example, $\sqrt[5]{243}$, which you read as "the 5th root of 243," represents the number that raised to an exponent of 5 equals 243. That number is 3 because $3^5 = 3 \times 3 \times 3 \times 3 \times 3 = 243$, so $\sqrt[5]{243} = 3$.

When there is no little number in the crook of the radical, a 2 is understood, as in $\sqrt{100}$, which can be read as "the *square root* of 100."

AVOID VAGUE ROOTS

When math heads first thought up the concept of the radical—finding the root of a number—they quickly ran into some confusing turf, particularly with the even roots. Take $\sqrt{100}$, for instance. That's the number that, squared, equals 100. Easy enough, right? Not so fast! The problem is that there are two such numbers—not just 10, but also –10. Positive numbers all have two real square roots, two real fourth roots, two real sixth roots, and so on. In every case the two roots are identical, except that one is positive and one is negative.

And if you go deeper, into *complex* numbers, *all* roots pose potential ambiguities in that every number (except 0) has two complex square roots, three complex cube roots, four complex fourth roots, five complex fifth roots, and so on. This can make an unsuspecting math student's head spin.

Luckily, math heads want to keep things simple, too. So they decided at some point to say that the radical represents what is called the *principal* root. Still, they had to define the principal root in two different ways, one way for even roots (like the square root and the fourth root) and another way for odd roots (like the cube root and the fifth root).

To Find the Principal Root of Even Roots: The principal root of even roots is the non-negative real root. Both 10 and –10 will give you 100 when they're squared, but only 10 is the *principal root*. And so, by convention, $\sqrt{100} = 10$. If you wanted to use the radical to represent the other square root, you'd put a minus sign in front *of the radical*: $-\sqrt{100} = -10$.

To Find the Principal Root of Odd Roots: The principal root of odd roots is the one real root. An odd root of a positive number is positive ($\sqrt[5]{32} = 2$, for example), and an odd root of a negative number is negative; or in this case, you put the minus sign in front *of the number* ($\sqrt[5]{-32} = -2$, for example).

For the rest of this chapter, we're going to go easy on you; we're just going to deal with principal roots.

Question: $-\sqrt{36} = ?$

Solution: The principal square root of 36 is 6. The opposite of that is –6.

Question: $\sqrt[13]{-1} = ?$

Solution: When you raise –1 to any odd exponent, you get –1. Therefore, an odd root of –1—*any* odd root of –1—will be –1.

IT'S HIP TO BE SQUARE

Like the rules of exponents, the rules of square roots are easiest to remember when you have an understanding of their derivation and their consistency. Put in plain lingo, it means figuring out where they come from, and what makes them tick. It may look confusing at first, but our Magical Mystery Tour of Square Roots is pretty easy to follow. Trust us; we care.

Let's take a couple of square roots and see what we can do with them. What, for example, is the *sum* of $\sqrt{2}$ and $\sqrt{3}$? Is it the same as $\sqrt{2+3}$? To test that hypothesis, take a couple of square roots whose value you know—say, $\sqrt{4}$ and $\sqrt{9}$. Do they add up to $\sqrt{4+9}$?

$$\sqrt{4} + \sqrt{9} \stackrel{?}{=} \sqrt{4+9}$$

$$2 + 3 \stackrel{?}{=} \sqrt{13}$$

$$5 \stackrel{?}{=} \sqrt{13}$$

No, unfortunately, 5 is *not* equal to $\sqrt{13}$. There is no more concise way to write $\sqrt{2} + \sqrt{3}$.

To Find the Sum of Square Roots: The sum of square roots is not the same as the square root of the sum. You can add square roots only if what's inside the radical signs is the same. For example:

$$\sqrt{2} + \sqrt{2} = 2\sqrt{2}$$

Notice that what's inside the radical doesn't change. Addition has no effect on what's inside the radical. The same goes for subtraction.

Times and Times Again

So, can you multiply square roots, if you cannot normally combine square roots by addition or subtraction? Is $\sqrt{2}$ times $\sqrt{3}$ equal to $\sqrt{2 \times 3}$? Again, let's check it out like we did before, with $\sqrt{4}$ and $\sqrt{9}$. Is their *product* equal to $\sqrt{4 \times 9}$?

$$\sqrt{4} \times \sqrt{9} \overset{?}{=} \sqrt{4 \times 9}$$

$$2 \times 3 \overset{?}{=} \sqrt{36}$$

$$6 \overset{?}{=} 6$$

Yes, they are equal. The product of $\sqrt{4}$ and $\sqrt{9}$ is equal to $\sqrt{4 + 9}$. Similarly, the product of $\sqrt{2}$ and $\sqrt{3}$ equal to $\sqrt{2 \times 3}$, and in general, the product of square roots is equal to the square root of the product. Who'd have thought: The math heads made this one easy! So, don't you feel a rule coming on?

To Combine Square Roots by Multiplication: The product of square roots is equal to the square root of the product.

Question: Express the product of $\sqrt{5}$ and $\sqrt{6}$ as a single square root.

Solution: The product of $\sqrt{5}$ and $\sqrt{6}$ is equal to the square root of 5 times 6:

$$\sqrt{5} \times \sqrt{6} = \sqrt{5 \times 6} = \sqrt{30}$$

Keeping It Simple

Suppose you wanted to simplify $\sqrt{108}$. To simplify any square root, you would re-express the number inside the radical as a product of a perfect square and something else. You can re-express 108 as the product of 4 and 27:

$$\sqrt{108} = \sqrt{4 \times 27} = \sqrt{4} \times \sqrt{27} = 2\sqrt{27}$$

You can do more, because the 27 inside the radical is a multiple of another perfect square, 9:

$$2\sqrt{27} = 2\sqrt{9 \times 3} = 2 \times \sqrt{9} \times \sqrt{3} = 2 \times 3 \times \sqrt{3} = 6\sqrt{3}$$

You're finished when the number inside the radical has no perfect square factors greater than 1.

To Simplify a Square Root: Factor out the perfect squares under the radical, unsquare them, and put the result in front.

Question: Simplify $\sqrt{68}$.

Solution: You can factor out a perfect square of 4 and re-express 68 as 4×17:

$$\sqrt{68} = \sqrt{4 \times 17}$$

Now, because the square root of a product is equal to the product of the square roots, you can break this square root apart and unsquare the perfect square:

$$\sqrt{4 \times 17} = \sqrt{4} \times \sqrt{17} = 2\sqrt{17}$$

A number written in front of the radical, like the 2 in $2\sqrt{17}$, is called a *coefficient*. To multiply square root expressions that include coefficients, you multiply the coefficients and the square roots separately. For instance, if you wanted to multiply $5\sqrt{2}$ and $4\sqrt{3}$, you'd multiply the 5 and the 4 to get the new coefficient 20, and you'd multiply the $\sqrt{2}$ and $\sqrt{3}$ to get the new radical part of $\sqrt{6}$:

$$5\sqrt{2} \times 4\sqrt{3} = (5 \times 4)(\sqrt{2} \times \sqrt{3}) = 20\sqrt{6}$$

To Multiply Square Root Expressions with Coefficients: Multiply the coefficients to get the new coefficient, and multiply the square roots to get the new square root. It's that easy.

Question: What is the product of $2\sqrt{6}$ and $3\sqrt{2}$?

Solution: Multiply the coefficients and the square roots separately:

$$2\sqrt{6} \times 3\sqrt{2} = (2 \times 3)(\sqrt{6} \times \sqrt{2}) = 6\sqrt{12}$$

This product can be expressed more simply. The 12 inside the radical has a perfect square factor, 4:

$$6\sqrt{12} = 6\sqrt{4 \times 3} = 6\sqrt{4} \times \sqrt{3} = 6 \times 2 \times \sqrt{3} = 12\sqrt{3}$$

Division Is a Snap

Dividing square roots is just as easy as multiplying them. The idea is much the same: The quotient of square roots is equal to the square root of the quotient. And if there are any coefficients, you just divide the coefficients and the square roots separately.

To Find the Quotient of Square Roots: The quotient of square roots is equal to the square root of the quotient.

Question: $\sqrt{6} \div \sqrt{3} = ?$

Solution: The quotient of $\sqrt{6}$ and $\sqrt{3}$ is equal to the square root of $6 \div 3$:
$$\sqrt{6} \div \sqrt{3} = \sqrt{6 \div 3} = \sqrt{2}$$

Question: $\dfrac{\sqrt{14}}{\sqrt{2}} =$

Solution: A fraction bar is the same thing as a division symbol. The quotient of $\sqrt{14}$ and $\sqrt{2}$ is equal to the square root of $14 \div 2$:
$$\frac{\sqrt{14}}{\sqrt{2}} = \sqrt{\frac{14}{2}} = \sqrt{7}$$

To Divide Square Root Expressions with Coefficients: When you need to divide square root expressions with coefficients, divide the coefficients to get the new coefficient, and divide the square roots to get the new square root.

Question: $10\sqrt{6} \div 5\sqrt{3} = ?$

Solution: Divide the coefficients, 10 and 5, to get the new coefficient, 2, and divide the square roots, $\sqrt{6}$ and $\sqrt{3}$, to get the new square root, $\sqrt{2}$:

$$10\sqrt{6} \div 5\sqrt{3} = (10 \div 5)(\sqrt{6} \div \sqrt{3}) = 2\sqrt{2}$$

Question: $\dfrac{12\sqrt{10}}{10\sqrt{6}} = ?$

Solution: This time the coefficients and square roots don't divide so neatly. The 12 over 10 you can reduce to 6 over 5, and the $\sqrt{10}$ over $\sqrt{6}$ you can reduce to $\sqrt{5}$ over $\sqrt{3}$:

$$\frac{12\sqrt{10}}{10\sqrt{6}} = \frac{6\sqrt{5}}{5\sqrt{3}}$$

One Big Rationalization

A self-respecting math head would not normally leave the answer $\dfrac{6\sqrt{5}}{5\sqrt{3}}$ in this form, because it has a square root in the denominator. There's nothing taboo about radicals in denominators—they're just not pretty, at least not to the eye of a math head. When you end up with such an answer, you generally want to *rationalize the denominator*. No, it's not some new head-shrinking technique, it just means you have to re-express the answer so there's no radical in the denominator.

To rationalize the denominator of a fraction, multiply the top and bottom of the fraction by the same number, which will not change the fraction's value. The number to multiply by is the number that will eliminate any radicals you see in the denominator. In the case of $\dfrac{6\sqrt{5}}{5\sqrt{3}}$, that number is $\sqrt{3}$:

$$\frac{6\sqrt{5}}{5\sqrt{3}} = \frac{6\sqrt{5} \times \sqrt{3}}{5\sqrt{3} \times \sqrt{3}} = \frac{6\sqrt{15}}{5 \times 3} = \frac{6\sqrt{15}}{15} = \frac{2\sqrt{15}}{15}$$

To Rationalize the Denominator of a Fraction: Just multiply the numerator and denominator by the radical or radical expression that will eliminate any radicals in the denominator.

Question: Rationalize the denominator of $\dfrac{10}{\sqrt{5}}$.

Solution: Multiply the top and bottom by $\sqrt{5}$:

$$\frac{10}{\sqrt{5}} = \frac{10 \times \sqrt{5}}{\sqrt{5} \times \sqrt{5}} = \frac{10\sqrt{5}}{5} = 2\sqrt{5}$$

Feel the Mighty Powers of Square Roots Raised to Exponents

Raising square roots to exponents is just as easy as multiplying and dividing them. The rule can be stated just as simply.

To Find a Square Root Raised to an Exponent: A square root is equal to the square root of the number under the radical sign raised to that exponent.

Question: $(\sqrt{3})^5 = ?$

Solution: $\sqrt{3}$ raised to the exponent 5 is equal to the square root of 3^5:

$$(\sqrt{3})^5 = \sqrt{3^5}$$

If you rewrite 3^5 as $3^2 \times 3^2 \times 3$, you can simplify the square root:

$$\begin{aligned}
\sqrt{3^5} &= \sqrt{3^2 \times 3^2 \times 3} \\
&= \sqrt{3^2} \times \sqrt{3^2} \times \sqrt{3} \\
&= 3 \times 3 \times \sqrt{3} \\
&= 9\sqrt{3}
\end{aligned}$$

EXPRESS YOUR SQUARENESS

Here are all the same rules for operations with square roots that we've just been working on, this time expressed in the fabulous language of algebra.

To Work with Square Roots: Our advice to you: Memorize these formulas!

Rule: Multiplying square roots
Formula: $\sqrt{a} \times \sqrt{b} = \sqrt{ab}$

Rule: Multiplying square roots with coefficients
Formula: $a\sqrt{b} \times c\sqrt{d} = ac\sqrt{bd}$

Rule: Dividing square roots

Formula: $\dfrac{\sqrt{a}}{\sqrt{b}} = \sqrt{\dfrac{a}{b}}$

Rule: Dividing square roots with coefficients

Formula: $\dfrac{a\sqrt{b}}{c\sqrt{d}} = \dfrac{a}{c}\sqrt{\dfrac{b}{d}}$

Rule: The power of a square root

Formula: $(\sqrt{a})^b = \sqrt{a^b}$

Radicals Rule (or Radical Rules)

The rules of multiplication and division of square roots apply to *all* radicals. The product of cube roots is equal to the cube root of the product; the product of fourth roots is equal to the fourth root of the product; and so on. Those math heads must've taken an early lunch on the day they made this stuff up; it's too easy!

To Find the Product of Radicals (of the Same Degree): The product of radicals is equal to the radical of the product.

Question: $\sqrt[5]{40} \times \sqrt[5]{3} = ?$

Solution: The product of fifth roots is equal to the fifth root of the product:

$$\sqrt[5]{40} \times \sqrt[5]{3} = \sqrt[5]{40 \times 3} = \sqrt[5]{120}$$

What you should *not* try to do is multiply radicals of different degrees. You cannot, for example, express the product of a square root and a cube root as a single radical. That would be like trying to mush Ralph Nader and Rush Limbaugh into one person.

Question: $\sqrt{2} \times \sqrt[3]{3} = ?$

Solution: You cannot combine $\sqrt{2}$ and $\sqrt[3]{3}$ by multiplication because the one's a square root and the other's a cube root.

Just like earlier in the chapter, dividing radicals is comparable to multiplying radicals.

To Find the Quotient of Radicals (of the Same Degree): The quotient of radicals is equal to the radical of the quotient.

Question: $\dfrac{\sqrt[4]{105}}{\sqrt[4]{21}} = ?$

Solution: $\dfrac{\sqrt[4]{105}}{\sqrt[4]{21}} = \sqrt[4]{\dfrac{105}{21}} = \sqrt[4]{5}$

To Find a Radical Raised to an Exponent: A radical raised to an exponent is equal to the radical of the number under the radical sign raised to that exponent.

Question: $(\sqrt[3]{5})^2 = ?$

Solution: $(\sqrt[3]{5})^2 = \sqrt[3]{5^2} = \sqrt[3]{25}$

When you start mixing exponents and radicals, it's often easier to put everything in terms of exponents. Remember, you can use fractional exponents to represent radicals.

Now you're ready to look at the Do the Math solution from chapter 8.

DO THE MATH

Which is greater, $\sqrt{999^5 \times 999^2}$ or $\sqrt[3]{(999^5)^2}$?

Solution: First use the rule for multiplying powers with the same base to simplify what's inside the first radical. To multiply powers with the same base, you add the exponents:

$$\sqrt{999^5 \times 999^2} = \sqrt{999^{5+2}} = \sqrt{999^7}$$

Next, use the rule for raising a power to an exponent to simplify what's inside the second radical:

$$\sqrt[3]{(999^5)^2} = \sqrt[3]{995^{5 \times 2}} = \sqrt[3]{999^{10}}$$

Now you're left comparing $\sqrt{999^7}$ and $\sqrt[3]{999^{10}}$. It's still not clear which is greater, is it? Now's the time to use fractional exponents:

$$\sqrt{999^7} = 999^{\frac{7}{2}} \text{ and } \sqrt[3]{999^{10}} = 999^{\frac{10}{3}}$$

The one with the greater exponent will be greater. The first exponent $\frac{7}{2}$ is greater than the second exponent $\frac{10}{3}$, so $999^{\frac{7}{2}}$ is greater than $999^{\frac{10}{3}}$.

Plug In

Since you've spent a whole chapter getting way radical with us, these follow-up questions should be as easy as . . . working for Greenpeace! For solutions to these "Plug-In" problems, turn to the solutions section at the back of the book. Good luck!

1. Express 81^{12} as a power of 3. _____

2. Express $3^7 + 3^7 + 3^7$ as a power of 9. _____

3. Which is greater, $(.999999999)^9$ or $(.999999999)^{10}$? _____

4. What is the product of $\sqrt[3]{100}$ and $\sqrt[6]{100}$? _____

5. Which is greater, $\sqrt[6]{888^2 \times 888^3}$ or $\sqrt[7]{(888^2)^3}$? _____

Monomials and Polynomials: Express Yourself!

Algebra. The mere mention of the word sends many young math heads running for cover, and has the *power* to turn sensible students into raving lunatics. Well, get a grip, because we're going to break it down for you, real easy-like. In fact, we already started

> ⌐◦ᴡᴡ◦ **DO THE MATH** ◦ᴡᴡ◦
>
> When $(x + 1)^8$ is expanded and expressed in simplest form, what is the coefficient of x^4? (See the solution near the end of this chapter.)

sneaking some basic algebra concepts into the last chapter. You're practically halfway there.

In this chapter you will review how to evaluate, add, subtract, multiply, and simplify algebraic expressions. In chapter 10 you will review how to factor algebraic expressions. Then you will be ready to tackle the equations and inequalities of chapters 11–13. Just sit back, relax, and enjoy the ride!

ALGEBRA, THE HANDY HELPER

Algebra is a mathematical system that enables you to work with *unknown* or *unspecified* numbers by representing those numbers with letters. These numbers may be unknown just because you haven't figured them out yet, or because you want to use them to express some rule or generalization. Letters that stand for numbers are called *variables*. In other words, algebra lets you take what you do know, and use it to figure out what you don't know.

 KAPLAN   109

Something that helpful can't be all bad, right?

As a simple example of what algebra can do for you, imagine the following situation: This week, Sal is psyched, because Shockwave Records is having a storewide sale. Every CD is 15 percent off. In addition, Sal has a coupon worth one dollar off the sale price, so he's doubly psyched. Let's just forget about tax for a minute and figure out how much Sal will have to pay for a CD.

Well, you say, that depends on the price. Exactly our point. There is no one answer to this question. The amount Sal will have to pay depends on the regular price of the CD chosen. One way to answer the question would be to list every possible regular price and for each one to determine how much Sal would have to pay.

Regular Price	Sale Price (15% off Regular Price)	Sal's Price ($1 off Sale Price)
$10.00	$8.50	$7.50
$11.00	$9.35	$8.35
$12.00	$10.20	$9.20
$13.00	$11.05	$10.05
etc.	etc.	etc.

This seems like a lot to do each time there's a sale! The algebraic way to answer the question is much simpler. If you use the letter x to represent any regular price (in dollars), then you can represent 15 percent less than that price (remember, "15 percent *off*" is the same as "85 percent *of*") as .85x. You can then represent one dollar off that as:

$$.85x - 1$$

This is no definite quantity. The value of .85x − 1 depends on the value of x. Yet what you have in .85x − 1 is a combination of symbols that communicates something, so you can call it an "expression." Now, we all know very well that Sal will probably just go to the store to buy CDs, but if he wanted one, he'd have an easy way to figure out how much money to take out of the bank, or how many CDs he could get for a given amount of money.

ALGEBRAIC EXPRESSIONS

When you smile, that's a "facial expression." A string of words, like, "Math makes my brain hurt," is a "verbal expression." A bunch of numbers and symbols, like 2 + 3, is an "arithmetic expression." When a combination of symbols includes a variable, what you have is an *algebraic expression*.

Believe it or not, there are times when it's much easier and clearer to express an idea using algebra instead of words. Here, for example, are two different ways to describe the same general math procedure:

What You Could Say: "The number of permutations of any number of objects taken a smaller number at a time is equal to the product of consecutive integers beginning with the larger number and decreasing until the number of factors is equal to the smaller number."

What You'd Rather Say: The number of permutations of n objects taken r at a time is $\dfrac{n!}{(n-r)!}$.

The second version is not only clearer, it's less of a mouthful, and you won't be standing there wagging your tongue for so long, while everyone else has fun.

Algebraic expressions are like arithmetic expressions except that in an algebraic expression, part of the quantity is not spelled out for you. The expression $x + 3$ clearly represents the sum of two numbers; the hard part is that one of the numbers is unknown. As long as the value of x is a secret, there is no way to find the value of $x + 3$.

Speaking Algebra-ese

The typical algebraic expression can look pretty intimidating: clusters of integers, variables, and exponents strung together with plus signs and minus signs like beads on a necklace no one would be caught dead wearing. Each of these clusters is called a term. The expression $3x^2 + 4x + 5$, for example, has three terms: $3x^2$, $4x$, and 5. The expression $x^2 - y^2$ has two terms: x^2

◦᚜᚛◦ **CONNECTION** ◦᚜᚛◦

In case you've forgotten already, go back and check out coefficients in chapter 8. You'll be glad you did!

and $-y^2$. The numerical part of a term, the part in front of the variable, is called the coefficient. The *coefficient* of $5x$ is 5. The coefficient of $-3x^2y$ is -3. The coefficient of x^2 is an implied 1. And the coefficient of $-ab^2$ is an implied -1. It's similar to the way we dealt with coefficients in the last chapter.

If coefficients, variables, and exponents are the "alphabet" of the language called algebra, then terms are the "words," and algebraic expressions are the "phrases." Looking ahead, when you add in "verbs" like " $=$ " and " $>$," you will be making "sentences"—equations and inequalities.

But, just like when you were little and learned to speak, you have to be comfortable with words and phrases before you can deal with whole sentences. So let's look at some phrases. You might find you like what you see.

CAN YOU SOLVE THE MYSTERY?

Because an algebraic expression contains variable quantities, the exact value of the expression as a whole will remain unknown as long as the variables remain unknown. Once you are given a precise value for each of the mystery elements of an expression, however, you can find the value of the entire expression by simply replacing each variable with the given number. Formally, this process is called *substitution*; informally it is called "plugging in."

To *evaluate* an expression means to plug in the given numbers for the variables and calculate the total value of the expression.

Question: If $a = -1$ and $b = -2$, what is the value of the expression $2a^2 - 2ab + b^2$?

Solution: Plug in -1 for each a and -2 for each b:

$$2a^2 - 2ab + b^2 = 2(-1)^2 - 2(-1)(-2) + (-2)^2$$
$$= 2 - 4 + 4$$
$$= 2$$

Make It Easy on Yourself

Just as with fractions, any algebraic expression has an infinite number of equivalent variations. Two expressions are *equivalent* if no matter what you plug in for the unknowns in one expression, you get the same result as when you plug them into the other expression. For example, "$x + x$" and "$2x$" are equivalent expressions—plug in $x = 5$ and you get 10 in both cases; plug in $x = -1$ and you get -2 in both cases; plug in anything and you'll get the same result in both cases.

Again, as is the case with fractions, one variation is the simplest. An expression is in *simplest form* when it has no parentheses and no terms that can be combined. In the case of "$x + x$" vs. "$2x$," the latter is in simplest form.

POWER SURGE

If you set aside roughly $19 a week (that's $1,000 a year) from age 25 to 34 in a retirement account with an 8% interest rate annually, and then didn't put any more in ever again, by the time you hit the ripe old age of 65, your $10,000 investment will have grown to almost $170,000! But if you don't start until you're 35, and *then* invest the same amount per year, for 30 years— that's a total of $30,000—you'll have only $125,228 at age 65. So, if you want to retire in style, you have to start thinking of your money exponentially.

—Beth Kobliner, *Get a Financial Life*

ONE-TERM WONDER

Algebraic expressions with just one term are called *monomials*. These are monomials:

$$3x \qquad 7ab \qquad c^2 \qquad -\frac{1}{2}x^2y^3z^5$$

Before you can get anywhere in algebra, you need to be unafraid of the basic rules of combining monomials. You need to be at the point where you don't hesitate for a second when faced with this, for example: $x + x$.

What does that equal? Is it x^2, or $2x$, or neither of these? You could pick a number for x and try it out. And this is a great way to start tackling algebra right now—just try stuff! See if it works. The worst that could happen is you'll be wrong, and have to try again. Experimenting is the key to success.

So suppose $x = 3$. Then $x + x = 3 + 3 = 6$. Now plug $x = 3$ into the possible equivalents. Plug it into x^2 and you get $3^2 = 3 \times 3 = 9$. That's not the same as 6, so $x + x$ is not the same as x^2. Plug $x = 3$ into $2x$, and you get $2 \times 3 = 6$, so in the case of $x = 3$, $2x$ and $x + x$ are the same. Plug anything you want for x

into $2x$ and $x + x$ and you'll get the same thing, so they're equivalent.

Obviously you don't want to have to go through this every time you want to combine monomials. You've got more important things to do! You want to know the rules of operations so well that you can apply them almost automatically.

Just like with the previous chapter, the rules are easier to learn and recall if you see where they come from. The rules of adding, subtracting, multiplying, and dividing monomials all derive from the basic expression we've just checked out:

$$x + x = 2x.$$

ADDING AND SUBTRACTING MONOMIALS

Suppose you wanted to add not just an x and an x, but something more like a $2x$ and a $3x$. Easy! $2x$, as you've already seen, is the same as $x + x$. And similarly you can think of $3x$ as $x + x + x$. Thus you can rewrite $2x + 3x$ this way:

$$2x + 3x = (x + x) + (x + x + x)$$
$$= x + x + x + x + x$$
$$= 5x$$

Notice that the *coefficient* of the result, 5, is equal to the sum of the original coefficients, 2 and 3. Notice also that the x itself is unchanged—it doesn't pick up an exponent or anything.

To Add/Subtract Monomials with the Same Variable Part: In this case, add or subtract the coefficients and keep the variable part the same.

Question: $13x + 5x = ?$

Solution: Add the coefficients 13 and 5, and keep the variable part x unchanged:

$$13x + 5x = (13 + 5)x = 18x$$

Question: $a^2b - 10a^2b = ?$

Solution: Subtract the coefficients, and keep the variable part unchanged.

The coefficient of the first term, a^2b, is understood to be 1, so when you subtract the coefficients you get $1 - 10 = -9$. The variable part that remains unchanged is a^2b:

$$a^2b - 10a^2b = (1 - 10)a^2b = -9a^2b$$

Monomials with the same variable part are called *like terms*. The number parts at the beginning of each term—the coefficients—can be anything, but the variable parts, including any exponents, must be exactly the same. Like terms are to monomials as common denominators are to fractions—you can't add or subtract without them.

To Add or Subtract Monomials: Here's the big rule: You can add or subtract monomials only if they are like terms.

Question: $3x + 4y = ?$

Solution: These monomials cannot be combined into one because the variable parts are different. One has x and the other has y. They are not like terms.

MULTIPLYING AND DIVIDING MONOMIALS

When it comes to multiplication, you can combine any two monomials, not just like terms. You just multiply everything. You multiply the coefficients and you multiply the variables, which often means adding exponents.

To Multiply Monomials: Whenever you multiply monomials, multiply the coefficients and multiply the variable parts.

Question: $(-3ax)(-5bx^2) = ?$

Solution: Multiply the coefficients, -3 and -5, to get a new coefficient of 15. The product of ax and bx^2 is abx^3. So the whole product is:

$$(-3ax)(-5bx^2) = 15abx^3$$

Dividing monomials is analogous.

Question: $\dfrac{18ab^2}{-6b} = ?$

KAPLAN   115

Solution: Divide the coefficients, 18 and –6, to get a new coefficient of –3. Divide ab^2 by b to get ab. So the whole quotient is:

$$\frac{18ab^2}{-6b} = \frac{18}{6} \times \frac{ab^2}{b} = -3 \times ab = -3ab$$

REELECTED: MORE THAN ONE TERM

Expressions that are the sum of more than one term are called *polynomials*. ("Poly" means "more than one.") These are polynomials:

$$x + 3 \qquad 7a + b + c + d \qquad -\frac{1}{2} + x^2 - y^3 + z^5$$

Polynomials that are the sum of two terms are called *binomials*, and look— here come a few right now:

$$x + 3 \qquad 7ab + cd \qquad -x^2y^3z^5 - \frac{1}{2}$$

To Add/Subtract Polynomials: To add or subtract polynomials, combine like terms.

$$(3x^2 + 5x - 7) - (x^2 + 12) = (3x^2 - x^2) + 5x + (-7 - 12)$$
$$= 2x^2 + 5x - 19$$

MULTIPLYING POLYNOMIALS

In algebra, parentheses usually indicate multiplication. Everything inside the parentheses is to be multiplied by whatever is right outside the parentheses. For example:

⌐√√√○ **MATH LAUGH** ○√√√⌐

A math head's two-word reply when asked what happened to his parrot:

"Polynomial. Polygon."

$$2(x + y) = 2x + 2y$$

The 2 is meant to be multiplied by both the x and the y. This process of multiplying something by every term inside a set of parentheses is often referred to as *distributing*.

The Distributive Property: Here's how we show the process of multiplying something by every term inside a set of parentheses:

$$a(b + c) = ab + ac$$

Question: Express $3x(x + 3)$ without parentheses.

Solution: Distribute the $3x$ over the $x + 3$ in parentheses:

$$3x(x + 3) = 3x \times x + 3x \times 3 = 3x^2 + 9x$$

If there are two adjacent sets of parentheses, then each term inside the first set is to be multiplied by each term inside the second set. Proceed systematically to be sure you get every match-up. The number of terms in the product (before you consolidate like terms) will be equal to the product of the number of terms in the original polynomials.

Question: $(x^2 + 3x + 4)(x + 5) =$

Solution: Systematically multiply each of the three terms in the first polynomial by each of the two terms in the second polynomial:

$$(x^2 + 3x + 4)(x + 5) = x^2(x + 5) + 3x(x + 5) + 4(x + 5)$$
$$= x^3 + 5x^2 + 3x^2 + 15x + 4x + 20$$

There were three terms in the first polynomial, and two terms in the second, so there are $2 \times 3 = 6$ terms in the product (before consolidation). Now combine like terms to express the answer in simplest form:

$$x^3 + 5x^2 + 3x^2 + 15x + 4x + 20 = x^3 + 8x^2 + 19x + 20$$

FOILed Again!

When both polynomials have exactly two terms—that is, when they're both binomials—you can take advantage of the famous mnemonic device, FOIL. FOIL stands for "First, Outer, Inner, Last." To multiply $(x + 3)$ by $(x + 4)$, for example, first multiply the First terms: $x \times x = x^2$. Next the Outer terms: $x \times 4 = 4x$. Then the Inner terms: $3 \times x = 3x$. And finally the Last terms: $3 \times 4 = 12$. Then add and combine like terms:

$$x^2 + 4x + 3x + 12 = x^2 + 7x + 12$$

 117

To Multiply Binomials: Try using the FOIL method (First, Outer, Inner, Last). When you multiply binomials, multiply the First terms of each, then the Outer terms, then the Inner terms, then the Last terms. Then add and combine like terms:

$$(a + b)(c + d) = ac + ad + bc + bd$$

FOIL isn't any kind of special rule. It's just a way to make sure you get every match-up of terms when multiplying binomials. But remember: FOIL works only when you're multiplying two binomials.

Question: $(2x + 4)(x + 5) = ?$

Solution: Use FOIL. The First terms are $2x$ and x, and their product is $2x^2$. The Outer terms are $2x$ and 5, and their product is $10x$. The Inner terms are 4 and x, and their product is $4x$. And the Last terms are 4 and 5, and their product is 20:

$$(2x + 4)(x + 5) = 2x^2 + 10x + 4x + 20$$

Combine the like terms $10x$ and $4x$ and you get:

$$2x^2 + 10x + 4x + 20 = 2x^2 + 14x + 20$$

BIGGER IS BETTER: BINOMIAL EXPANSION

Take a look at what you get when you raise the binomial $a + b$ to ever higher and higher exponents. Start with exponents of 0 and 1:

$$(a + b)^0 = 1$$
$$(a + b)^1 = a + b$$

Next, raise it to an exponent of 2—that is, square it—using FOIL:

$$(a + b)^2 = (a + b)(a + b) = aa + ab + ba + bb = a^2 + 2ab + b^2$$

So now you have the general form for the square of a binomial. When you get to factoring in the next chapter, this is something you should be able to recognize, like an old friend.

To Square a Binomial: The general form for the square of a binomial is:

$$(a + b)^2 = a^2 + 2ab + b^2.$$

Now, to get $a + b$ to the third power—that is, to cube it—multiply $a^2 + 2ab + b^2$ by $a + b$:

$$(a + b)^3 = (a^2 + 2ab + b^2)(a + b)$$
$$= a^2a + a^2b + 2aba + 2abb + b^2a + b^2b$$
$$= a^3 + 3a^2b + 3ab^2 + b^3$$

Now you have the general form for the cube of a binomial. Continue in this fashion and you can generate the general forms for as many powers of a binomial as you want. Here is what you'd get up to the eighth power.

$$(a + b)^0 = 1$$
$$(a + b)^1 = a + b$$
$$(a + b)^2 = a^2 + 2ab + b^2$$
$$(a + b)^3 = a^3 + 3a^2b + 3ab^2 + b^3$$
$$(a + b)^4 = a^4 + 4a^3b + 6a^2b^2 + 4ab^3 + b^4$$
$$(a + b)^5 = a^5 + 5a^4b + 10a^3b^2 + 10a^2b^3 + 5ab^4 + b^5$$
$$(a + b)^6 = a^6 + 6a^5b + 15a^4b^2 + 20a^3b^3 + 15a^2b^4 + 6ab^5 + b^6$$
$$(a + b)^7 = a^7 + 7a^6b + 21a^5b^2 + 35a^4b^3 + 35a^3b^4 + 21a^2b^5 + 7ab^6 + b^7$$
$$(a + b)^8 = a^8 + 8a^7b + 28a^6b^2 + 56a^5b^3 + 70a^4b^4 + 56a^3b^5 + 28a^2b^6 + 8ab^7 + b^8$$

There's a pattern here. The variable parts, including the exponents, come out according to the following system. In the expansion of $(a + b)^n$:

The number of terms is equal to $n + 1$.

The first term is a^n.

The variable part of the second term is $a^{n-1}b$.

In each succeeding term, the a exponent decreases by 1 and the b exponent increases by 1.

The sum of the a exponent and the b exponent in each term is equal to n.

Look at an example. In the case of $n = 5$, you see above that $(a + b)^5$ expands to $a^5 + 5a^4b + 10a^3b^2 + 10a^2b^3 + 5ab^4 + b^5$. According to the system, the number of terms should be $n + 1$. Yes, there are $n + 1 = 6$ terms in $a^5 + 5a^4b + 10a^3b^2 + 10a^2b^3 + 5ab^4 + b^5$. According to the system, the first term should be a^n, and it is indeed a^5. According to the system, the variable part of the

 119

second term should be $a^{n-1}b$, and in each succeeding term the a exponent should decrease by 1 and the b exponent should increase by 1, and indeed the variable part of the second term is a^4b, and after that the a exponent goes down by 1 and the b exponent goes up by 1. And, according to the system, the sum of the exponents in each term should be equal to n, and indeed in each term the exponents add up to 5.

Now this is quite a mouthful to digest—and you may have to go over it a couple times—but contained in the series of rules you've just learned are the basic keys to unsticking the mental blocks you may have about algebra!

PASCAL'S TRIANGLE

Now, we're sure you're already glued to your seat by this stuff, but we're going to up the ante one more exciting and informative level. Check out the pattern that develops in the coefficients in the binomial expansions above. This pattern is called *Pascal's Triangle*, named after its founder, Blaise Pascal. Keeping in mind that terms that look like they have no coefficients actually have implied coefficients of 1, Pascal put together this fabulous expanding triangle of coefficients.

```
                    1
                 1     1
              1     2     1
           1     3     3     1
        1     4     6     4     1
      1     5    10    10     5     1
    1     6    15    20    15     6     1
  1     7    21    35    35    21     7     1
1     8    28    56    70    56    28     8     1
```

Check out how each number in the pattern is equal to the sum of the two numbers just above. In the fifth line for example, the first 4 is the sum of the 1 and 3 above it, the 6 is the sum of the 3 and 3 above it, and the second 4 is the sum of the 3 and 1 above it. In the cases of the 1's, you can think of them each as the sum of the 1 and the nothing above them. Wow, huh!? Algebra—it's not just for figuring out CD sales, anymore!

Once you understand the pattern of binomial expansions, you're ready for the Do the Math solution.

DO THE MATH

When $(x + 1)^8$ is expanded and expressed in simplest form, what is the coefficient of x^4?

Solution: Think of the binomial $x + 1$ as $a + b$, where $a = x$ and $b = 1$. According to Pascal's Triangle, when the exponent is 8, the coefficients are 1, 8, 28, 56, 70, 56, 28, 8, and 1. The expansion of $(x + 1)^8$ then, is:

$$x^8 + 8x^7 + 28x^6 + 56x^5 + 70x^4 + 56x^3 + 28x^2 + 8x + 1$$

The coefficient of x^4 is 70.

Hedging Your Bets

You can also use Pascal's Triangle to find probabilities. Suppose you were to toss a coin eight times. You can take the numbers in the row of Pascal's Triangle for $n = 8$—that's 1, 8, 28, 56, 70, 56, 28, 8, and 1—as the various numbers of favorable outcomes, and the total of those numbers as the total number of possible outcomes. For all heads, there is 1 favorable outcome. For seven heads and one tails, there are 8 favorable outcomes:

HHHHHHHT

HHHHHHTH

HHHHHTHH

HHHHTHHH

HHHTHHHH

HHTHHHHH

HTHHHHHH

THHHHHHH

For six heads and two tails, there are 28 favorable outcomes; for five heads and three tails there are 56 favorable outcomes; and so on. The total number of possible outcomes is:

$$1 + 8 + 28 + 56 + 70 + 56 + 28 + 8 + 1 = 256$$

So the probability of all heads is $\dfrac{1}{256}$; the probability of seven heads and one-tails is $\dfrac{8}{256} = \dfrac{1}{32}$; the probability of six heads and two tails is $\dfrac{28}{256} = \dfrac{7}{64}$; the probability of five heads and three tails is $\dfrac{56}{256} = \dfrac{7}{32}$; and so on.

Pascal's Triangle and the Fibonacci Sequence

Remember our famous rabbit farmer, Fibonacci, from back in chapter 2? Now, are you ready to see something really cool about Pascal's Triangle? Look at what you get when you add up the triangle numbers diagonally. Do you recognize those numbers. It's the Fibonacci sequence!

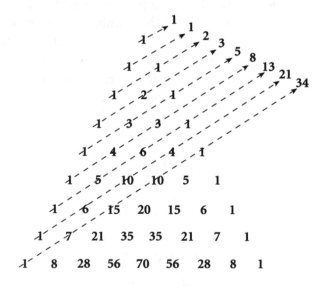

Plug In

Now that you're breezing through this algebra stuff like a pro (remember when it used to seem difficult?), try some of the review questions. For solutions, turn to the "Plug-In Solutions" section at the back of the book.

1. What is the product of $2x + 1$ and $3x + 2$? _____

2. What is the product of $x^2 - 4$ and $x + 2$? _____

3. What is the product of $x + 5$ and $x - 5$? _____

4. What is the square of $x + 3$? _____

5. What is the square of $x - 3$? _____

Factoring Polynomials: Just the Factors, Ma'am

Monomials, polynomials, factoring and variables . . . it's enough to make an aspiring math head want to throw in the towel! Well don't give up yet, because the fun is just beginning! Yeah, sure.

∿∿∿ DO THE MATH ∿∿∿

Simplify: $\dfrac{3x^2 - 11x + 6}{9 - x^2}$

(See the solution near the end of this chapter.)

Even if this section of *Math Power* isn't the most action-packed, we're filling you up with a lot of powerful facts and figures which will serve you for years to come. You'll thank us later, we swear! Anyway, in this chapter we'll get you deep into the heart of algebra, and you'll come out factoring like a pro!

PRESTO, CHANGE-O

Algebra is kind of like the kids' toys that switch from cars to robots: It's all about transformations. Learning the rules of algebra means learning how to make these changes.

When you get to solving equations and inequalities in the upcoming chapters, there will be times when you will want to take an expression in the form of a product, like $(x + 2)(x + 3)$, and transform it to standard form: $x^2 + 5x + 6$. To do that, you use the FOIL method we showed you in the last chapter.

There will be other times when you will want to do just the opposite—to take an expression in standard form like $x^2 - 7x + 12$ and transform it to a product: $(x - 3)(x - 4)$. This "de-multiplying" process is called *factoring*.

Both the standard form and the factored form have their own unique personality traits and flaws. It's just that the standard form is more useful in figuring some problems, and the factored form is more useful in others. To be a real algebra star, you need to be able to go between these two forms effortlessly, like quickly transforming the car into a robot! Keep reading and we'll show you how.

⌁⋀⋁⋀⋿ **SPARK** ⋿⋀⋁⋀⌁

If you want to explore algebra in the real world, maybe you should find out about the High School for the Physical City. In New York City, this school takes its work outside of the classroom and into the streets, playgrounds, and subways in order to work out their math and science problems in the *real* world.

Think of algebra as a kind of detective work: *Multiplying* polynomials is more like taking a "shoot first, ask questions later" approach. Once you know the rules, you just dive in and go, forging ahead with gusto until you solve the case. *Factoring* polynomials is like doing a thorough investigation to get to the heart of a crime. To factor successfully you have to ask more questions in order to reconstruct the monomials or polynomials that, multiplied, will give you the guilty polynomial.

THE FIVE FAMOUS FACTORABLES

You'll be a master factoring detective when you've learned to spot polynomials that fit certain profiles. Here are five "famous forms" that show up a lot:

1. The common monomial factor
2. The square of a binomial
3. The cube of a binomial
4. The difference of squares
5. The sum and difference of cubes

As you look at polynomials in these forms, one form at a time over the next few pages, it will generally be obvious what kind of Famous Factorable you're looking at and how to factor it.

But when you get away from the controlled setting of this book and into algebra in the real world, you'll be on your own. There won't be a *Math Power* safety net to tell you whether you're looking at one of these famous factorables, some other factorable, or a polynomial that's not factorable at all. "Art heads" cultivate an eye for beauty, and inquiring math heads like you need to develop a sharp eye for factorable forms.

FAMOUS FACTORABLE #1: THE COMMON MONOMIAL FACTOR

Whenever you're trying to factor a polynomial, the first thing to look for is a *common monomial factor*—that is, a monomial that can be factored out of each term in the polynomial.

Suppose, for example, you wanted to factor the polynomial $3x^3 + 12x^2 - 6x$. Since you've developed such hot skills at discerning common factors through the last few chapters, you can't help but notice right off the bat that all the coefficients are multiples of 3. That means you can "undistribute" the 3, taking it out of the picture. What you do is write a 3 in front of a set of parentheses, and then you write inside the parentheses what's left of the polynomial after you divide each term by 3:

$$3x^3 + 12x^2 - 6x = 3(x^3 + 4x^2 - 2x)$$

But wait; there's more! 3 is a factor common to all terms. But it's *not the only one*. There's also at least one x in each term, so you can undistribute one of those as well:

$$3(x^3 + 4x^2 - 2x) = 3x(x^2 + 4x - 2)$$

The three terms inside the parentheses have no more common factors.

Famous Factorable #1. Look for the common monomial factor(s):

$$ax + ay + az \ldots = a(x + y + z \ldots)$$

Question: Factor $2a^3b^2 + 4a^2b^3 + 2ab^4$.

Solution: Whenever you want to factor, look first for a common monomial factor. Here, all the coefficients are multiples of 2. Each term

also includes at least an a and a b^2, so the greatest common factor of the variable parts is ab^2, and the greatest common monomial factor of the whole polynomial is $2ab^2$. So you start by writing $2ab^2$ in front of an open parenthesis:

$$2ab^2($$

Now, after the parenthesis you write, term by term, what's left after getting rid of $2ab^2$. To divide the first term $2a^3b^2$ by $2ab^2$, you divide the 2 by 2—which gives you a 1 that you don't even have to write down—and you divide the a^3b^2 by ab^2—which gives you a^2.

So here's what you have so far:

$$2ab^2(a^2$$

Continue this way and you end up with:

$$2ab^2(a^2 + 2ab + b^2)$$

∽√w∘ **CONNECTION** ∘√w∽

To refresh your math power about the basics of exponents, you might want to review the "Rules of Exponents" section in chapter 8.

As it happens, this expression can be factored even further. What's left inside the parentheses at this point is a classic case of our next Famous Factorable. So without further ado . . .

FAMOUS FACTORABLE #2: THE SQUARE OF A BINOMIAL

Back in chapter 9, just before Pascal's Triangle, you saw the standard form for the *square of a binomial*:

$$(a + b)^2 = a^2 + 2ab + b^2$$

The right-hand side of this identity was generated by applying the FOIL method to the left-hand side. If you see something in the $(a + b)^2$ form, such as $(2x + 5)^2$, and you want to multiply it out, you can always follow FOIL. But if you see something that's already in the resulting $a^2 + 2ab + b^2$ form, like $4x^2 + 20x + 25$, and you want to trace it back to its factored form, there's no algorithm (our friend from chapter 3) comparable to FOIL that you can use. What you need now is a sharp eye for polynomials in this form. Here are some examples:

$$a^2 + 6ab + 9b^2$$
$$x^2 + 14x + 49$$
$$9n^2 + 24n + 16$$
$$9n^2 - 24n + 16$$

Here's how to recognize a polynomial in this form. First of all, in every case, there are three terms, and the first term is the square of a monomial, and the last term is the square of a monomial:

squares ———

a^2	$+ 6ab$	$+ 9b^2$
x^2	$+ 14x$	$+ 49$
$9n^2$	$+ 24n$	$+ 16$
$9n^2$	$- 24n$	$+ 16$

——— squares

That's not enough to make it an $a^2 + 2ab + b^2$ polynomial, though. Once you're sure the outer terms are squares, then check out the middle term. If the polynomial is the square of a binomial, the middle term will be equal to twice the product of the square roots of the outer terms. Huh? Okay, let's break it down together, step by step.

Take the case of $a^2 + 6ab + 9b^2$. The outer terms are squares. Here's how to check the middle term. Unsquare the outer terms, take the product of the results, and double it. Watch closely. Unsquare a^2 and you get $\pm a$. That "$\pm$" sign means for now, it could be either positive or negative. Unsquare $9b^2$ and you get $\pm 3b$. The product of those results is $\pm 3ab$. Double that and you get $\pm 6ab$. The middle term is indeed $+6ab$, so the terms of the binomial you're looking for are $+a$ and $+3b$, so the whole factorization looks like this:

$$a^2 + 6ab + 9b^2 = (a + 3b)^2$$

Not so hard once you learn to read the equations rather than the words, right? Here are the factorizations of the other examples listed above. If you're feeling brave, try doing the other three on your own first; if not, here are the answers (but don't expect us to do that on your trig test!):

$$x^2 + 14x + 49 = (x + 7)^2$$
$$9n^2 + 24n + 16 = (3n + 4)^2$$
$$9n^2 - 24n + 16 = (3n - 4)^2$$

Notice the differences between the last two examples. To be the square of a binomial, the outer terms must both be positive. But the inner term can be either positive or negative. A minus sign before the middle term of the expanded form means a minus sign in the middle of the factored form. Why's this? Because math heads say so!

Famous Factorable #2. Look for the square of a binomial:
$$a^2 + 2ab + b^2 = (a + b)^2$$
$$a^2 - 2ab + b^2 = (a - b)^2$$

Question: Factor $-5x^5 + 10x^3y^2 - 5xy^4$.

Solution: As always, look first for a common monomial factor. Here you can factor out $5x$:
$$-5x^5 + 10x^3y^2 - 5xy^4 = 5x(-x^4 + 2x^2y^2 - y^4)$$

What's left now inside the parentheses seems to have factoring potential, but the signs are all wrong. Try factoring out -1 as well:
$$5x(-x^4 + 2x^2y^2 - y^4) = -5x(x^4 - 2x^2y^2 + y^4)$$

Now the minus sign is in the right place for what's in the parentheses to be the square of a binomial. Unsquare the outer terms and you get $\pm x^2$ and $\pm y^2$. Multiply them, double the product, and you get $\pm 2x^2y^2$. Indeed, the middle term you're looking for is $-2x^2y^2$, so the part inside the parentheses is the square of $x^2 - y^2$, and now you have:
$$-5x(x^2 - y^2)^2$$

So the cool thing about algebra is that sometimes you can twist the arm off an expression in order to make it easier to work with. If only the rest of life were like that.

By the way, you can factor the above expression even further, because what's left inside the parentheses is a classic case of Famous Factorable #4, the difference of squares. But not so fast—before we get to that, let's take a look at Famous Factorable #3.

FAMOUS FACTORABLE #3: THE CUBE OF A BINOMIAL

Back in chapter 9, just before Pascal's Triangle, you also saw the general form for the *cube of a binomial*:

$$(a + b)^3 = a^3 + 3a^2b + 3ab^2 + b^3$$

Just like squaring a binomial, cubing a binomial is merely a matter of cranking it out according to a system. The method may not have a fab acronym like FOIL, but it's still a system. So if you have an expression in the $(a + b)^3$ form, like $(x + 2)^3$ and you want to transform it to the expanded $a^3 + 3a^2b + 3ab^2 + b^3$ form, you don't have to be clever or creative—you just do it.

But going from expanded form back to factored form means being able to recognize when a polynomial is in $a^3 + 3a^2b + 3ab^2 + b^3$ form, like:

$$x^3 + 6x^2 + 12x + 8$$

Here's how to do it. This time there are four terms, the first and last are cubes (of x and 2), and the coefficients of the middle terms are multiples of 3. That's not enough to say for sure that a polynomial is the cube of a binomial—but it's a start. If the expression you're working with fits this description, then you can just make a binomial by taking the sum of the cube roots of the outer terms, cube that binomial, and see if you get the polynomial you're trying to factor. (Factoring often entails some trial-and-error.)

Here are some polynomials in the $a^3 + 3a^2b + 3ab^2 + b^3$ form:

$$p^3 + 3p^2 + 3p + 1$$
$$8n^3 + 12n^2 + 6n + 1$$
$$27r^3 + 54r^2s + 36rs^2 + 8s^3$$

All three of these are cubes of binomials. Can you figure out what binomial is cubed in each case? And this time, no more Mr. Nice Book; it's up to you to figure them out.

Like the square of a binomial, the cube of a binomial also has its minus sign version. If, instead of $a + b$, you cube $a - b$, you get a similar form, but with minus signs before the second and last terms:

$$(a - b)^3 = a^3 - 3a^2b + 3ab^2 - b^3$$

Famous Factorable #3. Look for the cube of a binomial:

$$a^3 + 3a^2b + 3ab^2 + b^3 = (a + b)^3$$
$$a^3 - 3a^2b - 3ab^2 - b^3 = (a - b)^3$$

Question: Factor $2x^8y - 6x^6y^3 + 6x^4y^5 - 2x^2y^7$.

Solution: As always, look first for a common monomial factor. The greatest common monomial factor here is $2x^2y$. Factor that out and you have:

$$2x^2y(x^6 - 3x^4y^2 + 3x^2y^4 - y^6)$$

Now what's left inside the parentheses is in $a^3 - 3a^2b - 3ab^2 - b^3$ form, where a is x^2 and b is y^2, so a^3 comes out as x^6, and $-3a^2b$ comes out as $-3x^4y^2$, and so on. So what's inside the parentheses is the cube of $x^2 - y^2$, and you're down to:

$$2x^2y(x^2 - y^2)^3$$

Now it just so happens, you could factor this even further, because what's left inside the parentheses is another classic case of Famous Factorable #4.

FAMOUS FACTORABLE #4: THE DIFFERENCE OF SQUARES

This Famous Factorable sticks out like a sore thumb; it's probably the easiest to spot. Here are some examples:

$$4y^2 - 1$$
$$m^2 - 9n^2$$
$$16p^6 - q^4$$

Each of the above follows the classic $a^2 - b^2$ form. In each case, there are two terms separated by a minus sign. And in each case, what's before the minus sign is the square of a monomial, and what's after the minus sign is also the square of a monomial:

$$\text{squares} \quad \begin{array}{ccc} 4y^2 & - & 1 \\ m^2 & - & 9n^2 \\ 16p^6 & - & q^4 \end{array} \quad \text{squares}$$

What could be simpler? The factored form of $a^2 - b^2$ is $(a - b)(a + b)$. So to factor something in $a^2 - b^2$ form, you unsquare both terms and make two binomials out of the results—one with a minus sign and one with a plus sign. For example, to factor $4y^2 - 1$, you note that $4y^2$ is the square of $2y$, and that 1 is the square of 1, so you make two binomials out of $2y$ and 1, like this:

$$4y^2 - 1 = (2y - 1)(2y + 1)$$

Okay, you forced us to give away the answers again. Don't say we never did anything for you! Here are the factorizations of the other two examples listed above:

$$m^2 - 9n^2 = (m - 3n)(m + 3n)$$
$$16p^6 - q^4 = (4p^3 - q^2)(4p^3 - q^2)$$

Famous Factorable #4. Look for the difference of squares:
$$a^2 - b^2 = (a - b)(a + b)$$

Question: Factor $r^2 + 2rs - t^2 + s^2$

Solution: At first, this doesn't look like an $a^2 - b^2$ form, but if you rearrange the terms like $r^2 + 2rs + s^2 - t^2$ you can see that what comes before the minus sign is a square—this time the square of a binomial. Rewrite $r^2 + 2rs + s^2$ as $(r + s)^2$, and the whole expression becomes $(r + s)^2 - t^2$.

Now it looks like a case of the difference of squares. Unsquare the two parts and you get $r + s$ and t. Put them into $(a - b)(a + b)$ form and you get $(r + s - t)(r + s + t)$.

Since you can factor anything in the form of the difference of squares, you might think you can also factor anything in the form of the sum of squares—

that is, in $a^2 + b^2$ form. Sorry, but you can't. The sum of squares is generally not factorable. There is no plus sign variant for $a^2 - b^2 = (a - b)(a + b)$.

When it comes to cubes, however, you're in luck. There are both plus sign and minus sign variants.

FAMOUS FACTORABLE #5: THE SUM AND DIFFERENCE OF CUBES

Almost as easy to spot as the last Famous Factorable are the two variants of this factorable, the sum of cubes $a^3 + b^3$ and the difference of cubes $a^3 - b^3$. They both look like pairs of cubes. The sum of cubes has a plus sign between them. Here are some examples:

$$
\text{cubes} \quad
\begin{array}{c}
8x^3 \\
n^3 \\
p^6
\end{array}
\begin{array}{c}
+ \\
+ \\
+
\end{array}
\begin{array}{c}
27 \\
1 \\
q^9
\end{array}
\quad \text{cubes}
$$

The difference of cubes looks the same, except that it has a minus sign between the cubes:

$$
\text{cubes} \quad
\begin{array}{c}
8x^3 \\
n^3 \\
p^6
\end{array}
\begin{array}{c}
- \\
- \\
-
\end{array}
\begin{array}{c}
27 \\
1 \\
q^9
\end{array}
\quad \text{cubes}
$$

The factored forms of the sum and difference of cubes are similar. That's why it makes sense to think of them as two members of the same Famous Factorable family. Here are the formulas.

Famous Factorable #5. Look for the sum and difference of cubes.

$$a^3 + b^3 = (a + b)(a^2 - ab + b^2)$$
$$a^3 - b^3 = (a - b)(a^2 + ab + b^2)$$

If you're a good algebra detective, you'll notice both the similarities and the differences here. Both factorizations consist of a simple binomial and an almost familiar *trinomial*. In case you haven't figured it out yet, a trinomial is a polynomial that is the sum of three terms. (*Tri* and keep up, okay!?) The binomial is simply the sum or the difference of the cube roots—that is, $a + b$ or $a - b$. The trinomial in each case looks a lot like the square of a binomial—remember, $a^2 \pm 2ab + b^2$—except that it's missing the coefficient of 2 in the middle term. The trinomials $a^2 - ab + b^2$ and $a^2 + ab + b^2$ are not generally factorable. The only differences between the factorizations are the signs. The *sum* of the cubes yields a *plus* sign in the binomial and a *minus* sign before the middle term of the trinomial:

$$a^3 \oplus b^3 = \left(a \oplus b\right)\left(a^2 \ominus ab + b^2\right)$$

The *difference* of cubes yields a *minus* sign in the binomial and *plus* sign before the second term of the trinomial:

$$a^3 \ominus b^3 = \left(a \ominus b\right)\left(a^2 \oplus ab + b^2\right)$$

MORE FUN WITH FACTORING

Take a look at the first example of an $a^3 + b^3$ polynomial listed above:
$$8x^3 + 27$$

The first term is the cube of $2x$. The second term is the cube of 3. So plug $a = 2x$ and $b = 3$ into the general form:
$$a^3 + b^3 = (a + b)(a^2 - ab + b^2)$$
$$(2x)^3 + (3)^3 = (2x + 3)\,(4x^2 - 6x + 9)$$

The other two examples from the $a^3 + b^3$ list factor like this:
$$n^3 + 1 = (n + 1)(n^2 - n + 1)$$
$$p^6 + q^9 = (p^2 + q^3)\,(p^4 - p^2\,q^3 + q^6)$$

The three examples in $a^3 - b^3$ (difference of cubes) form factor similarly, but with a different pattern of plus and minus signs:

$$8x^3 - 27 = (2x - 3)(4x^2 + 6x + 9)$$
$$n^3 - 1 = (n - 1)(n^2 + n + 1)$$
$$p^6 - q^9 = (p^2 - q^3)\,(p^4 + p^2\,q^3 + q^6)$$

Question: Factor $x^3 - y^3 - z^3 - 3x^2z + 3xz^2$.

Solution: This does not at first look like an $a^3 + b^3$ or an $a^3 - b^3$ form, but with a little rearrangement and regrouping, it can be made to look more like a simple sum or difference of cubes:

$$x^3 - y^3 - z^3 - 3x^2z + 3xz^2 = (x^3 - 3x^2z + 3xz^2 - z^3) - y^3$$
$$= (x - z)^3 - y^3$$

It's the difference of cubes—that is, it's in $a^3 - b^3$ form, where $a = x - z$ and $b = y$. So that's what you plug into the general form:

$$a^3 - b^3 = (a - b)(a^2 + ab + b^2)$$
$$(x - z)^3 - (y)^3 = (x - z - y)\left[(x - z)^2 + (x - z)\,y + y^2\right]$$

That's not pretty, is it? And even when you alphabetize the first factor and re-express the second factor without parentheses inside brackets, it's still a big hairy mess:

$$(x - z - y)(x^2 + y^2 + z^2 + xy - 2xz - yz)$$

But it is a factored form. It's equivalent to the original, expanded form and may prove more useful in some contexts. Math is not always a beauty contest, so get used to messy figures like this.

Here's a chart that summarizes all the five Famous Factorables:

	Standard Form(s)	Factored Form
1. Common monomial factor	$ab + ac + ad + ...$	$a(b + c + d + ...)$
2. Square of a binomial	$a^2 + 2ab + b^2$ $a^2 - 2ab + b^2$	$(a + b)^2$ $(a - b)^2$
3. Cube of a Binomial	$a^3 + 3a^2b + 3ab^2 + b^3$ $a^3 - 3a^2b - 3ab^2 - b^3$	$(a + b)^3$ $(a - b)^3$
4. Difference of squares	$a^2 - b^2$	$(a - b)(a + b)$
5. Sum/difference of cubes	$a^3 + b^3$ $a^3 - b^3$	$(a + b)(a^2 - ab + b^2)$ $(a - b)(a^2 + ab + b^2)$

RECOGNIZING SOME NONFAMOUS FACTORABLES

As you probably realize, polynomials don't always lie down nicely and fit the profile of a Famous Factorable. When you do come across a Famous Factorable, think of it as a gift. Most factorable polynomials are not famous ones; they toil in obscurity their whole lives, and this can make them mean and uncooperative. And lots of polynomials are not factorable at all.

To factor obscure factorables, you have to be more like a persistent detective than a patient accountant. It takes a delicate balance of insight and trial-and-error to factor the obscure factorable. Suppose, for example, you're faced with factoring this polynomial:

$$6x^2 + 5x - 21$$

This polynomial looks like it might be the result of applying the FOIL method to a couple of binomials. If so, the two First terms would have to have a product—let's call it the "F-product"—of $6x^2$, and the two Last terms would have to have a product—the "L-product"—of -21.

There are only a few monomials with integer coefficients that will give you an F-product of $6x^2$: x and $6x$, $-x$ and $-6x$, $2x$ and $3x$, $-2x$ and $-3x$. And there are only a few integer pairs that will give you an L-product of -21: -3 and 7, 3

and –7, –1 and 21, 1 and –21. The correct factorization will be some kind of combination of these pairs, something like one of these:

$$(x - 3)(6x + 7)$$
$$(2x + 1)(3x - 21)$$
$$(-2x + 7)(-3x - 3)$$

The number of possibilities is limited—there are in fact 32—but it's still too many to check them all one by one. And anyway, the test would be over by the time you checked them all out! You know that all 32 possibilities will give you an F-product of $6x^2$ and an L-product of –21. It's only the middle term $+5x$ that you're concerned with now. That's the combined result of the O and the I in FOIL. The O-product and the I-product add up to $+5x$.

Here's where your ace math head crime-solving skills come into play. Instead of just blindly and systematically testing out all 32 possibilities, see if you can narrow down the possibilities first. Think about what kind of outer terms and inner terms will have products that add up to $+5x$.

First, notice that in all the possibilities, the O-product and the I-product have different signs—one is positive and the other is negative. Not only that, when you add the O-product and the I-product, you get a positive result ($+5x$), so you know the positive product outweighs the negative product—but not by all that much. It's not likely that either product will include +21 or –21. It's more likely that the binomials will end in +3 and –7, or –3 and +7. It also seems like they'll begin with $2x$ and $3x$. Here's a list of the possibilities to try first, along with their O- and I-products.

	O-product	I-product	O + I
$(2x + 7)(3x - 3)$	$-6x$	$+21x$	$+15x$
$(2x - 7)(3x + 3)$	$+6x$	$-21x$	$-15x$
$(2x + 3)(3x - 7)$	$-14x$	$+9x$	$-5x$
$(2x + 3)(3x + 7)$	$+14x$	$-9x$	$+5x$

The one that works is the last one. So the factorization looks like this:

$$6x^2 + 5x - 21 = (2x - 3)(3x + 7)$$

That's the FOIL method in reverse. Maybe we should call it the Plastic Wrap method!

Question: Factor $20ab + 14a - 10b - 7$

Solution: This looks like it might be the product of two binomials, one with an a plus or minus something, and the other with a b plus or minus something. To get a -7 at the end, the binomials must end either in $+1$ and -7 or in -1 and $+7$:

$$(\ +1)(\ -7)$$
$$(\ -1)(\ +7)$$

The first terms of the binomials have a product of $+20ab$, so they have to be one of these 12 possibilities:

a and $20b$	$-a$ and $-20b$
$2a$ and $10b$	$-2a$ and $-10b$
$4a$ and $5b$	$-4a$ and $-5b$
$5a$ and $4b$	$-5a$ and $-4b$
$10a$ and $2b$	$-10a$ and $-2b$
$20a$ and b	$-20a$ and $-b$

One good clue to which of these it will be is that $-10b$ is in the original polynomial. That suggests a product of either $+1$ and $-10b$ or -1 and $+10b$—which leaves the ±1 to be multiplied by the ±7. Thus the correct factorization turns out to be:

$$(2a - 1)(10b + 7) = 20ab + 14a - 10b - 7$$

SIMPLIFYING AN ALGEBRAIC FRACTION

Just when you thought it was safe to do algebra, we're throwing you a curve ball. One situation where *factored* forms are more useful than expanded forms is when you want to simplify an expression that makes a fraction out of polynomials.

 139

Simplifying an algebraic fraction is a lot like simplifying a numerical fraction. And we know you remember how to do that! (But in case you don't, turn back to chapter 3.)

The idea is to find factors common to the numerator and the denominator and cancel them. Simplifying an algebraic fraction begins with factoring. So, to simplify $\dfrac{x^2 - x - 12}{x^2 - 9}$, first factor the numerator and denominator:

$$\frac{x^2 - x - 12}{x^2 - 9} = \frac{(x - 4)(x + 3)}{(x - 3)(x + 3)}$$

Now you can cancel $x + 3$ from the numerator and denominator, which leaves you with $\dfrac{(x - 4)}{(x - 3)}$.

Now you're ready to look at chapter 10's Do the Math solution.

DO THE MATH

Simplify: $\dfrac{3x^2 - 11x + 6}{9 - x^2}$

Solution: To reduce a fraction, you get rid of factors common to the top and bottom. So the first step in reducing an algebraic fraction is to factor the numerator and denominator. Here the denominator is easy: it's the difference of squares $9 - x^2 = (3 - x)(3 + x)$. The numerator takes some thought and some trial-and-error. For the first term to be $3x^2$, the first terms of the factors must be $3x$ and x. For the last term to be $+6$, the last terms must be either $+2$ and $+3$, or -2 and -3, or $+1$ and $+6$, or -1 and -6. After a few tries, you should come up with: $3x^2 - 11x - 6 = (3x - 2)(x - 3)$. Now the fraction looks like this:

$$\frac{3x^2 - 11x + 6}{9 - x^2} = \frac{(3x - 2)(x - 3)}{(3 - x)(3 + x)}$$

In this form there are no precisely common factors, but there is a factor in the numerator that's the opposite (negative) of a factor in the denominator: $x - 3$ and $3 - x$ are opposites. Factor -1 out of the numerator and you get:

$$\frac{(3x-2)(x-3)}{(3-x)(3+x)} = \frac{(-1)(3x-2)(3-x)}{(3-x)(3+x)}$$

Now $(3-x)$ can be eliminated from both the top and the bottom:

$$\frac{(-1)(3x-2)(3-x)}{(3-x)(3+x)} = \frac{-(3x-2)}{3+x} = \frac{-3x+2}{x+3}$$

Plug In

Now that you've learned about that family of Famous Factorables, and about the not-so-famous obscure ones, try working out some problems on your own and flexing those math power muscles. Watch out—you're doing algebra!

1. Factor $4x^2 + 12x + 9$ _____

2. Factor $4x^2 + 8x + 4$ _____

3. Factor $4x^2 + 5x + 3$ _____

4. Factor $4x^3 - 12x^2 + 12x - 4$ _____

5. Simplify $\dfrac{8x^3 + 36x^2 + 54x + 27}{8x^3 - 12x^2 - 18x + 27}$ _____

Basic Equations: Be Fair to Both Sides

We're almost through with algebra, and you're coming through with flying colors! Hopefully by now, algebra is starting to make at least a little sense to you, and this chapter ought to just be icing on the cake. We're going to break down some basic rules of equations, and take you from the simplest to the more complex, step by step.

> ∿∿**DO THE MATH**∿∿
>
> Solve for N: $V = \dfrac{PN}{R + NT}$
>
> (See the solution near the end of this chapter.)

THE GOLDEN RULE OF EQUATIONS

The golden rule of solving algebraic equations is so simple a math head *couldn't* have made it up. Are you ready? Here goes: *do the same thing to both sides*. You can do almost anything you want to one side of an equation (beat it, kick it, make it write bad checks)—as long as you do the same thing to the other side. Think of an equation as a scale: as long as you treat both sides equally, you'll maintain the balance.

But how do you know what to do to both sides of an equation? That's what this chapter is all about. You will know what to do and when if you keep in mind your objective: to *solve* the equation, which means to isolate the variable—to get it all by itself on one side of the equation.

To Solve an Equation: Do whatever you need to do to both sides of the equation in order to isolate the variable you're solving for.

For starters, check out this very simple example: to solve the simple equation $x - 19 = -5$, the thing to do is add 19 to both sides. By doing so, you peel the "-19" away from the x on the left side, and you reach your objective:

$$x - 19 = -5$$
$$x - 19 + 19 = -5 + 19$$
$$x = 14$$

You've isolated the variable x—it's all by itself on one side—and so you've solved the equation.

To figure out what to do to both sides, look at what's cluttering up the side of the equation with the unknown, and peel that excess junk away, layer by layer, until the variable you're solving for is left alone. To peel away a layer, look at the operation that makes it stick, and apply the opposite operation to undo it.

In the example above, you wanted to peel that "-19" away from the x on the left side of the equation, so you *added* 19 to both sides. In general, to undo subtraction, you add (no kidding).

○⋀⋁○ **POWER SURGE** ○⋀⋁○

Thinking about going into graphic design? Think you can just take a quick course in Photoshop™ for Macintosh™, and you're on your way? Think again, friend! High-powered graphic designers may dress better than math heads, but they're using math skills all the time. Math, geometry, and algebra are all put into play when using computers to design logos, match color schemes, and let text interact with shapes and pictures in a cool way. This lets designers be precise with their work, in a way they couldn't possibly do without help from, you got it, math!

Similarly, to undo addition, you subtract:

Question: Solve for n: $n + 450 = 40$

Solution: To isolate n, you want to peel that "$+ 450$" away from the n on the left side. To do that, subtract 450 from both sides:

$$n + 450 = 40$$
$$n + 450 - 450 = 40 - 450$$
$$n = -410$$

To undo division, you multiply:

Question: Solve for x: $\dfrac{x}{1.1} = 900$

Solution: To isolate x, you want to peel that denominator of 1.1 away from the x on the left side. To do that, multiply both sides by 1.1:

$$\frac{x}{1.1} = 900$$

$$\frac{x}{1.1} \times 1.1 = 900 \times 1.1$$

$$x = 990$$

To undo multiplication, you divide:

Question: Solve for a: $.06a = 12$

Solution: To isolate a, you want to peel that coefficient of .06 away from the a on the left side. To do that, you divide both sides by .06:

$$.06a = 12$$

$$a = \frac{12}{.06} = 200$$

To Undo an Operation: Apply the inverse operation to both sides. Addition and subtraction are inverse operations. Multiplication and division are inverse operations.

Another thing you can do to both sides (as long as they're both nonzero) is take the reciprocal:

Question: Solve for k: $\dfrac{1}{k} = -5$

Solution: To isolate k, you want to flip the left side. To do that, flip both sides:

$$\frac{1}{k} = -5$$

$$k = \frac{1}{-5} = -\frac{1}{5}$$

Adding, subtracting, multiplying, dividing, and taking the reciprocal of both sides are usually all you need to do to solve a simple equation. There are a couple other steps you might need sometimes—like raising both sides to an

exponent or taking some root of both sides—but they can be a little problematic for now, and not much fun, either.

To undo a radical, you raise both sides to the same exponent:

Question: Solve for y: $\sqrt[3]{y} = -3$

Solution: To isolate y, you want to peel that cube root symbol away from the y on the left side. To do that, you cube both sides:

$$\left(\sqrt[3]{y}\right)^3 = \left(-3\right)^3$$
$$y = -27$$

Watch out though: if you raise both sides of an equation to an *even* exponent, you sometimes end up with a false solution.

Question: Solve for z: $\sqrt[4]{z} = -2$

Solution: To isolate z, you want to peel that fourth root symbol away from the z on the left side. To do that, you raise both sides to an exponent of 4:

$$\left(\sqrt[4]{z}\right)^4 = \left(-2\right)^4$$
$$z = 16$$

But that's not a correct solution. The fourth root of 16 is not –2. This equation has no solution among the real numbers.

When You Raise Both Sides of an Equation to an Even Power: Check your results—it's quite possible you will end up with a false solution, or what's officially called an *extraneous solution*.

To undo an exponent, you take the appropriate root of both sides:

Question: Solve for a: $a^3 = 16$

Solution: To isolate a, you want to peel that exponent of 3 away from the a on the left side. To do that, you take the cube root of both sides:

$$a^3 = 16$$
$$a = \sqrt[3]{16} = 2\sqrt[3]{2}$$

You can take an *even* root of both sides only when you know that both sides are positive. And when you know they're positive and take an even root, you have to attach a *plus-or-minus* sign ($\pm$) to one side:

Question: Solve for c: $c^4 = 16$

Solution: To isolate c, you want to peel that exponent of 4 away from the c on the left side. To do that, you take the fourth root of both sides. Remember, though, when you take an even root, to include the plus-or-minus sign:

$$c^4 = 16$$
$$c = \pm\sqrt[4]{16}$$
$$c = \pm 2$$

When You Take an Even Root of Both Sides of an Equation: Attach a plus-or-minus sign ($\pm$) to one side.

This last point about the plus-or-minus sign is important, and many aspiring math heads seem to have slept through it in school. Suppose you came across the following innocent-looking equation, minding its own business on a piece of paper:

$$y^2 = 25$$

You might think the solution is obvious. If you take the square root of both sides, you get:

$$y = 5$$

But that's only half right. It's true that $y = 5$ is a correct solution to this equation—but it's not the only one. An equally valid solution is $y = -5$. Remember, when you take an even root of both sides of an equation, you have to attach a plus-or-minus sign to one side. Here's the correct solution:

$$y^2 = 25$$
$$\sqrt{y^2} = \pm\sqrt{25}$$
$$y^2 = \pm 5$$

There are *two* solutions because this is a *second-degree equation*—that just means the unknown y is raised to an exponent of 2. Second-degree equations

are often called *quadratic equations*—a term you've probably run away from before—and we will review how to solve them in the next chapter. For the rest of this chapter, we're just going to worry about *first-degree equations*, also called *linear equations*, which are equations with one variable, with no exponents, and with one solution. They're a piece of cake.

ONE STEP AT A TIME: DOING MULTISTEP SOLUTIONS

Every equation you've seen so far in this chapter has been solvable in one step. Don't you wish all of algebra was that easy? We do too, but life ain't fair, kid. That kind of equation is almost too easy to solve. It gets more, um, interesting (that's one word for it) when it takes more than one step—when you have to do more than one thing to both sides to isolate the unknown. When this happens, you have to be a better algebra sleuth—you have to figure out what's the best order in which to apply the steps. Take a look at this equation:

$$5x = 2 - x\sqrt{3}$$

You might think that you want to peel that coefficient of 5 away from the x on the left side by dividing both sides by 5. But look what that gets you:

$$5x = 2 - x\sqrt{3}$$
$$x = \frac{2 - x\sqrt{3}}{5}$$

That step didn't get you any closer to a solution. You haven't really isolated x. There may be an x all by itself on the left side, but there's still an x on the right side. To isolate a variable means to get it all by itself on one side *and* cleared away completely from the other side. Whoops, did we forget to mention that? Sorry.

From Soup to Nuts: Transposing the Terms

A better first step to take towards solving the equation $5x = 2 - x\sqrt{3}$ would be to add $x\sqrt{3}$ to both sides:

$$5x = 2 - x\sqrt{3}$$
$$5x + x\sqrt{3} = 2 - x\sqrt{3} + x\sqrt{3}$$
$$5x + x\sqrt{3} = 2$$

That gets every term with an x in it on one side. Now you can factor the left side, and then divide both sides by $5 + \sqrt{3}$:

$$5x + x\sqrt{3} = 2$$
$$x(5 + \sqrt{3}) = 2 \text{ (and voilà!)}$$
$$x = \frac{2}{5 + \sqrt{3}}$$

That's the solution. (Yeah, we know—there's a *radical* lurking in the denominator. Rationalize it for yourself, if you want to. We have other things to talk about right now.)

To Solve a Linear Equation: Try to get every term with the variable you're solving for on one side and everything else on the other.

Question: Solve for w: $11w + 40 = 34 - 7w$

Solution: Add $7w$ and subtract 40 from both sides in order to get all terms with a w on the left and all terms without a w on the right.

$$11w + 7w = 34 - 40$$

Then combine like terms.

$$18w = -6$$

Then divide both sides by 18 to get the solution.

$$w = \frac{-6}{18} = -\frac{1}{3}$$

No Second Thoughts: Removing Parentheses

Before you can transpose the various terms to the appropriate sides of the equation, you have to deal with any parentheses there might be. Take this equation, for example:

$$3(x - 5) = -4(x + 3)$$

Before you can doing any transposing, you need to multiply out both sides. That means distributing the 3 on the left and the -4 on the right.

$$3x - 15 = -4x - 12$$

Now you can transpose.

$$3x + 4x = -12 + 15$$

Combine like terms.

$$7x = 3$$

And divide by 7.

$$x = \frac{3}{7}$$

When Solving a Linear Equation: Try first to remove all parentheses by multiplying everything out.

Question: Solve for b: $2 - (5b + 7) = 11 - b$

Solution: Before you do anything else, remove the parentheses. The minus sign applies to both terms inside the parentheses.

$$2 - 5b - 7 = 11 - b$$

Then you can transpose and solve as usual.

$$-5b + b = 11 - 2 + 7$$
$$-4b = 16$$
$$b = \frac{16}{-4} = -4$$

In the Clear: Clearing Denominators

A more complicated kind of linear equation is one that includes one or more fractions. The easiest thing to do whenever you have fractions in an equation is to multiply both sides by whatever necessary to get rid of all denominators. Look at this example:

$$\frac{1}{4}a - 3 = \frac{1}{5}a + 2$$

Multiply both sides by 20 and you'll clear both denominators.

$$\left(\frac{1}{4}a - 3\right) \times 20 = \left(\frac{1}{5}a + 2\right) \times 20$$

$$\frac{20}{4}a - 3 \times 20 = \frac{20}{5}a + 2 \times 20$$

$$5a - 60 = 4a + 40$$

Now you have what you like to see—an equation with no fractions. From what we've gone over before, you know how to solve for a now—transpose the a-terms to one side and the other terms to the other side.

$$5a - 4a = 40 + 60$$

$$a = 100$$

If There Are Any Fractions in the Equation: Multiply both sides by a common multiple of the denominators.

It's super important to clear denominators like this when there are variables in the denominators:

Question: Solve for n: $\dfrac{n + 11}{n + 3} = 4$

Solution: To clear the denominator on the left side, multiply both sides by $n + 3$.

$$\left(\frac{n + 11}{n + 3}\right)(n + 3) = 4(n + 3)$$

$$n + 11 = 4n + 12$$

Now you know what to do—subtract $4n$ from both sides and subtract 11 from both sides.

$$n - 4n = 12 - 11$$

$$-3n = 1$$

$$n = \frac{1}{-3} = -\frac{1}{3}$$

The CerTiFieD Method

If you like swell acronyms like FOIL, here's another one for you: the CeRTiFieD method. You can use the consonants in the word "certified" to help you remember a step-by-step

ᴧᴧᴧ POWER SURGE ᴧᴧᴧ

Clear all denominators.

Remove parentheses.

Transpose.

Factor.

Divide.

approach that will help you solve almost any linear equation:

The CeRTiFieD Method. Here's how it works.

Suppose you wanted to solve this equation for z:

$$\frac{3(z + 1)}{2(z - 1)} = -2$$

According to the CeRTiFieD method, you want first to *Clear* any denominators. Here there's a denominator on the left side. To clear it, multiply both sides by $2(z - 1)$.

$$\frac{3(z + 1)}{2(z - 1)} \times 2(z - 1) = -2 \times 2(z - 1)$$

$$3(z + 1) = -4(z - 1)$$

Next step is to *Remove* the parentheses—distribute the 3 on the left side and the −4 on the right side.

$$3z + 3 = -4z + 4$$

Next, to *Transpose,* add $4z$ to both sides and subtract 3 from both sides.

$$3z + 4z = 4 - 3$$

$$7z = 1$$

There's nothing to *Factor* here, so you just go ahead and *Divide* both sides by the coefficient of z:

$$z = \frac{1}{7}$$

And there's the solution. You're a CeRTiFieD algebra sleuth now!

Coming to Terms: Solving "In Terms Of"

To "solve" an equation for x doesn't necessarily mean to find a numerical value for x. To solve for x means to get x alone on one side of the equation. As long as there are then no x's on the other side, what you have on the other side is the solution, even if it looks like something the cat dragged in. If there are other unknowns in the equation, the solution will be an algebraic expression that includes those other unknowns.

Take, for example, the equation $y = \frac{1}{2}x - \frac{3}{10}$. This equation expresses y in terms of x—in other words, it's an equation that has y alone on one side and has an algebraic expression that includes x on the other side. When you solve an equation like this for x, what you end up with is an equation that expresses x in terms of y. Now, you might be wondering why you'd ever care what x is when you don't even know what y is in the first place. Hey, we're not sure either, we just do what the math heads tell us to.

So, to solve this equation for x:

$$y = \frac{1}{2}x - \frac{3}{10}$$

First thing you do is clear denominators by multiplying both sides by 10.

$$y \times 10 = \left(\frac{1}{2}x - \frac{3}{10}\right) \times 10$$

$$10y = 5x - 3$$

The next thing is transpose—that is, move any term with an x in it to one side, and any term without an x to the other side.

$$10y - 10y - 5x = 5x - 3 - 10y - 5x$$

$$-5x = -10y - 3$$

All you have left to do now is divide both sides by –5.

$$\frac{-5x}{-5} = \frac{-10y - 3}{-5} =$$

$$x = 2y + \frac{3}{5}$$

Now you have x in terms of y. Bravo!

To Solve for One Unknown in Terms of One or More Others: Isolate the variable you're solving for. The solution will be an algebraic expression that includes the other unknowns.

Question: The formula $C = \frac{5}{9}(F - 32)$ expresses the Celsius temperature reading C in terms of the Fahrenheit temperature reading F. Rewrite the formula so that it expresses F in terms of C.

Solution: To solve for F, you want to get F all by itself on one side.

You can peel away the $\frac{5}{9}$ by multiplying both sides of the equation by $\frac{9}{5}$.

$$C \times \frac{9}{5} = \frac{5}{9}(F - 32) \times \frac{9}{5}$$

$$\frac{9}{5}C = F - 32$$

Now all you have left to do is add 32 to both sides.

$$\frac{9}{5}C + 32 = F - 32 + 32$$

You end up with F in terms of C.

$$\frac{9}{5}C + 32 = F$$

The CeRTiFieD method is especially useful when you're solving an equation that has lots of unknowns, as in this chapter's Do the Math question.

DO THE MATH

Solve for N: $V = \dfrac{PN}{R + NT}$

Solution: According to the CeRTiFieD method, you begin by clearing the denominator. Multiply both sides by $R + NT$.

$$V(R + NT) = PN$$

Next, remove parentheses.

$$VR + VNT = PN$$

Now transpose the terms with an N to one side and the terms without an N to the other.

$$VNT - PN = -VR$$

Then factor out the variable you're solving for.

$$N(VT - P) = -VR$$

And lastly, divide both sides by $VT - P$ to get N all by itself on one side of the equation.

$$N = \frac{-VR}{VT - P}$$

That's the solution. You're on easy street!

SOLVING "UNCERTIFIABLE" EQUATIONS

The CeRTiFieD method is no substitute for thinking (wouldn't that be nice). It doesn't really work on some equations. How would you use it in this equation, for example?

$$3^{3n + 2} = 9^{2n - 3}$$

There aren't any denominators to clear. There aren't any parentheses to remove. But you can't transpose anything yet either. What do you do? Throw up your arms and walk away? We think not. The way to solve an equation with the unknown in an exponent is to re-express one or both sides to give them the same base.

Here, the 9 on the right side can be reexpressed as 3^2.

$$3^{3n + 2} = (3^2)^{2n - 3}$$

Now the right side shows a power raised to an exponent. To do that, you multiply the exponents. That's 2 times $2n - 3$.

$$3^{3n + 2} = 3^{2(2n - 3)}$$
$$3^{3n + 2} = 3^{4n - 6}$$

Now that the two sides have the same base, you can forget the base and focus on the exponents. If 3 to an exponent of $3n + 2$ is the same as 3 to an exponent of $4n - 6$, then the two expressions in the exponents are equal.

$$3n + 2 = 4n - 6$$

Now you can transpose and solve as usual.

$$3n - 4n = -6 - 2$$
$$-n = -8$$
$$n = 8$$

Sometimes the CeRTiFieD method is longer and more involved than necessary. Look at what happens if you unquestioningly apply the CeRTiFieD method to the following equation:

$$\frac{17\pi + 97}{x + 2} = \frac{3(17\pi + 97)}{7}$$

According to the method, you first clear denominators. Here you'd multiply both sides by $x + 2$ to clear one denominator, and you'd multiply both sides by 7 to clear the other.

$$(7)(x + 2)\,\frac{17\pi + 97}{x + 2} = \frac{3(17\pi + 97)}{7}\,(7)(x + 2)$$

$$7(17\pi + 97) = 3(17\pi + 97)(x + 2)$$

Next thing to do, according to the method, is remove parentheses. Multiply out both sides and look at what you get.

$$119\pi + 679 = 51\pi\,x + 102\pi + 291x + 582$$

Next, transpose all the terms with an x to one side and all other terms to the other side.

$$119\pi + 679 - 102\pi - 582 = 51\pi x + 291x$$

Then combine like terms on the left side and factor out the x on the right side.

$$17\pi + 97 = (51\pi + 291)x$$

And finally, divide both sides by the coefficient of x, which is $51\pi + 291$.

$$\frac{17\pi + 97}{51\pi + 291} = x$$

All that business on the left simplifies to $\frac{1}{3}$.

That solution method is much messier than necessary. You'd have been much better off with a completely different first step.

Notice that the two numerators in the original equation include $17\pi + 97$.

$$\frac{17\pi + 97}{x + 2} = \frac{3(17\pi + 97)}{7}$$

If you divide both sides by that expression . . .

$$\frac{17\pi + 97}{x + 2} \div (17\pi + 97) = \frac{3(17\pi + 97)}{7} \div (17\pi + 97)$$

you end up with a much simpler equation.

$$\frac{1}{x + 2} = \frac{3}{7}$$

The thing to do now is to take the reciprocal of both sides.

$$x + 2 = \frac{7}{3}$$

Now all you have to do is subtract.

$$x = \frac{7}{3} - 2 = \frac{7}{3} - \frac{6}{3} = \frac{1}{3}$$

So solving equations is not a mindless process. Your objective is always to isolate the variable you're solving for. But the means to that objective varies from equation to equation. Don't rely unthinkingly on an easy algorithm like the CeRTiFieD method. Use your (math) head, and do some of these questions.

🔌 *Plug In*

1. Solve for x: $\sqrt[3]{8x + 6} = -3$ _____

2. Solve for x: $\dfrac{19}{5x + 17} = \dfrac{19}{31}$ _____

3. Solve for x: $8^x = 16^{x-1}$ _____

4. Solve for x: $a = \dfrac{b + x}{c + x}$ _____

5. Solve for x: $2(x - 1) = (2 - x)\sqrt{2}$ _____

KAPLAN

Advanced Equations: Advancing the Cause

"Do the same thing to both sides." That was about all you needed to know to solve the equations you saw back in chapter 11. Now you'll see some more complex equations that call for special sleuthing techniques, and you'll learn methods for solving simultaneous

∿**DO THE MATH**∿

Find the positive number x for which $x - 1$ is equal to the reciprocal of x. (See the solution near the end of this chapter.)

equations, equations with absolute value, inequalities, and quadratic equations. Sound a little like gibberish? We'll translate as we go along. And next chapter, we'll start working with word problems; after that it's on to Geometry. So sit back, relax and enjoy the algebra sleuthing!

ALL AT ONCE: SOLVING SIMULTANEOUS EQUATIONS

If a *linear* equation has only one variable, you know from the last chapters that you can get a numerical solution, or, in other words, you can find out what number the variable represents. If there's more than one variable, the best you can do for a solution is an algebraic expression. To get numerical solutions for more than one variable, you need more than one equation.

To take a simple example, look at this equation:

$$x + y = 10$$

 KAPLAN   159

What are the values of x and y? You don't know yet, do you? There are lots of pairs of numbers that add up to 10—infinitely many. One equation's not enough to establish the numerical values of x and y. You can say that $x = 10 - y$, and that $y = 10 - x$, but if you want to know exactly what numbers x and y are, you need more information.

Now, suppose you are given this additional piece of information:

$$x = y + 2$$

By itself, this equation's no help at all. It says that x is 2 more than y, but there are still infinitely many pairs of numbers that fit that description.

But if it's understood that the x and y in the second equation are the same as the x and y in the first, then we're in business! By considering the two equations simultaneously, you can figure out the values of x and y. In the case of $x + y = 10$ and $x = y + 2$, you can probably figure it out in your head that $x = 6$ and $y = 4$. Those are the only values for x and y that will work in both equations.

A group of two or more equations that share variables is called a set of *simultaneous equations*. There are two standard methods for solving a pair of simultaneous equations:

1. substitution method
2. adding-equations method

The basic aim in both methods is the same—combine the equations so you can get rid of one variable temporarily. You can solve for only one variable at a time.

To Solve Simultaneous Equations: You cannot normally solve one equation at a time. Instead, you have to combine the equations so that you can solve for one *variable* at a time.

The Substitution Method

One way to get rid of one variable so you can solve for the other is to use the *substitution method*. You switch around one equation so that it expresses one variable in terms of the other, and then you plug that expression into the other equation. Check out this pair of equations:

$$\begin{cases} 3m + 5n = -1 \\ 5m + n = 13 \end{cases}$$

The substitution method is a good one to use here because it's very easy to manipulate the second equation into a useful form. Subtract $5m$ from both sides and you get an expression for n in terms of m:

$$5m + n = 13$$
$$n = 13 - 5m$$

What you have now is a new way of looking at n. So in place of n in the first equation you can substitute this new name, $13 - 5m$:

$$3m + 5n = -1$$
$$3m + 5(13 - 5m) = -1$$

Now you have one equation with one variable, so you can solve for m using the methods you've learned in the last chapters.

$$3m + 5(13 - 5m) = -1$$
$$3m + 65 - 25m) = -1$$
$$-22m + 65 = -1$$
$$-22m = -66$$
$$m = \frac{-66}{-22} = 3$$

Now that you know what m is, plug it into the expression for n in terms of m to solve for n:

$$n = 13 - 5m$$
$$= 13 - 5(3) = 13 - 15 = -2$$

So, you've figured out that $m = 3$ and $n = -2$. That wasn't so bad, now, was it?

The Substitution Method for Solving Simultaneous Equations

1. Manipulate one equation so as to isolate one variable.
2. Plug the new expression for that variable into the other equation.
3. Solve for the one variable that's left.

4. Plug the one solution back into the expression of the other variable and solve.

The Adding-Equations Method

Another excellent way to solve a pair of simultaneous equations is the *adding-equations method*. As the name ever-so-subtly suggests, you add equations, but not without some preliminary investigation.

Take a gander at these two equations:

$$\begin{cases} 6a - 7b = -2 \\ 3a + 2b = -23 \end{cases}$$

Each is a statement of equality (kind of like the E.R.A.), and if you add equals to equals you get equals (you also get a tongue twister), so you can add the two left sides and add the two right sides and say that the sums are the same:

$$6a - 7b = -2$$
$$\underline{3a + 2b = -23}$$
$$9a - 5b = -25$$

The resulting equation $9a - 5b = -25$ is a true statement, but it doesn't get you any closer to a numerical solution. The way to go instead is first to manipulate one or both equations so that when you add them one of the variables drops out. That will happen if you can arrange it so that one variable has equal but opposite coefficients in the two equations. That's a cinch if you multiply both sides of the second equation by -2:

$$(-2)(3a + 2b) = -23(-2)$$
$$-6a - 4b = 46$$

Now the a-coefficient is 6 in the first equation and -6 in the second. When you add the equations with the second one in this new form, look what happens:

$$6a - 7b = -2$$
$$\underline{-6a - 4b = 46}$$
$$-11b = 44$$

Presto! Now you have one equation with one variable, so you can solve for b using our tried and true "do-the-same-thing-to-both-sides" method. Divide both sides by -11 and you see that $b = -4$. Plug $b = -4$ back into either of the original equations to solve for a:

$$3a + 2b = -23$$
$$3a + 2(-4) = -23$$
$$3a - 8 = -23$$
$$3a = -23 + 8$$
$$3a = -15$$
$$a = -5$$

So you've figured out that $a = -5$ and $b = -4$.

The Adding-Equations Method for Solving Simultaneous Equations

1. Manipulate one or both equations so that one of the variables has opposite coefficients in the two equations.
2. Add the two equations to eliminate the one variable and form one equation in one variable.
3. Solve for the one variable that's left.
4. Plug the one solution back into either of the original equations and solve for the other variable.

Question: Solve for s and t: $\begin{cases} 5s - 3t = 2 \\ 7s - 2t = 16 \end{cases}$

Solution: Multiply both sides of the first equation by 2, and both sides of the second by -3, and you'll get two equations that will combine nicely:

$$5s - 3t = 2 \qquad\qquad 7s - 2t = 16$$
$$2 \times (5s - 3t) = 2 \times 2 \qquad\qquad -3 \times (7s - 2t) = 16 \times (-3)$$
$$10s - 6t = 4 \qquad\qquad -21s + 6t = -48$$

When you add the equations in this form, the *t*-terms drop out:

$$10s - 6t = 4$$
$$-21s + 6t = -48$$
$$\overline{}$$
$$-11s = -44$$
$$s = 4$$

Now that you know that $s = 4$, you can plug that back into either of the original equations to find t.

$$5s - 3t = 2$$
$$5(4) - 3t = 2$$
$$20 - 3t = 2$$
$$-3t = 2 - 20$$
$$-3t = -18$$
$$t = 6$$

And so the correct solution is $s = 4$ and $t = 6$.

⌇⌇⌇ **POWER SURGE** ⌇⌇⌇

Trying to choose between health care plans? You'll need those powerful math skills we've been teaching you. Let's say you're trying to choose between plan A, with a monthly premium of $200, a yearly deductible of $500 and then a 50% copayment for the next $2,500 and plan B, with a $140 monthly premium, a $1,000 deductible and a 50% copayment for the next $5,000. It's going to make sense (and cents) to break it down, dollar by dollar, and "do the math" to figure out what's best for you. Now aren't you feeling healthier for having read this book?

How Do I Know Which Method to Use?

It takes a sharp algebra detective to figure out which is the better method to use to solve a notorious pair of simultaneous equations. Often, either method will work eventually; one's just going to do it for you more quickly and easily. In textbooks and standardized tests, simultaneous equation problems are often deliberately designed to be solvable by the *adding-equations* method without too much manipulation. That's just a little tidbit, we hope you'll find useful in your travels. Now don't say we never did anything for you.

Always look closely at what *exactly* a math problem is asking you for. And always be on the lookout for quick and easy shortcuts to the solution. In answering the following question, for example, you might get stuck doing more work than you have to, if you're not careful; and we know you don't want to do that.

Question: If $2p - 9q = 11$ and $p + 12q = -8$, what is the value of $p + q$?

Solution: If you insist on following methods without thinking things through first, you can end up doing a lot more figuring and calculating than you have to. And on a timed, standardized test, that can make or break your math power score.

You might think that to answer the question above you have to solve for each variable, one at a time. You could do that by multiplying both sides of the second equation by -2, which will make the p-terms cancel when you add the equations:

$$2p - 9q = 11$$
$$\underline{-2p - 24q = 16}$$
$$-33q = 27$$

Divide both sides by -33, and you find that $q = -\dfrac{27}{33}$ or $-\dfrac{9}{11}$. Now you'd have to plug that back into one of the original equations to find p. Then you'd add p and q to get the answer the question is looking for.

But there's a much easier way. Look what happens if you add the equations as originally presented:

$$2p - 9q = 11$$
$$\underline{p + 12q = -8}$$
$$3p + 3q = 3$$

Now all you have to do is divide both sides by 3 and you get $p + q = 1$. That's the answer to the question asked. You were able to bypass the actual solutions for p and q. Why do more work than you have to? You're not getting paid to do this stuff, are you?

NO-WIN SITUATIONS: SIMULTANEOUS EQUATIONS THAT CAN'T BE SOLVED

When is a pair of equations *not* a pair of equations? When they're really two versions of the *same* equation. To take a really simple example, look at the following pair:

$$\begin{bmatrix} x + y = 10 \\ \quad x = 10 - y \end{bmatrix}$$

There are infinitely many pairs of numbers that will fit both equations. Any number that fits one will fit the other. It doesn't take a genius algebraic mind to see that these are two variants of the same equation, and you can't do much with them. But sometimes it's not so obvious.

Question: Solve for r and s: $\begin{bmatrix} 6r - 2s + 1 = -3 \\ \quad 5s - 3 = 15r + 7 \end{bmatrix}$

Solution: Manipulate one or both equations so that when you add them one of the variables will drop out. Let's move all the r- and s-terms to the left and numbers to the right in both. Subtract 1 from both sides in the first. Subtract $15r$ from both sides and add 3 to both sides in the second:

$$6r - 2s + 1 = -3 \qquad\qquad 5s - 3 = 15r + 7$$
$$6r - 2s = -4 \qquad\qquad\quad -15r + 5s = 10$$

Now you can simplify both equations. Divide everything in the first by 2, and divide everything in the second by 5:

$$6r - 2s = -4 \qquad\qquad -15r + 5s = 10$$
$$3r - s = -2 \qquad\qquad\quad -3r + s = 12$$

Now the equations look very similar. If you try adding the equations at this point, look what happens:

$$3r - s = -2$$
$$\underline{3r + s = -2}$$
$$0 = 0$$

In an effort to get rid of one variable, you ended up losing both. Because the end result "0 = 0" is a true statement (now that's stating the obvious!), the original equations were actually two variants of the same equation. Any pair of numbers that works in one will also work in the other.

Another time when you cannot get numerical solutions for what look like simultaneous equations is when the equations are *inconsistent*. That's when you have a pair of equations that cannot possibly describe the same unknowns. To take a simple example, look at the following pair:

$$\begin{bmatrix} x + y = 10 \\ x + y = 11 \end{bmatrix}$$

There are infinitely many pairs of numbers that will fit the first equation, and there are infinitely many pairs of numbers that will fit the second equation, but there is no pair of numbers that will fit both. There's no such thing as a pair of numbers that add up to 10 and also add up to 11. And if you didn't know that, there's a bridge in Brooklyn we'd like to sell you.

Sometimes the inconsistency isn't so easy to spot.

Question: Solve for t and u: $\begin{bmatrix} 8u = 7 - 2t \\ 3t + 7u = 5 - 5u \end{bmatrix}$

Solution: Manipulate one or both equations so that when you add them one of the variables will drop out. Let's try moving all the t- and u-terms to the left and numbers to the right in both. Add $2t$ to both sides in the first. Add $5u$ to both sides in the second:

$$8u = 7 - 2t \qquad\qquad 3t + 7u = 5 - 5u$$
$$2t + 8u = 7 \qquad\qquad 3t + 12u = 5$$

To give the t's equal and opposite coefficients, multiply both sides of the first equation by 3, and both sides of the second equation by –2:

$$3 \times (2t + 8u) = 7 \times 3 \qquad (-2) \times (3t + 12u) = 5 \times (-2)$$
$$6t + 24u = 21 \qquad\qquad -6t - 24u = -10$$

Now the equations look very similar. If you try adding the equations at this point, look at what happens:

$$6t + 24u = 21$$
$$\underline{-6t - 24u = -10}$$
$$0 = 11$$

In an effort to get rid of one variable, you ended up losing both. And this time the end result, "$0 = 11$," is a *false* statement (and it doesn't take a detective to figure that out), so the original equations were actually inconsistent. There is no pair of numbers that will work in both equations.

INEQUALITIES AND ABSOLUTE VALUE

If you've ever seen absolute value bars and learned what they meant, you probably thought, "What a cinch!" All it means is strip away the negative sign if there is one. Thus, $|12|$ is 12, and $|-12|$ is also 12.

Absolute value is easy when there's only a number between the bars. It's easy when you know the sign of what you are "absolute-valuing." It gets more complicated when there's a variable in there, because you don't know yet whether what's inside is positive or negative.

To solve an equation that includes absolute value signs, think about the two different cases. For example, to solve the equation $|x - 12| = 3$, think of it as two equations:

$$x - 12 = 3 \text{ or } x - 12 = -3$$
$$x = 15 \text{ or } 9$$

Lucky for you, solving an inequality is a lot like solving an equation, where you just do whatever is necessary to both sides to isolate the variable. Just remember that when you multiply or divide both sides by a negative number, you have to reverse the sign. To solve $-5x + 7 < -3$, subtract 7 from both sides to get: $-5x < -10$. Now divide both sides by -5, remembering to reverse the sign: $x > 2$.

Some of the most complicated algebraic solving you'll ever encounter will involve inequalities and absolute value signs. Suppose you wanted to solve the following:

$$|2x - 3| < 7$$

What does it mean if $|2x - 3| < 7$? It means that if the expression between the absolute value bars is positive, it's less than +7, or, if the expression between the bars is negative, it's greater than –7. In other words, $2x - 3$ is between –7 and +7:

$$-7 < 2x - 3 < 7$$
$$-4 < 2x < 10$$
$$-2 < x < 5$$

That's the solution.

Here's a general rule: To solve an "absolute-value-is-*less*-than" inequality—that is, an inequality in the form $|\text{thing}| < p$, where $p > 0$—just put that "thing" *inside* the range $-p$ to p: For example, $|x - 5| < 14$ becomes $-14 < x - 5 < 14$.

$|\text{thing}| < p$ implies: $-p < \text{thing} < p$

And here's another general rule: To solve an "absolute-value-is-*greater*-than" inequality—that is, an inequality in the form $|\text{thing}| > p$, where $p > 0$, just put that "thing" *outside* the range $-p$ to p: For example, $\left|\frac{3x + 9}{2}\right| > 7$ becomes $\frac{3x + 9}{2} < -7$ OR $\frac{3x + 9}{2} > 7$.

$|\text{thing}| > p$ implies: $\text{thing} < -p$ or $\text{thing} > p$

A REAL SQUARED DEAL: QUADRATIC EQUATIONS

All the equations you've seen so far in the last two chapters have been linear equations. That means the variables are not squared or cubed or raised to any higher exponents; they just are

MATH LAUGH

A statistician will have his head in the oven, and his feet on ice, and say that, on average he feels fine.

what they are. A *quadratic equation* is an equation with a variable that's squared. These equations have been amped to the next power, and only the cleverest detectives get to the bottom of them. And we're here to make you the cleverest!

Quadratic equations with one variable can have as many as two solutions. To make your job easier, the first thing to do when you find yourself faced with a quadratic equation, get it into standard $ax^2 + bx + c = 0$ form. Once you have an equation in that form, you have three solution methods to choose from:

1. factoring method
2. complete-the-squares method
3. quadratic formula method

The Factoring Method

A popular way to solve quadratic equations is the *factoring method*. When you see a way to factor the left side of the equation, then you can do so and set each factor separately equal to 0. The idea is that, when you know the product of two quantities is 0, then you know that one of those quantities must be 0—there's no other way to get a zero product.

Take this equation:

$$x^2 - 5x + 6 = 0$$

The left side is easy to factor, so do it!

$$(x - 2)(x - 3) = 0$$

Now, if the product of $x - 2$ and $x - 3$ is 0, then it must be true that either $x - 2$ or $x - 3$ is 0.

$$x - 2 = 0 \text{ or } x - 3 = 0$$

Add 2 to both sides of one equation and add 3 to both sides of the other and you have the solutions.

$$x = 2 \text{ or } x = 3$$

The Factoring Method for Solving Quadratic Equations
1. Put the equation into $ax^2 + bx + c = 0$ form.
2. Factor the left side of the equation.
3. Set each factor separately equal to 0.
4. Solve for the values of x.

You can't use the factoring method if you don't see a way to factor the left side. But when you *do* see a way to factor, this method is usually the best way to go.

The "Complete-the-Square" Method

The second ace quadratic equation-solving method is the *complete-the-square* method. Think of it like an especially hard line of detective questioning. Here, you manipulate the equation to get a polynomial in the form of the square of a binomial on one side. Then you solve by taking the square root of both sides. You remember *square roots*, right?

Here's an example. Take this equation:
$$x^2 - 6x - 2 = 0$$

Add the opposite of the third term (the term without an x) to both sides.
$$x^2 - 6x - 2 + 2 = 0 + 2$$
$$x^2 - 6x = 2$$

Take the coefficient of x, which is -6. Divide it by 2 to get -3, and square the result to get $+9$. Add that to both sides.
$$x^2 - 6x + 9 = 2 + 9$$

Now the left side is the square of the binomial $x - 3$.
$$(x - 3)^2 = 11$$

Take the square root of both sides. Don't forget the $\pm$ sign.
$$\sqrt{(x-3)^2} = \pm\sqrt{11}$$
$$x - 3 = \pm\sqrt{11}$$

Solve for x.

$$x = 3 \pm \sqrt{11}$$

But wait, there's more! This method is only a little more complicated when the coefficient of x^2 is something other than 1. Yeah, we know you've heard that "just a little more complicated" song and dance before. Just start by dividing everything by that first coefficient.

Surprise! Here's an example:

$$2x^2 + 5x + 1 = 0$$

Divide everything by the coefficient of the first term.

$$x^2 + \frac{5}{2}x + \frac{1}{2} = 0$$

Add the opposite of the third term (the term without an x) to both sides.

$$x^2 + \frac{5}{2}x = -\frac{1}{2}$$

Now take the coefficient of x, $\frac{5}{2}$, divide it by 2, which gives you $\frac{5}{4}$, and square that to get $\frac{25}{16}$. Add $\frac{25}{16}$ to both sides.

$$x^2 + \frac{5}{2}x + \frac{25}{16} = -\frac{1}{2} + \frac{25}{16}$$

Now the left side is the square of the binomial $x + \frac{5}{4}$.

$$\left(x + \frac{5}{4}\right)^2 = \frac{17}{16}$$

Take the square root of both sides. Don't forget the $\pm$ sign.

$$\sqrt{\left(x + \frac{5}{4}\right)^2} = \pm\sqrt{\frac{17}{16}}$$

Solve for x.

$$x + \frac{5}{4} = \frac{\pm\sqrt{17}}{4}$$

$$x = \frac{-5 \pm\sqrt{17}}{4}$$

Here's a quick recap of all those crazy steps:

The Complete-the-Square Method for Solving Quadratic Equations

1. Put the equation into $ax^2 + bx + c = 0$ form.
2. Divide everything by the coefficient of x^2.
3. Add the opposite of the third term (the term without an x) to both sides.
4. Take the new coefficient of x, divide it by 2, square what you get, and add the result to both sides of the equation.
5. Take the square root of both sides—don't forget the $\pm$ sign.
6. Solve for the values of x.

Now look at what happens when you use the complete-the-square method on the general form of a quadratic equation $ax^2 + bx + c = 0$.

Divide everything by the coefficient of x^2.

$$x^2 + \frac{b}{a}x + \frac{c}{a} = 0$$

Add the opposite of the third term (the term without an x) to both sides.

$$x^2 + \frac{b}{a}x = 0 - \frac{c}{a}$$

Take the new coefficient of x, $\frac{b}{a}$, divide it by 2 to get $\frac{b}{2a}$, and square that to get $\frac{b^2}{4a^2}$. Add $\frac{b^2}{4a^2}$ to both sides of the equation.

$$x^2 + \frac{b}{a}x + \frac{b^2}{4a^2} = -\frac{c}{a} + \frac{b^2}{4a^2}$$

$$\left(x + \frac{b}{2a}\right)^2 = -\frac{4ac}{4a^2} + \frac{b^2}{4a^2}$$

Take the square root of both sides—don't forget the ± sign.

$$\sqrt{\left(x + \frac{b}{2a}\right)^2} = \pm\sqrt{\frac{b^2 - 4ac}{4a^2}}$$

Solve for the values of x.

$$x + \frac{b}{2a} = \pm\frac{\sqrt{b^2 - 4ac}}{2a^2}$$

$$x = -\frac{b}{2a} \pm \frac{\sqrt{b^2 - 4ac}}{2a}$$

$$x = \frac{-b \pm \sqrt{b^2 - 4ac}}{2a}$$

This is the solution to any equation of the form $ax^2 + bx + c = 0$, where $a \neq 0$.

This solution should look familiar, from your exciting math classes in high school. (What do you mean you missed that day!) Anyway, it's called the *quadratic formula*.

The Quadratic-Formula Method

The quadratic formula is a like a shiny new socket wrench set for your bike—it's an excellent tool that enables you to solve *any* quadratic equation—without the hassle of factoring, or completing the square.

The Quadratic-Formula Method for Solving Quadratic Equations

1. Put the equation into $ax^2 + bx + c = 0$ form.
2. Plug the values of a, b, and c into the formula:

$$x = \frac{-b \pm \sqrt{b^2 - 4ac}}{2a}$$

3. Solve for the values of x.

Question: Solve for y: $2y^2 = 4 - 5y$

Solution: First put the equation into $ax^2 + bx + c = 0$ form.

$$2y^2 + 5y - 4 = 0$$

Plug $a = 2$, $b = 5$, and $c = -4$ into the quadratic formula.

$$y = \frac{-5 \pm \sqrt{25 - (-32)}}{4}$$

Simplify.

$$y = \frac{-5 \pm \sqrt{57}}{4}$$

POWER SURGE

Using the quadratic formula, you can find solutions to quadratic equations even when those solutions are not real numbers. Suppose, for example, you used the quadratic formula on this equation:

$$x^2 - x + 1 = 0$$

Plug $a = 1$, $b = -1$, and $c = 1$ into the quadratic formula:

$$x = \frac{-b \pm \sqrt{b^2 - 4ac}}{2a} = \frac{1 \pm \sqrt{1-4}}{2} = \frac{1 \pm \sqrt{-3}}{2}$$

If you define i as $\sqrt{-1}$,

then you can express the above solutions as $\dfrac{1 \pm i\sqrt{3}}{2}$.

A number of the form ai, in which a is a real number and i is $\sqrt{-1}$, is called an *imaginary number*. A number of the form $a + bi$, in which a and b are real numbers and i is $\sqrt{-1}$ is called a *complex number*. Imaginary and complex numbers are a logical extension of the number system, and in a sense they are just as real as the misleadingly named "real" numbers. They might have just been theoretical notions at first, born of math heads' nagging desire to have *all* the answers for equations with integer coefficients. But eventually, since they needed something to do with this whole new system they'd dreamed up, imaginary and complex numbers developed some practical, applications here on planet Earth, particularly in electrical theory and the physical sciences.

Math heads are not primarily motivated by practical applications. (If you've been reading the last couple chapters, you've figured that one out already.) They're more like explorers than engineers, pioneers on the frontier of knowledge (ooh, neat), motivated by a desire to find out fundamental math truths, and they're so into what they're doing, that they're sure that the truth will lead to usefulness.

Equations with Variables Inside Square Root Symbols

Sometimes quadratic equations don't look like quadratic equations at first. A case in point is the type of equation that has a variable lurking inside a square root symbol.

You can turn such an equation into a more familiar-looking equation form by the following means: isolate the radical, square both sides of the equation, and solve it as usual. You've got to

ᴧᴧᴧ∘**CONNECTION** ∘ᴧᴧᴧ

To find out more about these *Extraneous Solutions*, turn to chapter 11.

remember, though, that squaring both sides of an equation can give you a false answer, that is, an *extraneous solution*. Talk about finding out more than you want to . . .

Check out this example:

$$x + \sqrt{x + 1} = 5$$

First thing to do is get the radical alone on one side. To do so, subtract x from both sides.

$$\sqrt{x + 1} = 5 - x$$

Now square both sides to get rid of the radical.

$$\sqrt{(x + 1)^2} = (5 - x)^2$$
$$x + 1 = 25 - 10x + x^2$$

Now you have an equation form that you know how to solve. It's a quadratic equation, so put it into $ax^2 + bx + c = 0$ form.

$$x^2 - 11x + 24 = 0$$

Plug $a = 1$, $b = -11$, and $c = 24$ into the quadratic formula and simplify.

$$x = \frac{11 \pm \sqrt{11^2 - 4(1)(24)}}{2}$$

$$x = \frac{11 \pm \sqrt{121 - 96}}{2}$$

$$x = \frac{11 \pm \sqrt{25}}{2} = \frac{11 \pm 5}{2}$$

$$x = \frac{16}{2} = 8 \ \text{ or } \ x = \frac{6}{2} = 3$$

Once you get through the machinations of applying the quadratic formula and end up with $x = 3$ or 8, you might forget that early in the solution process you squared both sides, and so you need to double-check your solutions. Plug $x = 3$ back into the original equation:

$$x + \sqrt{x + 1} = 5$$

$$3 + \sqrt{3 + 1} = 5$$

$$3 + \sqrt{4} = 5$$

$$3 + 2 = 5 \ \text{ Yes.}$$

So $x = 3$ works. What about $x = 8$?

$$x + \sqrt{x + 1} = 5$$

$$8 + \sqrt{8 + 1} = 5$$

$$8 + \sqrt{9} = 5$$

$$8 + 3 = 5 \ \text{ No.}$$

So $x = 8$ does *not* work. It's an extraneous solution.

How Do You Know Which Method to Use?

When you want to solve a quadratic equation and you see a way to do it by factoring, just go ahead and do it that way. Otherwise, use the quadratic-formula method. If there's a way to factor the left side but you just don't see it, no matter. The quadratic-formula method will work just fine. One of the great things about the quadratic-formula method is that it *always* works, eventually. Don't you wish your car was like that?

You're not likely to want to use the complete-the-squares method very often. Once you've used it to derive the quadratic formula, you've already done the work and you might as well just use the formula from then on.

With the quadratic formula under your belt, you're ready for this chapter's "Do the Math" Question:

DO THE MATH

Find the positive number x for which $x - 1$ is equal to the reciprocal of x.

Solution: The reciprocal of x is $\dfrac{1}{x}$.

If $x - 1$ is equal to the reciprocal of x, then this is the equation:

$$x - 1 = \frac{1}{x}$$

Multiply both sides by x.

$$(x - 1)(x) = \left(\frac{1}{x}\right)(x)$$

Remove parentheses.

$$x^2 - x = 1$$

Subtract 1 from both sides to get $ax^2 + bx + c = 0$ form.

$$x^2 - x - 1 = 0$$

Plug $a = 1$, $b = -1$, and $c = -1$ into the quadratic formula.

$$x = \frac{-(-1) \pm \sqrt{(-1)^2 - 4(1)(-1)}}{2(1)}$$

Solve for x.

$$x = \frac{1 \pm \sqrt{1 + 4}}{2}$$

$$x = \frac{1 \pm \sqrt{5}}{2}$$

The question asks for the *positive* number that meets the given criteria, and so the answer is $\frac{1 + \sqrt{5}}{2}$. This is an especially exciting irrational number.

Use your calculator to approximate it. Enter 5, take the square root, add 1, and divide the result by 2. What you should end up with is approximately 1.618033989; if you didn't, then it's time to get a new calculator. Now, take the reciprocal of that and see what you get. You get the same number, but without the 1 in front of the decimal point. Take the reciprocal again and the 1 comes back. Keep taking the reciprocal over and over again and you can watch the 1 come and go and come and go. (The last digit might toggle, too, but that's just because of rounding off.)

Here's another calculator trick you can do with this number. Take your approximation of $\frac{1 + \sqrt{5}}{2}$ again—that's about 1.618033989—and square it.

What happens? What do you get? Now, take the square root of the result. What happens? What do you get? Keep squaring and square-rooting and watch it toggle. What you're demonstrating is that this is also the positive number x for which the square of x is equal to $x + 1$.

This number has a lot of wacky properties and applications. For one thing, it is the value of what is called the *golden ratio*, which is the ratio of the length to the width of the *golden rectangle*.

○◦ᴡᴡᴡ◦ **CONNECTION** ◦ᴡᴡᴡ◦

Golden Rectangle (chapter 15).

And another thing: this number also relates to the Fibonacci sequence (remember those). Who knew? The ratio of any number in the sequence to its immediate predecessor is approximately equal to this number. And the deeper you get into the sequence—that is, the bigger the numbers you take the ratio of, the closer the ratio will be to $\frac{1 + \sqrt{5}}{2} \approx 1.618033989$. Here, for example, are the ratios of consecutive Fibonacci numbers up to 1,597:

$$\frac{1}{1} = 1.0$$

$$\frac{2}{1} = 2.0$$

$$\frac{3}{2} = 1.5$$

$$\frac{5}{3} \approx 1.666666667$$

$$\frac{8}{5} = 1.6$$

$$\frac{13}{8} = 1.625$$

$$\frac{21}{13} \approx 1.615384615$$

$$\frac{34}{21} \approx 1.619047619$$

$$\frac{55}{34} = 1.617647059$$

$$\frac{89}{55} \approx 1.618181818$$

$$\frac{144}{89} \approx 1.617977528$$

$$\frac{233}{144} \approx 1.618055556$$

$$\frac{377}{233} = 1.618025751$$

$$\frac{610}{377} \approx 1.618037135$$

$$\frac{987}{610} \approx 1.618032787$$

$$\frac{1{,}597}{987} \approx 1.618034448$$

As the Fibonacci numbers get larger, the ratio of consecutive numbers approaches a limit of $\dfrac{1 + \sqrt{5}}{2}$. So important is this irrational number, so wide-reaching are its applications, that mathematicians have given it a Greek-letter name—just like π. By convention, the irrational number $\dfrac{1 + \sqrt{5}}{2}$, which is approximately equal to 1.618033989, is called ϕ, or "phi" (rhymes with "hi" and "why" as in "why do I have to learn this stuff").

Do you want to see another cool characteristic of the number ϕ? Don't answer that, because you know we're going to show you anyway. Look at the pattern that develops when ϕ is raised to successively higher exponents:

$$\phi^1 = \frac{1 + \sqrt{5}}{2}$$

$$\phi^2 = \frac{3 + \sqrt{5}}{2}$$

$$\phi^3 = \frac{4 + 2\sqrt{5}}{2}$$

$$\phi^4 = \frac{7 + 3\sqrt{5}}{2}$$

$$\phi^5 = \frac{11 + 5\sqrt{5}}{2}$$

$$\phi^6 = \frac{18 + 8\sqrt{5}}{2}$$

$$\phi^7 = \frac{29 + 13\sqrt{5}}{2}$$

$$\phi^8 = \frac{47 + 21\sqrt{5}}{2}$$

Do you see the pattern? Each power is equal to the sum of the two preceding powers. For example, ϕ^8 is equal to $\phi^6 + \phi^7$. There is no other positive real number x for which it is true that $x^n + x^{n+1} = x^{n+2}$ for all values of n.

And did you notice all the Fibonacci numbers in the above forms? As presented above—always with a denominator of 2, even when the fraction can be further reduced—the coefficient of each $\sqrt{5}$ is a Fibonacci number. And further-

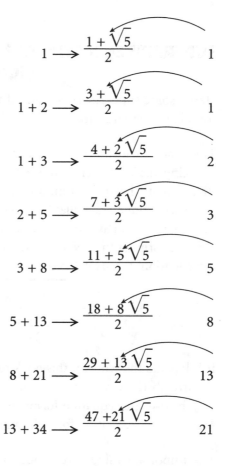

$$1 \longrightarrow \frac{1 + \sqrt{5}}{2} \qquad 1$$

$$1 + 2 \longrightarrow \frac{3 + \sqrt{5}}{2} \qquad 1$$

$$1 + 3 \longrightarrow \frac{4 + 2\sqrt{5}}{2} \qquad 2$$

$$2 + 5 \longrightarrow \frac{7 + 3\sqrt{5}}{2} \qquad 3$$

$$3 + 8 \longrightarrow \frac{11 + 5\sqrt{5}}{2} \qquad 5$$

$$5 + 13 \longrightarrow \frac{18 + 8\sqrt{5}}{2} \qquad 8$$

$$8 + 21 \longrightarrow \frac{29 + 13\sqrt{5}}{2} \qquad 13$$

$$13 + 34 \longrightarrow \frac{47 + 21\sqrt{5}}{2} \qquad 21$$

more, the other number in the numerator is equal to the sum of the preceding and succeeding Fibonacci numbers. Even math heads couldn't get that complex by themselves. They were just watching nature work. Whoever thought raising rabbits could be such an intellectual pursuit?

In the case of $\phi^8 = \dfrac{47 + 21\sqrt{5}}{2}$, for example, the coefficient of $\sqrt{5}$ is 21, which is the eighth Fibonacci number. And the other number in the numerator, 47, is equal to the sum of 13 and 34, the seventh and ninth Fibonacci numbers. Fibonacci numbers—they're everywhere you look!

SUPERPOWER MATH: THE SEARCH FOR FORMULAS FOR HIGHER-DEGREE EQUATIONS

Here's some superpowered math, if the detective work we've been doing in this chapter wasn't enough for you.

The quadratic formula enables you to solve a second-degree equation just by plugging the coefficients into a formula. In the 16th century, a group of Italian math heads, Geronimo Cardane, Niccolò Tartaglia, and Lodovico Ferrari, developed formulas for solving third-degree and fourth-degree equations. They're not as neat and clean as the quadratic formula. Here, for example, is a formula that, when used correctly, will lead you to the solutions of the equation $x^3 + ax + b = 0$:

$$x = \sqrt[3]{\dfrac{-b + \sqrt{b^2 + \dfrac{4a^3}{27}}}{2}} + \sqrt[3]{\dfrac{-b - \sqrt{b^2 + \dfrac{4a^3}{27}}}{2}}$$

It is beyond the scope of this book to explain exactly how to use this formula correctly (hey, even powered-up people like us have our limits). As you can see, third-degree equation formulas are complicated. Can you imagine what fourth-degree equation formulas must be like?

The important thing here is not so much to understand the mechanics of these formulas as it is just to know they exist. Once it was known that there are formulas for second-, third-, and fourth-degree equations, it was expected that there would be formulas for equations of higher degrees as well. That's the kind of generality mathematicians live for. "Great" minds worked for centuries, staying up late, drinking endless cups of coffee, to derive formulas for fifth- and higher-degree equations. But they never pulled it off.

Finally, in the 19th century, French math student Évariste Galois proved that no such formulas exist. Boy were the last three hundred years' worth of math heads steamed about that! Fortunately Galois had the presence of mind to jot down some of his ground-breaking ideas the night before he was killed in a duel at age 21. Don't you think it was one of those old guys who got him for proving them wrong?

Plug In

After an invigorating chapter on advanced algebra equations, what better way to unwind than with a few of our review questions!

1. Solve for x and y: $\begin{cases} ax - by = 1 \\ 2ax + by = 8 \end{cases}$ _____

2. Solve for $x + y$: $\begin{cases} 2x - 3y = 6 \\ x - 4y = 4 \end{cases}$ _____

3. Solve for x: $|x + 4| < 5$ _____

4. Solve for x: $x^2 + 2x = 1$ _____

5. Solve for x: $\sqrt{x + 9} = x + 7$ _____

Word Problems: Words of Wisdom

Let's face it, people: Algebraic word problems are some of the concrete proof that this stuff is useful in the real world. Even if some of these problems seem a little simplified compared to your own life (in the Do the Math problem, if Albert and Bertha *fall in love*, while painting, for instance; it could take a lot longer to do the job), think of them as blueprints for things that will really come up in your life.

> ～ﾊﾟ**DO THE MATH**ﾊﾟ～
>
> Albert could paint the living room all by himself in *x* hours. If Bertha helped, the job would get done 2 hours faster. How many hours, in terms of *x*, would it take Bertha to paint the living room all by herself? (See the solution near the end of this chapter.)

In this, our last chapter of algebra, we're going to get into basic word problem scenarios, and variations on the most common themes you'll find. Some of these situations are so awesome, they'll take the *words* right out of your MATH!

WORD UP!

The finest algebra detective has to be able to see through problems that are too tricky to solve just by manipulating numbers and variables. This is when your old friend and fellow detective, the English language comes in handy. Here's a look at a prime example:

Question: Let's say you're planning to put some money into an account that increases at an effective annual interest rate of 9.85 percent. If you want have one million dollars at the end of 40 years, how much should you put in?

If you tried to find the answer by trial-and-error, you'd be broke by the time you expected to have your million in the bag. You'd have to start by picking a number out of thin air, and try applying a 9.85 percent increase 40 times, and see how close to a million you end up. If you end up with more than a million after 40 increases, then your first guess was too big, so you'd try a smaller number. Just testing out each guess takes too long to even think about.

It makes more sense to translate the problem to an algebraic equation and solve. The initial investment is what you're looking for, so call it x. Each year the amount increases by 9.85 percent. That means, in the course of the first year, x dollars becomes $1.0985x$ dollars. And in the course of the next year, $1.0985x$ dollars becomes $(1.0985)(1.0985)x$ dollars—you can think of that as 1.0985^2x dollars. And in the course of the next year, $(1.0985)(1.0985)x$ dollars becomes $(1.0985)(1.0985)(1.0985)x$ dollars—you can think of that as 1.0985^3x dollars. Do you see the pattern? We sure hope so.

after 1 year	$1.0985x$
after 2 years	1.0985^2x
after 3 years	1.0985^3x
after n years	1.0985^nx

So after 40 years, x dollars will have become $1.0985^{40}x$ dollars. To find out what x has to be to make 1.0985^{40} equal to a million, solve this equation:

$$1.0985^{40}x = 1,000,000$$

Compared to making the equation, solving the equation is easy. Remember? You just divide both sides by 1.0985^{40}:

$$x = \frac{1,000,000}{1.0985^{40}}$$

Use your handy-dandy calculator (remember those?) to find 1.0985^{40}. Enter "1.0985." Then hit the "y^x" key and enter "40." When you hit the "=" key, you should get something like "42.85509382":

$$x = \frac{1,000,000}{42.85509382}$$

Punch the division into your calculator: 1,000,000 divided by 42.85509382 is about 23,334.44897. Thus you would want to invest \$23,334.45. (Pretty amazing, how you can start with less than \$24,000 and end up with a million? And you'd have never known if you hadn't started pumping up your own math power!)

An Age-Old Problem

Sometimes word problems can be a big fat bummer to have to untangle. Here's an example of the kind of word problem that causes math-headaches world-wide:

Question: Five years ago, the sum of the ages of Abby's two daughters was 22. Five years from now the older daughter will be exactly twice as old as the younger daughter. How old is the older daughter now?

One way to do this problem would be just to try out many different possibilities for the older daughter's current age until you found the one that works. Even here, however—where you know the solution will probably be less than 100—the trial-and-error approach would take longer than even die-hard math heads want to spend.

⌇⌇ POWER LINE ⌇⌇

"Do not worry about your difficulties in mathematics, I assure you that mine are greater."

–Albert Einstein

You'll get to the answer much more quickly and painlessly if you take an algebraic approach.

Let's start at the beginning. The word problem consists of three sentences—two statements and a question. Read the whole problem once through just to get the overview, and to figure out what the heck you're being asked to find. The two statements provide key clues as to the relative ages of Abby's daugh-

ters, and the question asks for the older daughter's current age. Let x represent the older daughter's age, and let y represent the younger daughter's age.

Now go back to the beginning of the problem, and translate each statement into an equation. The first statement reads: "Five years ago, the sum of the ages of Abby's two daughters was 22." To translate that statement, think about what the daughters' ages were back then in terms of their current ages x and y. They were each 5 years younger, and so their ages were $x - 5$ and $y - 5$. The sum of those two ages was 22, so your first equation is:

$$(x - 5) + (y - 5) = 22$$

The above equation is the algebraic equivalent of the English sentence, "Five years ago, the sum of the ages of Abby's two daughters was 22," but it's not a complete translation. It doesn't say anything about Abby, or daughters, or ages, or years. It deals only with the *underlying quantitative equality* (that means, "the math") presented in the sentence, and says the sum of 5 less than one number and 5 less than another number is the same as the number 22. The equation doesn't even reflect the fact that the unknown numbers have to be integers. The equation actually contains less information than the sentence, but the information it contains will prove more useful mathematically.

Now look at the next sentence: "Five years from now the older daughter will be exactly twice as old as the younger daughter." If the older daughter is x years old now, then she will be five more than that, or $x + 5$ years old five years from now. Likewise, the younger daughter will be $y + 5$ years old. The quantitative equality that underlies this sentence is this: the older daughter's age will be equal to two times the younger daughter's age. Thus the equation looks like this:

$$x + 5 = 2(y + 5)$$

Now that you've distilled the verbiage to its mathematical essence, you have two equations in two variables, which means you can pretty much forget the text and concentrate on the algebra. All you really need to remember is that it's the older daughter's age you're looking for, and so it's x that you're solving for.

To solve for x, look for a way to combine the equations and lose all the y's.

First remove the parentheses and express the equations in parallel form:

$$(x-5) + (y-5) = 22 \qquad\qquad x+5 = 2(y+5)$$
$$x+y-10 = 22 \qquad\qquad x+5 = 2y+10$$
$$x+y = 32 \qquad\qquad x-2y = 5$$

Now multiply both sides of the first equation by 2, and you'll get $2x + 2y = 64$, which will combine the second equation just the way you want it to:

$$2x + 2y = 64$$
$$\underline{x - 2y = 5}$$
$$3x = 69$$

Now just divide both sides by 3 and you end up with $x = 23$.

Now that you have a solution in numbers, it's time to go back to the text and try it out. If the older daughter is now 23, then five years ago she was 18. And if the two daughters' ages added up to 22, then the younger daughter was 4 years old five years ago and is therefore 9 years old now. Five years from now the daughters will be $23 + 5 = 28$ and $9 + 5 = 14$. The older daughter, at 28, will indeed be twice as old as the younger daughter, at 14. The solution was correct. The older daughter is 23. And POW! You're a math-word-head extraordinaire!

What Am I Supposed to Do?!

Here's a bare bones summary of the four-step approach to solving word problems algebraically:

1. **Read the problem straight through once quickly, zeroing in on the question at the end.** In this first read-through, just get a general feel for the situation—get a mental picture—and focus on what you are asked to figure out. What the problem's asking for is usually found at the end. Don't get bogged down in the details of the given information during the first read-through.

2. **Go back and read the problem again, translating each verbal statement into algebra.** Make sure you keep track of what variables you're using

and what they represent. Sometimes a mental note is good enough, but when the problems get complicated, it helps to write down explicitly what each variable represents. Look for the quantitative equality that underlies each statement and translate it carefully into an equation. Remember, to get numerical solutions, you generally need as many equations as you have variables.

3. **Forget the text and solve the equation.** Just do the algebra—this is usually the easiest step in the process. It takes a lot less creativity and insight to solve equations than to create them.

4. **Go back to the text and check your answer.** Make sure your answer makes sense. If it's a distance you're looking for and you get a negative solution, then something must be wrong (or you're dealing with black holes, or something). If it's a number of people you're looking for and you get a fractional solution, then something must be wrong.

How to Do Word Problems: Read a word problem at least twice. First time read quickly, just getting the broad view, and zooming in carefully on the last part—the question. Don't start translating until the second read-through.

Question: If the sum of four consecutive multiples of 3 is 498, what is the largest of the four?

Solution: **Step 1:** Read the problem straight through once quickly, zeroing in on the question at the end. This problem is just one sentence, but that sentence breaks down to a statement and a question. What you're looking for is the largest of four consecutive multiples of 3. What you're given is the fact that the four multiples add up to 498.

Step 2: Go back and read the problem again, translating each verbal statement into algebra. The problem concerns four numbers, but you're only looking for the largest of them, and you can express the other three in terms of the one you're looking for. Let n represent what you're looking for: the largest of four consecutive multiples of 3. Then the other three multiples, in decreasing order, are $n - 3$, $n - 6$, and $n - 9$. According to the given information, these four numbers add up to 498. There's your equation:

$$n + (n - 3) + (n - 6) + (n - 9) = 498$$

Step 3: Solve the equation:

$$n + (n - 3) + (n - 6) + (n - 9) = 498$$
$$4n - 18 = 498$$
$$4n = 498 + 18$$
$$4n = 516$$
$$n = \frac{516}{4} = 129$$

Step 4: Go back to the text and check your answer. If the largest of the four consecutive multiples of 3 is 129, then the other three are 126, 123, and 120. The sum of those is 129 + 126 + 123 + 120 = 498. The solution was correct. The answer is 129.

Start Making Sense

Let's say you've got mad foreign language power, and you tried to translate this sentence from French: *Elles s'en sont allées il n'y a que deux heures.* If you did it word for word, you might come up with a result something like, "They themselves of it are gone it not there has that two hours." That's not just uni-diomatic—it's gibberish. With foreign languages, you don't translate word by word, but idea by idea. *Elles s'en sont allées* translates more idiomatically and clearly to "They left," and *il n'y a que deux heures* translates to "only two hours ago." So the whole sentence means "They left only two hours ago." Now that's better, *n'est-ce pas?*

It's the same deal when you translate English into math. Don't try to translate word for word. Translate whole phrases or statements at a time. A chart like the following has its uses, but it doesn't tell you the whole story:

English	Math
equals, is, was, will be, has, costs, adds up to, is the same as	=
times, of, multiplied by, product of, twice, double, half, triple	×
divided by, per, out of, each, ratio of __ to ___	÷
plus, added to, sum, combined, and, more than, total	+
minus, subtracted from, less than, decreased by, difference	−
what, how much, how many, a certain number	x, n, etc.

If you just try and translate this stuff without thinking it through, you're going to get into trouble. Take the word "of," for example. The chart says "of" means multiplication. Well, that's true sometimes, as in "50 percent *of* the population" or "five groups *of* 24 students." But it's *not* true in cases like "the sum *of* two consecutive integers" or "the ratio *of* wins to losses."

Learning the Classics

If you've been near an algebra textbook sometime in your life, you probably have had nightmares about the following three scenarios:

1. The Two-Trains Scenario
2. The Alcohol-Solution Scenario
3. The Working-Together Scenario

The *Two-Trains Scenario* goes something like this: A train leaves point *A* at a certain time and heads towards point *B* at a certain speed. Another train leaves point *B* at a certain time and heads towards point *A* at a certain speed. When will they collide? (And how do you make sure you're not on either one?)

The *Alcohol-Solution Scenario* goes like this: A certain amount of a solution that is a certain percent alcohol is added to a certain amount of another solution that is a certain percent alcohol. The resulting solution is what percent alcohol?

The *Working-Together Scenario* goes something like this: If one person can do a job in a certain amount of time, and another person can do the same job in a certain amount of time, how long will it take the two persons together to do the job?

Remember these things? Still hate them? Well, it's probably because they're really hard! Rest assured, you aren't alone: a lot of people hate these problems. Many never get over their hatred, or need years of counseling to work it out. Luckily you've got us, your Math Power therapists.

Look at it this way. If you're a musician, then you know how every song you write or learn to play has at least one part to it that's really difficult. The way you deal with those parts is to spend extra time rehearsing them, so you look and sound smooth and sassy the next time you hit the stage. That's turning your musical weakness into strength, while also taking your playing to the next level.

Well now, you can do the same thing with algebra. Want potential dates to swoon at your rocking math solos, and complex algebraic harmonies? Instead of running away from a problem type you can't seem to figure out, try facing it head on. You can master all three of the scenarios we've been dealing with; it just takes a little more rehearsal.

Be careful, though. You're not going to learn simplistic rote methods here (those are so 1980's). There are so many possible variations within each of the three classic scenarios, you can't really expect to get a formula that will apply to every variation. If all *two-trains* problems were the same except for the numbers—or if all *alcohol-solution* problems were the same, or if all *working-together* problems were the same—then you could use formulas to solve them.

But formulas get boring after a while. These problems take a little more in-depth sleuthing to figure out. The way to learn how to do each of them is to learn the standard setup for a typical example, and then to learn how to adapt the standard setup to common variations.

Two Trains Running

Let's use the following as our typical example of a two-trains question:

Typical Two-Trains Problem: A train leaves Town A and heads for Town B at an average speed of 45 miles per hour. A second train leaves Town B at the same time and heads for Town A along the same route at an average speed of 30 miles per hour. If the route is 450 miles long, how many hours will it take for the trains to meet?

Here's how to set up the solution. As always, look for the underlying equality. In this case it's that the distance traveled by train 1 up to the moment they meet, added to the distance traveled by train 2 up to the same moment, is equal to the total distance from A to B:

Use the standard "distance-equals-rate-times-time" formula to express each distance in terms of x, the number of hours it takes for the trains to meet. Train 1, traveling at 45 miles per hour, will have traveled a total of $45x$ miles in x hours. Train 2, traveling at 30 miles per hour, will have traveled $30x$ miles in x hours. Those two distances, $45x$ miles and $30x$ miles, add up to the total A-to-B distance of 450 miles. So the equation is:

$$45x + 30x = 450$$

As usual, it's a lot easier to solve the equation than to come up with it. Add the like terms $45x$ and $30x$ and you get $75x$. Then divide both sides by 75 to get x alone:

$$45x + 30x = 450$$
$$75x = 450$$
$$x = \frac{450}{75} = 6$$

It will take 6 hours for the trains to meet.

So the standard setup for the typical two-trains problem is this:

The Two-Trains Setup

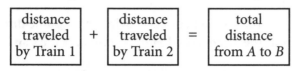

| distance traveled by Train 1 | + | distance traveled by Train 2 | = | total distance from A to B |

More Trains of Thought

Of course, problems of this type don't have to be about trains at all. They can be about anything that moves, like motorcycles, skateboards or hockey pucks. A trickier version of the two-trains problem has the moving objects leaving at different times:

Question: A guy driving a car leaves Town A at 12:00 noon and heads for Town B at an average speed of 60 miles per hour. Another guy driving another car leaves Town B at 2:00 P.M. the same day and heads for Town A along the same route at an average speed of 50 miles per hour. If the route is 450 miles long, how far will they be from Town A when they pass each other?

Solution: The underlying equality is the same: the distance traveled by the guy in the first car added to the distance traveled by the guy in the second car equals the total distance from A to B. Let t represent the number of hours since the first guy's departure. Going 60 miles per hour for t hours, the first guy travels $60t$ miles. The second guy hasn't been traveling for the whole t hours. He left two hours later, so he's been traveling for $t - 2$ hours. Going 50 miles per hour for $t-2$ hours, the second guy travels $50(t - 2)$ miles. Those two distances, $60t$ miles and $50(t-2)$ miles, add up to the total A-to-B distance of 450 miles. So the equation is:

$$60t + 50(t - 2) = 450$$

$$60t + 50t - 100 = 450$$

$$110t = 550$$

$$t = \frac{550}{110} = 5$$

They will pass each other 5 hours after the first guy's departure. The question asks how far they will be from Town A. After 5 hours, the first guy will have traveled 60 × 5 = 300 miles from Town A.

Another variation has the moving objects moving in the same direction. You might think of this as the *Tortoise-and-Hare Variation*. Here's an example:

Question: In a foot race, the tortoise is given a merciful 30-minute head start. If the tortoise runs at 2 miles per hour, and the hare runs at 8 miles per hour, how many minutes after the hare starts running will he catch up to the tortoise?

The difference in the setup here is that the two distances don't add up to a total distance. This time, the two distances are the same. When the bunny catches up to the turtle, they will both have traveled the same distance from the starting point.

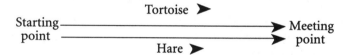

Let x represent the number of *hours* it will take the hare to catch up. (Remember that the question asks for the answer in minutes.) The tortoise is traveling 2 miles per hour, but he's been traveling for more than x hours. He had a 30-minute head start, so he's been traveling for $x + \dfrac{1}{2}$ hours. Traveling 2 miles per hour for $x + \dfrac{1}{2}$ hours, the tortoise travels $2\left(x + \dfrac{1}{2}\right)$ miles. The hare, traveling 8 miles per hour for x hours, travels $8x$ miles. Those two distances, $2\left(x + \dfrac{1}{2}\right)$ and $8x$, are equal:

$$2\left(x + \frac{1}{2}\right) = 8x$$

Now all you have to do is solve the equation:

$$2\left(x + \frac{1}{2}\right) = 8x$$

$$2x + 1 = 8x$$

$$6x = 1$$

$$x = \frac{1}{6}$$

The hare needs only $\frac{1}{6}$ of an hour to catch up. That's 10 minutes.

Drinking's Not the Answer: The Alcohol-Solution Scenario

Let's use the following as our typical example of an alcohol-solution problem.

Typical Alcohol-Solution Problem: Four liters of a solution that is 20 percent alcohol is mixed with 8 liters of a solution that is 50 percent alcohol. What percent of the resulting mixture is alcohol?

Here's how to set up a solution (so to speak) to this typical problem. Think of it as the "solution solution." As always, look for the underlying equality in the wording. In this case it's that the actual amount of alcohol in the first solution, added to the actual amount of alcohol in the second solution, equals the actual amount of alcohol in the final mixture.

The Alcohol-Solution Setup

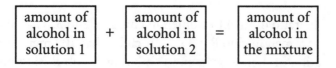

You can find the actual amount of alcohol in each of the two original solutions by multiplying the percents by the quantities. You have 4 liters of solution 1, and 20 percent of that is alcohol, so the actual amount of alcohol in solution + is .20(4) liters. Similarly, the actual amount of alcohol in solution 2 is .50(8) liters. The total volume of the final mixture is 4 + 8 = 12 liters, x percent of which is alcohol. The two actual amounts of alcohol, .20(4) and .50(8), add up to the amount of alcohol in the final mixture, which is x percent of 12, or $\frac{x}{100}(12)$. Now you have your equation, and you can solve for x:

$$.20(4) + .50(8) = \frac{x}{100}(12)$$

$$.8 + 4.0 = .12x$$

$$x = \frac{4.8}{.12} = 40$$

The resulting mixture is 40 percent alcohol.

The typical alcohol solution problem concerns five numbers—the quantity of solution 1, its percent alcohol, the quantity of solution 2, its percent alcohol, and the percent alcohol of the resulting mixture. (The *quantity* of the resulting mixture is just the sum of the two original quantities.) If you know any four of these numbers, you can figure out the fifth. They are related this way:

$$\left(\frac{\text{percent 1}}{100} \times A\right) + \left(\frac{\text{percent 2}}{100} \times B\right) = \left(\frac{\text{new percent}}{100}\right) \times (A + B)$$

More Mixed Drinks:
Variations on Alcohol-Solution Problems

Of course, problems of this type don't have to be about alcohol at all. They can be about all kinds of mixtures. And they don't have to be expressed in terms of percents, either. Here's a related situation that mixes men and women and expresses the mixtures in terms of *ratios*:

Question: The ratio of men to women in club A is 2 to 3. The ratio of men to women in club B is 3 to 7. If club A has 100 members and the ration of men to women in club A and club B combined is 8 to 17, how many members does club B have?

Solution: First, turn the ratios into fractions. The ratio of men to women in club A is 2 to 3, so you can say that club A is $\frac{2}{2+3} = \frac{2}{5}$ male. Similarly, the ratio of men to women in club B is 3 to 7, so you can say that club B is $\dfrac{3}{3+7} = \dfrac{3}{10}$ male. Similarly again, when club A and club B are combined, the ration of men to women is 8 to 17, so you can say that club A and club B combined is $\dfrac{8}{8+17} = \dfrac{8}{25}$ male. Two-fifths of the 100 members of club A added to $\dfrac{3}{10}$ of the x numbers of club B equals $\dfrac{8}{25}$ of the $100 + x$ members of club A and club B combined.

So the equation is: $\dfrac{2}{5}(100) + \dfrac{3}{10}x = \dfrac{8}{25}(100 + x)$

To solve, first clear all the denominators by multipying both sides by the LCM of 5, 10, and 25, which is 50.

$$50 \times \left[\dfrac{2}{5}(100) + \dfrac{3}{10}x \right] = \dfrac{8}{25}(100 + x)$$

$$20(100) + 15x = 16(100 + x)$$

$$2{,}000 + 15x = 1{,}600 + 16x$$

$$400 = x$$

$$x = 400$$

There are 400 members in club B.

Punch the Clock: The Working-Together Scenario

Finally, here's our example of a typical working-together problem:

Typical Working-Together Problem: If Alice can do the job alone in 30 hours, and if Betty can do the job alone in 20 hours, how many hours will it take the two of them working together to do the job?

Here's how to set up the solution to this typical problem. As always, look for the underlying equality (sound like a broken record?). In this case it's that the fraction of the job that Alice can do in an hour, added to the fraction of the job that Betty can do in an hour, equals the fraction of the job that they can do together in an hour.

The Working-Together Setup

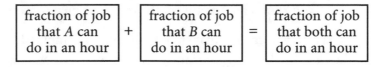

If Alice can do the whole job in 30 hours, then she can do $\frac{1}{30}$ of the job in one hour. Similarly, if Betty can do the whole job in 20 hours, then she can do $\frac{1}{20}$ of the job in one hour. Together then, they can do $\frac{1}{30} + \frac{1}{20}$ of the job in one hour. Add $\frac{1}{30}$ and $\frac{1}{20}$ and you get $\frac{1}{30} + \frac{1}{20} = \frac{2}{60} + \frac{3}{60} = \frac{5}{60} = \frac{1}{12}$. (We're taking you way back to fractions to handle this stuff.) So together they can do $\frac{1}{12}$ of the job in one hour, which means they can do the whole job in the reciprocal of $\frac{1}{12}$, or 12 hours.

So, the setup for this typical problem is:

$$\frac{1}{A \text{ alone}} + \frac{1}{B \text{ alone}} = \frac{1}{A \text{ and } B \text{ together}}$$

Doing Overtime: Working-Together Variations

Since we're living in the age of automation, we're throwing a variation at you that involves machines instead of people; see if you can handle it. You're given the time it would take for the first machine, and the time for the two machines together, and you're asked to find the time it would take for the second machine alone:

Question: If Machine A alone can produce 100 widgets in 30 minutes, and if Machines A and B together can produce 100 widgets in 24 minutes, how many minutes would it take Machine B alone to produce 100 widgets?

Solution: Use the standard working-together setup. Here you know the time for A alone and for A and B together:

$$\frac{1}{A \text{ alone}} + \frac{1}{B \text{ alone}} = \frac{1}{A \text{ and } B \text{ together}}$$

$$\frac{1}{30} + \frac{1}{x} = \frac{1}{24}$$

Now solve for x. First clear denominators by multiplying both sides by the LCM of 30, x, and 24—that's $120x$:

$$120x \times \left(\frac{1}{30} + \frac{1}{x}\right) = \left(\frac{1}{24}\right) \times 120x$$

$$4x + 120 = 5x$$

$$120 = 5x - 4x$$

$$x = 120$$

It would take Machine B 120 minutes (i.e., two hours) to do the job alone.

In this chapter's "Do the Math" question, you're given one person's time and some information about the time it would take the two people together. Here's where it gets tricky. One problem is that the one person's time is given, not as a specific number of hours, but as x. The other is that, instead, of telling you how long it would take the two together, the problem tells you they'd do it two hours faster. When you own your own company, you're going to need this stuff, so you know who to hire.

DO THE MATH

Albert could paint the living room all by himself in x hours. If Bertha helped, the job would get done 2 hours faster. How many hours, in terms of x, would it take Bertha to paint the living room all by herself?

Solution: According to the standard setup:

$$\frac{1}{A \text{ alone}} + \frac{1}{B \text{ alone}} = \frac{1}{A \text{ and } B \text{ together}}$$

This time, "A alone" is x; "B alone" is what you're looking for; and "A and B together" is 2 less than "A alone," so it's $x - 2$:

$$\frac{1}{x} + \frac{1}{b} = \frac{1}{x - 2}$$

Now you want to solve this equation for b. To do that, you begin by clearing denominators. First, multiply both sides by x:

$$x\left(\frac{1}{x} + \frac{1}{b}\right) = \left(\frac{1}{x - 2}\right)x$$

$$1 + \frac{x}{b} = \frac{x}{x - 2}$$

Then multiply both sides by $x - 2$:

$$(x - 2)\left(1 + \frac{x}{b}\right) = \left(\frac{x}{x - 2}\right)(x - 2)$$

$$x - 2 + \frac{x^2 - 2x}{b} = x$$

$$\frac{x^2 - 2x}{b} = 2$$

$$x^2 - 2x = 2b$$

$$b = \frac{x^2 - 2x}{2}$$

That's the answer. The actual amount of time it takes Bertha depends on the value of x. If Albert could do the job in 6 hours by himself, then $x = 6$ and it would take Bertha this many hours:

$$b = \frac{x^2 - 2x}{2} = \frac{(6)^2 - 2(6)}{2} = \frac{36 - 12}{2} = 12$$

On the other hand, if Albert could do the job in 3 hours by himself, then $x = 3$ and it would take Bertha this many hours:

$$b = \frac{x^2 - 2x}{2} = \frac{(3)^2 - 2(3)}{2} = \frac{9 - 6}{2} = 1\frac{1}{2}$$

Algebra, it's not just for math heads anymore! To check out whether you've got the hang of this stuff, use the Plug-In Questions. The answers are at the back of the book.

Plug In

1. If the sum of five consecutive positive integers is equal to exactly 6 times the smallest of those integers, what is the largest of those integers?

2. Village *A* currently has a population of 6,800, and its population is decreasing at a steady rate of 120 persons per year. Village *B* currently has a population of 4,200, and its population is increasing at a steady rate of 80 persons per year. After how many years will the two populations be the same?

3. A street vendor sells two types of newspapers, one for 25 cents and the other for 40 cents. If in one day she sold 100 newspapers and took in exactly 28 dollars, how many of the 25-cent newspapers did she sell?

4. John could stuff all the envelopes in 2 hours. Peter could stuff them all in 1 hour and 20 minutes. How many minutes will it take the two of them working together to stuff all the envelopes?

5. After Charles gives Darla *x* dollars, he still has *y* dollars more than she does. How much more than she did he have before he gave her the *x* dollars?

The Elements of Geometry: Are Euclid-ing Me?

If the algebra we've been studying recently can be likened to detective work, then try thinking of Geometry as Art Appreciation. It's about seeing some fundamental laws of nature, through points, lines and shapes. And if the previous chapters made you wonder whether you'd ever need them in the real world, basic

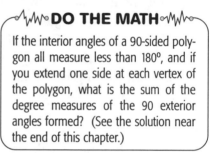

⌐₩₩₩ **DO THE MATH** ₩₩₩⌐

If the interior angles of a 90-sided polygon all measure less than 180°, and if you extend one side at each vertex of the polygon, what is the sum of the degree measures of the 90 exterior angles formed? (See the solution near the end of this chapter.)

Geometry shows up everywhere you look . . . literally! From maps to paintings, from pool halls to gymnastics, and from coastlines to mountains, this branch of science has a powerful relationship to the way we look at things. Geometry It's not just for math heads any more!

In this chapter, we're going to get down to basics, and get into the most important concepts in this branch of math. Don't forget them, you'll be needing them later on.

THE BEAUTY OF GEOMETRY (NO, REALLY, WE MEAN IT)

Geometry is the most beautiful branch of mathematics. Come again? It's beautiful not just because of the pretty pictures. It's also the oldest, purest, and most carefully thought-out branch of math. And in recent years, it's played an important role in understanding the cool new study of Chaos Theory.

Who do we have to thank for all this fabulous Geometry? His name was Euclid, the granddaddy of math heads. He was the guy who invented the notion of a *system of pure logical consistency* (that's a long-winded way to describe math). He also figured out that any logical system has to be based on precise definitions—that means you have to be able to prove stuff—and at least a few basic precepts that one just has to take on faith. Today, all branches of mathematics use Euclid's systems of proving things, but geometry was the first one on the block.

Euclid didn't figure it all out by himself. The book he's best known for, the *Elements*, is not wholly original. It's more like a Cliff's Notes for all that was known of geometry by the Greeks of the 4th century B.C. It's also highly structured and systematic in the way it's put together. Euclid took volumes of information and arranged it so that it flowed in a logical sequence, just like what we're doing for you!

By the 20th century's more rigorous standards, Euclid's geometry is far from perfect. But the *Elements* was the standard geometry text for over 2,000 years, and, according to math heads, one of the most influential books ever written. Think of it like this: *Elements* is to math what *Star Wars* is to movies.

WHAT DO YOU MEAN BY THAT: EUCLID'S DEFINITIONS

Because he was an ambitious guy, Euclid started with 23 definitions, 5 common notions, and 5 postulates. Here are some of his definitions:

point—that which has no part

line—breadthless length

straight line—a line which lies evenly with the points on itself

surface—that which has length and breadth only

plane surface—a surface which lies evenly with the straight lines on itself

angle—the inclination to one another of two lines in a plane which meet one another and do not lie in a straight line

right angle—one of the angles formed when a straight line set up on a straight line makes the adjacent angles equal to one another

perpendicular—a straight line which set up on a straight line makes adjacent right angles

acute angle—an angle less than a right angle

obtuse angle—an angle greater than a right angle

parallel lines—straight lines in a plane which, extended indefinitely in both directions, do not meet in either direction

triangle—a figure contained by three straight lines

equilateral triangle—a triangle that has its three sides equal

isosceles triangle—a triangle that has two of its sides alone equal

circle—a plane figure contained by a line such that all straight lines falling upon it from one point among those lying within the figure are equal to one another

One could write a book about these definitions alone (though it might not be a bestseller). There's a lot to say, and a lot to explain. Some of Euclid's definitions are pretty much useless by now. Does it mean anything to you when you read that a point is "that which has no part"? Doesn't say much, does it? But hey, could you do any better?

Today math heads don't even bother trying to define things like *point, line,* or *plane.* There's no satisfactory way to define every term without some trouble maker somewhere making definitions that go around and around in circles. But there is still general agreement about what those words mean; this general agreement comes essentially from talking about these things a lot. Sort of like group therapy for math heads.

At first it's a little hard to adjust to the seeming abstract notion of a point as a location in space so infinitesimally small as to have *no dimension*—or to the notion of a straight line as an array of points that has infinite length but no breadth or depth (it's there but it's not there)—or to the notion of a plane as a flat surface that has infinite length and breadth but no depth. But after you hear the words used that way a few times, and then use them yourself a few times, you get accustomed to the ideas, and you're ready to forge ahead. Basically, Euclid was simplifying our crazy, 3-D world down to 1- and 2-D, just for studying purposes.

Getting to Know Euclid: His Notions and Postulates

After defining his terms, Euclid presents his precepts. These are statements that Euclid thinks to be so self-evident and fundamental that they can be accepted without proof and serve as the basis of all geometric deductions from then on. Five of these precepts Euclid calls *common notions*—fundamental mathematical truths that go beyond mere geometry.

Euclid's Five Common Notions

1. Two things both equal to a third thing are equal to each other.
2. Equals added to equals are equal.
3. Equals subtracted from equals are equal.
4. Things that coincide are equal.
5. The whole is greater than the part.

The other five precepts, which Euclid calls *postulates*, are fundamental truths that are just about geometry itself.

Euclid's Five Common Postulates

1. You can connect two points to make a line segment.
2. You can extend a line segment as far as you want in either direction.
3. You can make a circle given a center point and a distance.
4. All right angles are equal.
5. If a line segment connecting two straight lines makes two interior angles on the same side that add up to less than two right angles, then the two straight lines will intersect somewhere on that side.

Postulate #5 is a little hard to grasp at first. Hopefully, this diagram will help. Take a look. You have two lines and a segment that connects them:

Euclid's postulate says that if the two angles on the right side of the connecting segment add up to less than two right angles (less than 180 degrees), then the two lines will intersect somewhere to the right. That seems believable enough, but clearly this postulate feels quite different from the other four. It's different enough and has a history interesting enough to warrant the nickname *Euclid's Famous Fifth Postulate*. But you can also think of it as its logical equivalent, called Playfair's Axiom:

Playfair's Axiom: Given a line and a point not on that line, there exists in the plane determined by that point and line exactly one line that includes the given point and is parallel to the given line.

Now, the language of geometry can sound like it's running in circles, which is because, in this case, a picture is worth a thousand math-head words.

Are You Going to Give Me That Old Tired Line: Euclid's Propositions

Beginning with just a few definitions and a handful of precepts, Euclid aimed to gather a huge collection of *propositions*—no he wasn't asking anyone on a date—statements that are proven to be true based on accepted precepts and previously-proven propositions. Basically, he wanted to take his math power to the next level.

The first three propositions were elementary (my dear Watson).

- Proposition #1 said that it was possible to construct an equilateral triangle from a given length.

- Proposition #2 said that it was possible to transfer a given length from one place to another in a plane.

- Proposition #3 showed that it was possible to cut off a given length from a longer line segment

The first three propositions might seem just as obvious as some of the five postulates. How come turning a line into a circle is a postulate—something you just believe to be true without proving—while turning a line segment into an equilateral triangle is a proposition—requiring proof?

Euclid wanted to take for granted as little as possible, because you know what happens when you *assume* too much. His conception of a perfect system called for the most elemental set of postulates he could get away with. He wasn't about to call something a postulate if it could already be deduced from postulates that came before it.

Still, the first three propositions are really just building blocks for proving later propositions; they aren't so exciting on their own. It's with Proposition #4 that Euclid began to deduce statements that were not so self-evident. Proposition #4 states that, if two triangles have two sides equal, respectively, and have the angle contained by the equal sides equal, then the two triangles are *congruent*—that is they have the same side lengths and the same angle measures. *Congruent* is math heads' fancy word for "identical."

Euclid's Proposition #4: If two triangles have two sides equal to two sides respectively, and have the angles contained by the equal sides equal, then the triangles are congruent.

For example, in these figures, the little hatchmarks show that $AB = XY$, $BC = YZ$, and angle $B =$ angle Y:

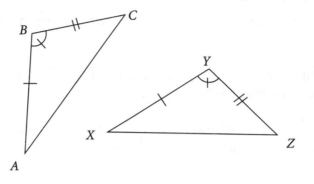

With two sides and the included angle equal, these triangles are congruent.

Today Euclid's propositions are called *theorems*, and Proposition #4 is now widely known as the *Side-Angle-Side Theorem*, or *SAS Theorem*. Recently, though the SAS Theorem is considered to be one of Euclid's biggest goofups. He thought he proved it, but there's that unsupported concept of picking up a triangle and putting it down on another to say they're congruent. It's especially difficult to use Euclid's postulates to justify picking up a triangle and flipping it onto another to say they're congruent:

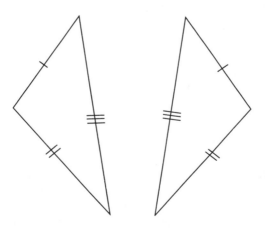

The modern view is that the Side-Angle-Side Theorem is really a postulate.

But at the time, SAS opened the floodgates. Once Euclid had a way to prove the congruence of triangles, there was no stopping him.

The Proof Is in the Euclidean Punch

Euclid's next proposition is another famous one: that the base angles of an isosceles triangle are equal.

Euclid's Proposition #5: If a triangle has two equal sides, then the angles opposite the equal sides are equal.

Euclid's proof of this proposition will serve as a good example of how he uses postulates and previous propositions in his reasoning.

Given: Triangle *ABC* with *AB* = *BC*:

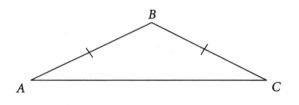

Prove: That angle *BAC* is equal to angle *CBA*.

Here's how he did it. First, he invoked Postulate #2 to extend the equal sides like this:

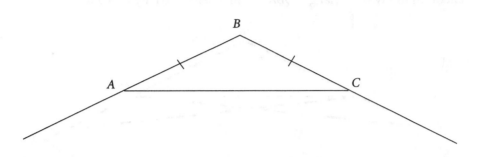

Then he invoked Postulate #3 to make a circle centered at the vertex of the triangle and thereby locating points *P* and *Q* on the extended legs:

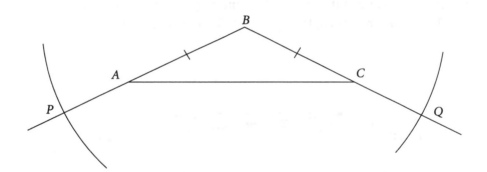

Then he invoked Postulate #1 to draw line segments *AQ* and *PC*:

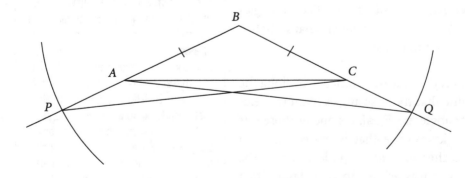

Now, because $AB = BC$ (given), $BQ = BP$ (two radii of the same circle), and because angle B is equal to itself, Euclid was able to use the Side-Angle-Side Theorem to say that triangle QBA is congruent to triangle BCP:

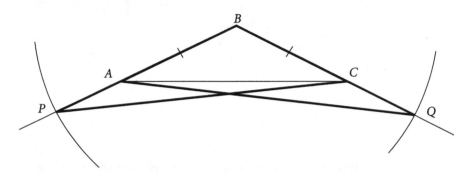

Because triangles QBA and BCP are congruent, Euclid could say that sides AQ and PC are equal and that angles APC and CQA are equal. Therefore, by the SAS Theorem again, triangles APC and CQA are congruent:

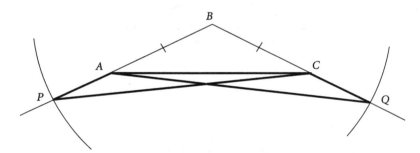

That makes angles PAC and ACQ equal, and therefore adjacent angles BAC and BCA are equal. That's what he set out to prove.

Everybody learns somewhere along the line that the base angles of an isosceles triangle are equal. It's one of those bits of knowledge that is passed on from teacher to student (unless one or the other was asleep on that day!) Often

⸰ᴡᴠ⋅ SPARK ⋅ᴡᴠ⸰

The diagram Euclid ended up with in the proof of Proposition #5 has taken on the nickname *pons asinorum* ("bridge of asses"). To some extent the diagram *does* look like a bridge, though what it is that makes it a bridge for *asses* is a matter for speculation. Self-congratulatory math heads like to think this is the point in Euclid's system where not-so-bright people (asses) get lost—they're unable to cross the bridge into the wonderful world of Euclidean geometry. Don't worry, we won't leave you stranded.

it's tossed off like trivia, like it's a magical fact of nature that doesn't deserve any further thought. It's also the sort of thing most of us don't remember very well, so in this and the next few chapters you will get a succinct summary of *all* the key facts and formulas about lines, angles, polygons, circles, and solids.

The thing to remember is that these facts and formulas are not just meaningless tidbits, imposed by some random math heads and plopped in your lap to be memorized one by one. Everything you'll read about lines, angles, polygons, circles, and solids one way or another follows logically from Euclid's postulates and early propositions.

We don't have room in these pages for all the proofs (and we're sure you're really bummed about that), but we will try to give you an idea of how all these formulas and facts and stuff fit together. To understand how a whole system of math follows from just a few basic precepts, go to the source. Why not read the *Elements* for yourself, in the tons of spare time we're sure you have? It's a real page turner.

Why Prove the Obvious?

Euclid's Proposition #20 is another one that has made some folks scratch their (math) heads over the millennia. It says that any two sides of a triangle will add up to more than the third side.

Euclid's Proposition #20: In any triangle, two sides taken together in any manner are greater than the remaining side.

Euclid's detractors say that it's so obvious, even a donkey knows that it's shorter to go directly from A to B than to go by way of point C if C is not on a straight line between A and B. Suppose you had a fence around a triangular piece of your lawn and you put a donkey outside the fence at one corner and put his food outside the fence at another corner:

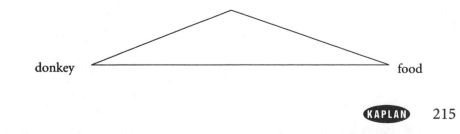

You think the donkey would go around the third corner to get to his food? Even a donkey would know better than that. What is the point of proving something that even a donkey could figure out?

Euclid's reason for proving something is often just because it *can* be proved. It's like people who say they climb Mount Everest, "because it's there." Sometimes that means corroborating the obvious. Sometimes, however, Euclid's methods can lead to propositions that are surprising.

We're getting a little ahead of ourselves here, but, let's take a peek at an example of a logical deduction that's a little unexpected. It has to do with the exterior angles of a convex polygon—that is, the angles you get when you extend one side at each vertex, like so:

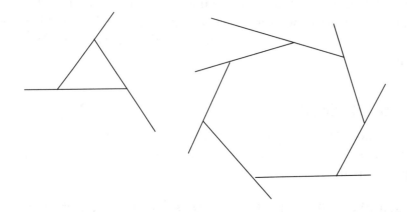

(A *convex polygon* is one whose interior angles all measure less than 180°— which means the polygon has no indentations.) Do you know how to figure out what the exterior angles of an *n*-sided polygon will add up to? What is the sum of the exterior angles of a triangle? Of a heptagon?

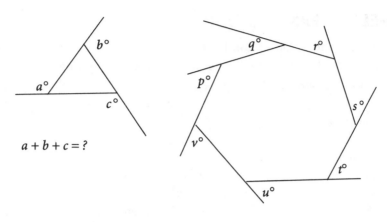

$$p + q + r + s + t + u + v = ?$$

The fact is—and it can be proven by Euclidean methods—that the sum of the exterior angles of *any* convex polygon, no matter how many sides, is the same: 360 degrees. In the figure above, $a + b + c = 360$, and $p + q + r + s + t + u + v = 360$.

Now that you know this fact, you can answer this chapter's Do the Math question in a try:

DO THE MATH

If the interior angles of a 90-sided polygon all measure less than 180°, and if you extend one side at each vertex of the polygon, what is the sum of the degree measures of the 90 exterior angles formed?

Solution: The sum of the exterior angles is the same for all convex polygons, even one that has as many as 90 sides. The exterior angles add up to 360 degrees.

NON-EUCLIDEAN GEOMETRY

There's yet another good reason for attempting to prove even that which is obvious to a donkey. Sometimes the donkey might be wrong. Sometimes it turns out that something that is obvious to everyone is actually unprovable. When that happens, one should start to wonder whether this "obvious" fact has to be true at all.

For an excellent case in point, let's return to Euclid's Famous Fifth Postulate and its logical equivalent, Playfair's Axiom.

Euclid's Famous Fifth Postulate: If a line segment connecting two straight lines makes two interior angles on the same side that add up to less than two right angles, then the two straight lines will intersect somewhere on that side.

Playfair's Axiom: Given a line and a point not on that line, there exists in the plane determined by that point and line exactly one line that includes the given point and is parallel to the given line.

Of all the postulates, the fifth feels the least elemental. It reads more like a proposition than a postulate. But that's because Euclid was so smart! He recognized the unprovability of this assertion.

Actually, Euclid was so full of himself, he never imagined that Postulate #5 might not have to be true. In Euclid's mind, Postulate #5 accorded with reality. Its validity could not be disputed.

Trying to prove Postulate #5—Playfair's Axiom—was one of those problems that mathematicians worked on for centuries; math heads live a long time, you know. Some tried to do it with indirect proof.

CONNECTION

Find out more than you'd ever need to know about indirect proof. For an example of an indirect proof, check out Euclid's answer to the question, "Are there infinitely many prime numbers?" in chapter 2.

An *indirect proof* is one that begins by assuming the opposite of what's to be proven, and concludes when it reaches an inconsistency. Playfair's Axiom asserts that, given a line and a point not on that line, there is exactly one line that goes through that point and is parallel to the given line. To prove this indirectly, you would start with the assumption that there is either more than one such line, or that there is no such line. Unfortunately for Euclid and his buddy Playfair, neither of these assumptions leads to an inconsistency. Meaning Postulate #5 can't be proven.

For centuries, frustrated math heads attacked Postulate #5 with attempts at indirect proof, never hitting an inconsistency. But it wasn't until the 1820's that anyone dared to propose an alternative to Euclid's Fifth.

When Nikolai Lobachevsky postulated instead that there's *more than one* parallel line through that point and then figured out what the consequences would be, he did far more than just create a new geometry. He revolutionized the whole concept of the axiom.

Axiom is the preferred word today for a common notion or a postulate. Euclid was so full of himself, that he figured all his axioms were just the way things were, and that everything that followed from them must also be true. After the Russian guy got done with him, the understanding is that, *if* you take his axioms to be true, then everything that logically follows from them is also true. But you can decide to experiment and learn beyond Euclid if you want.

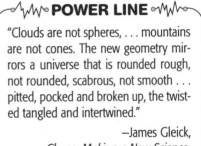

POWER LINE

"Clouds are not spheres, . . . mountains are not cones. The new geometry mirrors a universe that is rounded rough, not rounded, scabrous, not smooth . . . pitted, pocked and broken up, the twisted tangled and intertwined."

—James Gleick,
Chaos: Making a New Science,
1987, Penguin Books.

You're thinking, big deal, right? It is, though, really. See, Euclid believed that his geometry described reality—that it was the only possible geometry. Lobachevsky and others finally realized in the early 19th century that one need not accept Euclid's axioms, or anybody's axioms, as the only true axioms. By taking a different turn when faced with Postulate #5, Lobachevsky was able to carry through and devise a non-Euclidean geometry that was just as consistent as Euclid's geometry. And what's remarkable is that Lobachevsky's geometry is sometimes a better description of reality than Euclid's—particularly when working with astronomically great distances, speeds, and periods of time.

Euclid and his geometry have taken a bit of a bad rap in the last 150 years, but he's still the man in many ways. The geometry we all learn in high school is still basically Euclid's. And the dream we all have of a systematic and rational universe with self-evident truths is still basically Euclid's.

Polygons: The Shapes of Things to Come

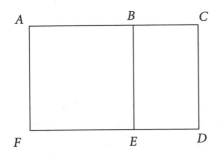

⌐Ѡ⌐ DO THE MATH ⌐Ѡ⌐

In the figure to the left, *ABEF* is a square of area 1. If rectangle *BCDE* is similar to rectangle *ACDF*, what is the length of *AC*? (See the solution near the end of this chapter.)

People tend to be either algebra heads or geometry heads. If you're not a fan, geometry is scary business, too many shapes and theorems and lines (oh my!), too many triangles, quadrilaterals, and polygons. So many exotic names and esoteric facts and formulas to remember; so little time! But in fact, once you have the names and definitions under your belt, just about everything else follows so logically—that it becomes easy to remember.

But you do have to know the lingo. There's no getting around it. Fortunately the meanings of many geometric terms are pretty obvious. Take the word *polygon* itself. *Polygon* is the general word for any closed figure with straight sides. *Poly-* means "many" and *-gon* means "angle," so a polygon is a "figure with many angles." The same combination form *-gon* is used in the specific names of polygons of five or more sides and angles:

- A *pentagon* has five sides and five angles.
- A *hexagon* has six sides and six angles.
- A *heptagon* has seven sides and seven angles.
- An *octagon* has eight sides and eight angles.
- A *nonagon* has nine sides and nine angles.
- A *decagon* has ten sides and ten angles.

The forms *poly-*, *-gon*, *penta-*, *hexa-*, *hepta-*, *octa-*, *nona-*, and *deca-* all come from Greek. If the way math heads named stuff were totally consistent, a polygon with three sides and three angles would be called a "trigon," and a polygon with four sides and angles would be called something like a "tesseragon." In fact, they are called a *triangle* and a *quadrilateral*. These two types of polygons get by far the most attention, which can sometimes make the other polygons jealous.

ALL ABOUT TRIANGLES

The triangle is the fundamental polygon in more ways than one. It's the polygon with the fewest sides, but it's also the polygon with the most *implications*. There is more to say about triangles than there is to say about any other type of polygon. (The quadrilateral is the first runner-up.) There are all kinds of special triangles, and there's a lot to be said about them as well; they're often the subject of polygon party gossip.

Euclid had a thing about triangles. He was the one who established the two different ways of dividing them all up into three categories.

His first way to divide them up is according to how many equal sides they have. If all sides are equal, it's *equilateral*. If only two sides are equal, it's *isosceles*. And if no sides are equal, it's *scalene*.

Actually, here's a rare moment when math heads disagree (so let's make the most of it). The isosceles triangle is often defined ambiguously as a triangle "with two equal sides." What this definition fails to address is the case of

three equal sides. Does "with two equal sides" mean "with two, *and no more than two*, equal sides"? Or does it mean "with *at least* two equal sides"? Euclid insisted isosceles triangles have *only* two equal sides. He considered isosceles and equilateral triangles to be nonoverlapping categories.

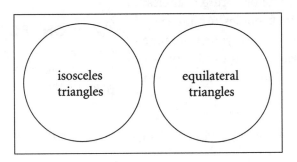

But today a lot of geometry books define isosceles triangles the second way—as having *at least* two equal sides—so they consider the equilateral triangle to be a special case of the isosceles triangle. Go figure!

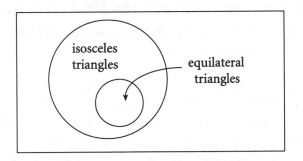

So even in the world of mathematics, where it seems like everyone's always bending over backwards to be precise, there are differing opinions about what some words mean.

Euclid's other way of dividing triangles into three categories is according to the measure of the biggest angle. If the biggest angle is less than 90°, it's an *acute triangle*. If the biggest angle is more than 90°, it's an *obtuse triangle*. If the biggest angle is exactly 90°, it's a *right triangle*.

As it happens, there's not a whole lot to say about acute or obtuse triangles; they're one-trick ponies. About right triangles, however, everyone wants the last word. Most significantly, there's Euclid's Proposition #47, better known as the *Pythagorean Theorem*. Call the two sides that meet at the right angle the *legs*, and call the side opposite the right angle the *hypotenuse*. Then:

> ‑◦ᴸᴸᴸᴸᴼ **SPARK** ◦ᴸᴸᴸᴼ‑
>
> Did you know, for another example, that the Americans and the British have different names for numbers over a million? What Americans call a "billion"—1 followed by nine zeroes—the British call a "milliard." And what Americans call a "trillion"—1 followed by 12 zeroes—the British call a "billion." Can't we all just get along?

> ‑◦ᴸᴸᴸᴼ**CONNECTION** ◦ᴸᴸᴸᴼ‑
>
> If you want to skip ahead and learn more about the Pythagorean Theorem, flip up to chapter 16.

💡 **Pythagorean Theorem**
In any right triangle, the sum of the squares of the legs is equal to the square of the hypotenuse.

Pretty Much the Same: Congruent and Similar Triangles

Euclid's first 40-some propositions include a whole ton of statements about triangles. Like we said, he was fixated.

There are theorems that can be used to prove that two triangles are *congruent*—which means they have the same side lengths and the same angles. The first of these theorems was the Side-Angle-Side (SAS) Theorem. After that came the Angle-Side-Angle, the Side-Angle-Angle, and the Side-Side-Side. Sounds like a bunch of cheerleaders working out, huh? Anyway, any time you have three equalities between triangles in one of the above sequences, you can say the triangles are congruent. In the triangles below, for example, the sequence of equalities is Angle-Angle-Side:

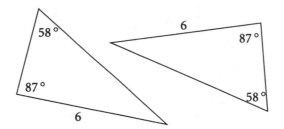

But now look at these two triangles:

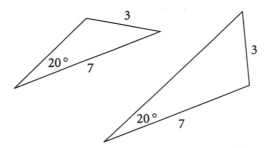

The sequence of equalities here is Angle-Side-Side. As you can see, though, the triangles are not equivalent. That's because there's is no such thing as the Angle-Side-Side Theorem. (Which is too bad, because you could have quite a field-day with the abbreviation for that one.) In fact, rather than trying to remember the four sequences that work to prove congruence, it's easier just to remember the two that *don't* work: ASS and AAA (the donkey and the Auto Club).

If the sequence of equalities is AAA, you can't say the triangles are congruent. (They still might be—but you need to know something about at least one side to decide.) But if the angles are all the same, you can at least be sure the triangles are *similar*—which means they have the same shape. Corresponding angles are equal and corresponding sides are proportional. The triangles below are similar because they have the same angles:

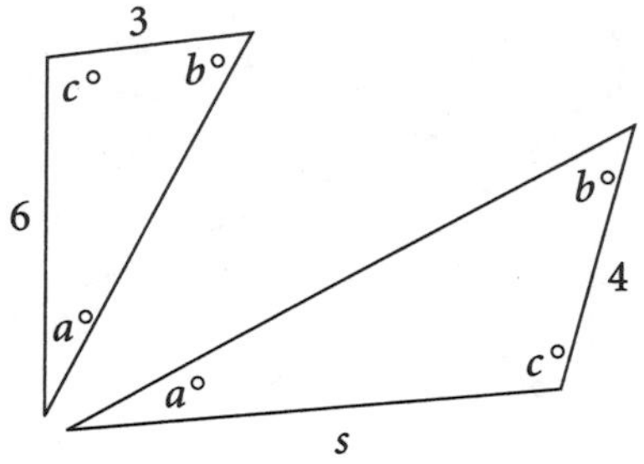

The side of length 3 corresponds to the side of length 4, and the side of length 6 corresponds to the side of length *s*.

$$\frac{3}{4} = \frac{6}{s}$$

$$3s = 24$$

$$s = 8$$

Three: That's the Magic Number

Other Euclidean propositions about triangles had to do with the relationships among the sides and angles. As you saw in the last chapter, Euclid demonstrated that any two sides of a triangle will always add up to more than the third side. Many have said that this is obvious even to a donkey.

CONNECTION

To review the answer to the age old question, Why Prove the Obvious? go back to chapter 14.

It boggles the math head mind how often students forget this fact when they're working on a problem like the following:

Question: If the three sides of a triangle are all integers, and if exactly two of the sides are equal, what is the least possible perimeter of the triangle?

Solution: The *perimeter* of a polygon is the sum of its side lengths. The minimal perimeter of a triangle with integer side lengths is 1 + 1 + 1 = 3, but that's not the answer to this question—it says that exactly *two* sides are equal. So then what about 1 + 1 + 2 = 4? Do you see why that doesn't work? You can't make a triangle out of those side lengths! The longest side has to be *less* than the sum of the other two—here they're *equal*. No good. The smallest perimeter that fits the given conditions and satisfies the "little bro' theorem" is 1 + 2 + 2 = 5.

Whenever you know two sides of a triangle, you know something about the third side. You know that, whatever it is, it must be greater than the positive difference between the other two sides, and it must be less than the sum of the other two sides. For example, if you know that one side is 3 and another side is 7, then you know that the third side must be greater than 7 – 3 = 4, and less than 7 + 3 = 10. If you tried to make a triangle out of sides of length 3, 7, and 2, you won't be able to get the ends to meet:

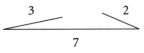

You run into similar difficulties when you try to make a triangle out of 3, 7, and 12:

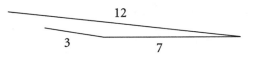

Euclid also showed that, within any triangle, the longest side will be found opposite the biggest angle, and that the shortest side will be found opposite the smallest angle. When two sides are the same (an isosceles triangle), the opposite angles are equal. And when all three sides are the same (an equilateral triangle), all three angles are the same (60°). That Euclid was some guy, huh?

One of the most basic facts about triangles is that the interior angles of any triangle will add up to 180°. Whenever you know two angles, you can easily figure out the third angle. And sometimes, if you know something else about the triangle, all you need to know is one angle and you can figure out the other two.

Question: If the measure of one of the base angles of an isosceles triangle is 55°, what is the degree measure of the vertex angle?

Solution: You're given just one angle, but because it's the base angle of an isosceles triangle, you know another angle. The two base angles each measure 55°, so they add up to 110°, which leaves 180° − 110° = 70° for the vertex angle.

An *exterior angle* is what you get when you extend one side of a polygon. Here, you get an exterior angle by extending one side of a triangle:

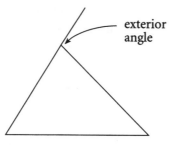

exterior
angle

An exterior angle of a triangle is equal to the sum of the remote interior angles. In the figure below, the exterior angle labeled $x°$ is equal to the sum of the remote angles: $x = 50 + 100 = 150$.

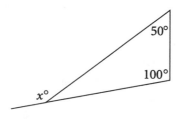

50°

100°

$x°$

The three exterior angles of a triangle add up to 360°. In the figure below, $a + b + c = 360$.

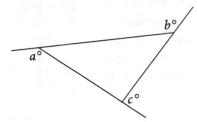

IT TAKES FOUR TO TANGO

There's a lot to talk about with quadrilaterals. There's not a lot to say about them in general—they have four sides, four angles, 360 degrees, no big deal—but there are all kinds of special quadrilaterals with their own sets of facts and formulas.

Just like he did with triangles, that wacky Euclid divided all quadrilaterals into three nonoverlapping categories. The way he separated quadrilaterals was by the number of parallel sides. A quadrilateral with no parallel sides is a *trapezium*. A quadrilateral with *one* pair of parallel sides is a *trapezoid*. And a quadrilateral with *two* pairs of parallel sides is a *parallelogram*. So trapezoids and parallelograms are nonoverlapping sets:

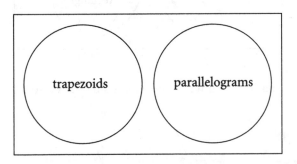

Trapezoids are cute (sure they are), but parallelograms have a lot more going for them, especially because the category of parallelograms includes as subcategories three extra-special quadrilateral types: rectangles, rhombi, and squares.

A *rectangle* is a quadrilateral that has four equal angles—that is, four right angles. Opposite sides are equal. Diagonals are equal. Quadrilateral *ABCD* is shown to have three right angles. The fourth angle therefore also measures 90°, and *ABCD* is a rectangle:

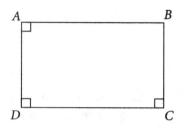

All rectangles are parallelograms, but not all parallelograms are rectangles. In other words, the rectangles are a *subset* of parallelograms:

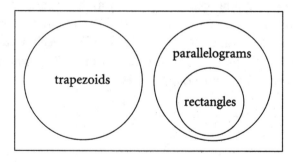

A *rhombus* is a quadrilateral with four equal sides. It's also a fun word to say.

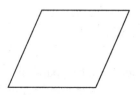

Because opposite sides are parallel and equal, a rhombus is also a parallelogram, but it's a parallelogram with some special properties of its own. For example, each of the diagonals of a rhombus will divide it into a pair of congruent isosceles triangles:

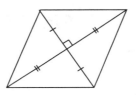

As a pair, the diagonals are perpendicular bisectors:

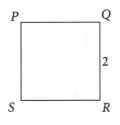

A *square* is a quadrilateral with four equal angles and four equal sides. In other words, a square is both a rectangle and a rhombus. In the figure below, if *PQRS* is a square, all sides are the same length as *QR*.

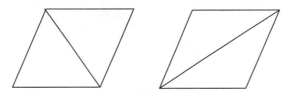

Everything that's true of rectangles in general is true of this special rectangle: four right angles, equal diagonals, etc. And everything that's true of rhombi in general is true of this special rhombus: four equal sides, perpendicular diagonals, etc. Rectangles and rhombi are both subsets of parallelograms, and the intersection of those two subsets is the set of squares:

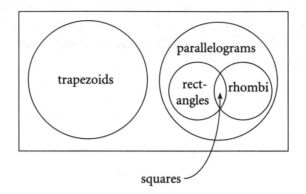

squares

BUT WAIT, THERE'S MORE! OTHER POLYGONS

Any polygon can be divided up into triangles like this:

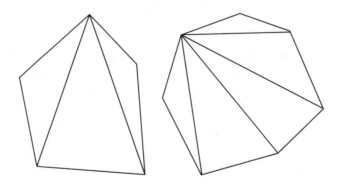

This way you divide a 5-sided polygon into 3 triangles, you divide a 7-sided polygon into 5 triangles, and you divide an n-sided polygon into $n - 2$ triangles. The angles inside each triangle add up to 180°, so the angles inside an n-sided polygon add up to the number of triangles inside it times 180°. That's $(n - 2)$ times 180°.

Sum of the angles $= (n - 2) \times 180$

Question: What is the sum of the degree measures of the angles of an octagon?

Solution: An octagon has eight sides, so plug $n = 8$ into the formula:

$$\text{Sum of the angles} = (n - 2) \times 180$$
$$= (8 - 2) \times 180$$
$$= 6 \times 180$$
$$= 1{,}080$$

To find one angle of a regular polygon, divide the sum of the angles by the number of angles (which is the same as the number of sides). The formula, therefore, is:

Interior angle $= \dfrac{n-2}{n} \times 180$

Question: What is the measure of angle A in the regular octagon below?

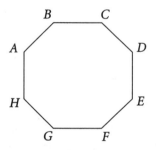

Solution: Plug $n = 8$ into the formula:

$$\text{Measure of angle A} = \frac{(n - 2) \times 180}{n}$$
$$= \frac{(8 - 2) \times 180}{8}$$
$$= \frac{1{,}080}{8}$$
$$= 135$$

GETTING INTO THE RIGHT AREA

For a lot of people, finding the areas of various polygons means memorizing dozens of boring formulas. Formulas are useful, but you're better off ultimately if you can see how they're related to each other, if you have some idea where they come from.

Into the Four: The Area of a Rectangle

The basis of all polygon area formulas is the fundamental idea that the area of a rectangle is equal to the product of its length and width:

Area of rectangle = length × width

The area of the 7-by-3 rectangle below, for example, is 7 × 3 = 21.

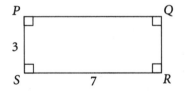

Here's something to keep an eye out for. Which dimension is the "length" and which is the "width"? There's no formal definition. Some say the *vertical* dimension is the length and the *horizontal* dimension is the width. Some say the *longer* dimension is the length and the *shorter* dimension is the width. It doesn't really matter. What does matter is the fundamental idea that area is equal to the product of two dimensions.

To avoid ambiguity, it's better to use this version of the formula:

Area of rectangle = base × height

You can use either dimension for the base, in which case the other dimension is the height, but conventionally the base is the horizontal dimension as the figure is shown.

Square-Off: The Area of a Square

The square is just a special kind of a rectangle. In this case, the base and height are the same, so you can express the area formula in terms of the length of a side, like this:

Area of square = $(\text{side})^2$

The square below, with sides of length 5, has an area of $5^2 = 25$.

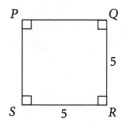

Parallel Universe: The Area of a Parallelogram

To see where the formula for the area of a parallelogram comes from, imagine slicing off one end of the parallelogram with a perpendicular like this:

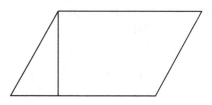

Imagine then moving that lopped-off triangle to the other end and making a rectangle out of the parallelogram:

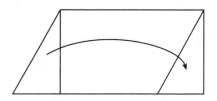

The area of this rectangle is base times height. The base of the rectangle is the same as the base of the original parallelogram. The height of the rectangle is the same as the height of the parallelogram, as long as you remember that *height* means the *perpendicular distance* between the base and the top. So the area formula for a parallelogram is the same as that for a rectangle.

Area of parallelogram = base × height

The only difference is that the height of a parallelogram is not normally the length of its lateral sides. It's the *perpendicular distance*. The height is the same as the length of the lateral sides only in the case of the rectangle. Here's a bunch of parallelograms, beginning with a rectangle, that all have the same area:

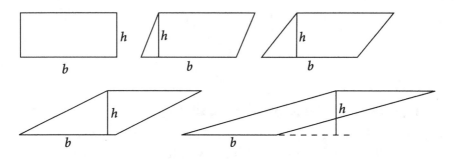

In parallelogram *KLMN* below, 4 is the height when *LM* or *KN* is used as the base. Base × height = 6 × 4 = 24:

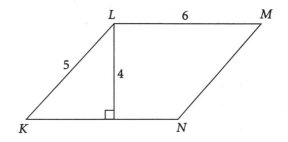

The height is also called the altitude.

Trapped!: The Area of a Trapezoid

To see where the formula for the area of a trapezoid comes from, imagine slicing off each end of the trapezoid like you just did with the parallelogram:

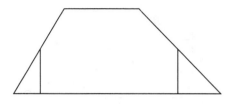

Then imagine rotating those lopped-off triangles to the top and making a rectangle out of the trapezoid:

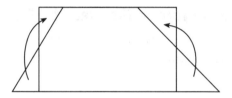

The height of the rectangle you've made is the same as the height of the original trapezoid. The base of the rectangle is equal to the *mean* of the original trapezoid's *two* bases. And so you just have to vary the basic base-times-height formula by replacing "base" with "base$_1$ plus base$_2$ over 2."

> **Area of trapezoid** $= \left(\dfrac{\mathbf{base_1} + \mathbf{base_2}}{2}\right) \times \mathbf{height}$

In the trapezoid *ABCD* below, you can use side *AD* for the height:

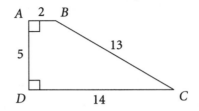

The average of the bases is $\dfrac{2 + 14}{2} = 8$, so the area is 5×8, or 40.

Good Things Come in Threes: The Area of a Triangle

To see where the formula for the area of a triangle comes from, think of a triangle as half of a parallelogram:

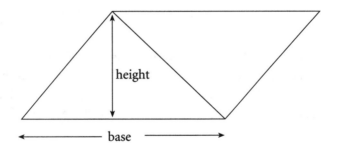

The parallelogram and the triangle have the same base and height. The triangle is half the parallelogram, so the area of the triangle is half the base times the height:

> **Area of triangle** $= \dfrac{1}{2} (\mathbf{base} \times \mathbf{height})$

So this Euclid guy really figured some stuff out!

As you have seen, the facts and formulas of polygons are interrelated. They're easiest to remember if you think of them as consistent parts of a sensible system, rather than as a whole great long list of unrelated items to be committed to memory.

Now that we've immersed you in the world of shapes, sizes and relationships between them, let's take a look at the Do the Math problem from this chapter:

DO THE MATH

In the figure below, *ABEF* is a square of area 1. If rectangle *BCDE* is similar to rectangle *ACDF*, what is the length of *AC*?

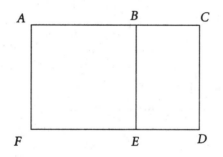

Solution: If the area of the square is 1, then all its sides are 1, and *CD* is also 1. You're looking for *AC*, so call that *x*. That makes *BC* equal to $x - 1$:

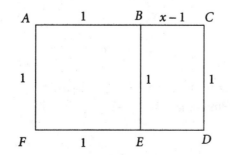

Now, if rectangle *BCDE* is similar to rectangle *ACDF*, then corresponding sides are proportional. It can really help to separate and reorient the similar rectangles to bring out the correspondences, like this:

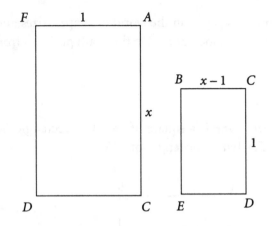

The respective shorter sides are *BC* = *x* − 1 and *AF* = 1. The respective longer sides are *CD* = 1 and *AC* = *x*. Now you can set up a proportion and solve for *x*:

$$\frac{BC}{AF} = \frac{CD}{AC}$$

$$\frac{x-1}{1} = \frac{1}{x}$$

$$(x-1)x = 1$$

$$x^2 - x = 1$$

$$x^2 - x - 1 = 0$$

Now you have a quadratic equation in standard form, so you can use the quadratic formula. Plug in *a* = 1, *b* = −1, and *c* = −1:

$$x = \frac{-b \pm \sqrt{b^2 - 4ac}}{2a}$$

$$= \frac{-(-1) \pm \sqrt{(-1)^2 - 4(1)(-1)}}{2(1)}$$

$$= \frac{1 \pm \sqrt{1 + 4}}{2}$$

$$= \frac{1 \pm \sqrt{5}}{2}$$

This is a geometry problem. The length you're looking for has to be a positive number, so the answer is $\frac{1 + \sqrt{5}}{2}$.

Do you recognize that number? It's ϕ—remember?

FINDING THE GOLDEN RECTANGLE

No, it's not a new Indiana Jones flick: the *Golden Rectangle* is any rectangle in which the ratio of the longer dimension to the shorter dimension is equal to ϕ. As you saw in the problem above, when you cut away a square from a Golden Rectangle, what you're left with is another, smaller Golden Rectangle. Thus, if you were to cut away another square, you'd have yet another Golden Rectangle, and you could continue this way *ad infinitum* (that means forever in Euclid-speak). The result isn't bad to look at:

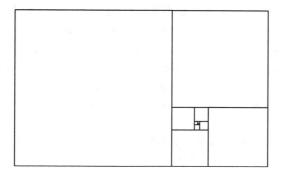

Looks like some funky modern art, doesn't it? And look what you get if you put a quarter circle inside each of the squares:

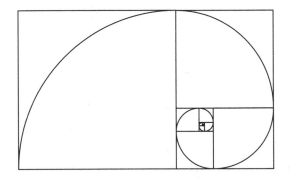

This is a very accurate representation of the pattern you can see in certain seashells. Some art theorists have said some pretty deep things about the Golden Rectangle over the centuries. They claim that it's the rectangle *most* harmonious and pleasing to the eye. The most famous example of the Golden Rectangle in art and architecture is the facade of the Parthenon. The ratio of the width to the height is very close to ϕ. In other words, you can fit it inside a Golden Rectangle.

The temple atop the Acropolis in Athens is pretty dang beautiful. To what extent that beauty is a result of the ratio of the width to the height, however, is maybe a little hard to tell.

But there does seem to be an aesthetic preference in our world for a rectangle roughly shaped like the Golden Rectangle. Sheets of paper, pages in books, standard photo print sizes, TV screens and computer monitors, index cards and credit cards, parking spaces and windows—they're all in the general shape of a rectangle with a ratio of anywhere between about 1.4 to 1 and 1.8 to 1. Take a look around you—you don't see a lot of squares, do you? And think about it; to call someone a "square" is an insult. Calling them a "Golden Rectangle" isn't so bad.

But enough about that. Let's see how well you got with this program. Try these review questions and see how you do.

🐝 Plug In

1. The largest angle of a triangle measures 10 degrees more than the middle-sized angle and twice as much as the smallest angle. What is the degree measure of the largest angle?

2. In Figure 1, $AB = BC$. If the area of $\triangle ABE$ is x, what is the area of $\triangle ACD$?

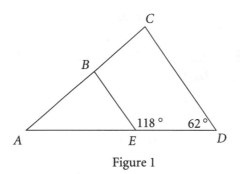

Figure 1

3. In Figure 2, QS and PT are parallel, and the lengths of segments PQ and QR are as marked. If the area of $\triangle QRS$ is x, what is the area of $\triangle PRT$ in terms of x?

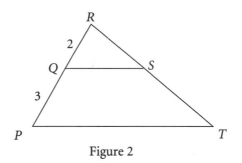

Figure 2

4. In Figure 3, if ABC is a straight line, $x = ?$

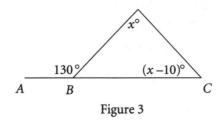

Figure 3

5. If the two squares shown in Figure 4 are identical, what is the degree measure of angle ADE?

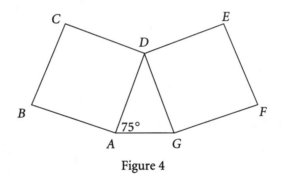

Figure 4

CHAPTER SIXTEEN

The Pythagorean Theorem: Know Your Rights

Something about the name Pythagoras scares even the bravest. If math heads had been more user-friendly, they would have called it something like "Joe's Way-Easy Theorem." Don't let the name fool you, though. This is really one of the most basic concepts you'll need to be a powerful geometry head;

⌇⩊⩊⌇**DO THE MATH**⌇⩊⩊⌇

Use the Pythagorean Theorem to derive the formula for area of a regular hexagon in terms of the length of one of its sides s. (See the solution near the end of this chapter.)

and we're here to demystify it for you, until it becomes as easy as *three-four-five*. Huh? Hang on and you'll see what we mean!

PYTHAGORAS' TRIPLE-HEADER

Way before Pythagoras, somebody figured out that if you take three sticks, one 3 units long, one 4 units long, and one 5 units long, and make a triangle out of them, the result will be a *right* triangle:

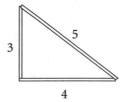

 245

But Pythagoras and his sixth-century B.C. number gurus must have had better P.R., because they got all the credit! Okay, they actually did a little more than that. They're the ones who discovered the more general rule that we now call the *Pythagorean Theorem*. Remembering that the legs are the two shorter sides—the sides that form the right angle—and that the *hypotenuse* (one of your favorite words, we know) is the longest side, the side opposite the right angle—you can say:

In *any* right triangle: The sum of the squares of the legs is equal to the square of the hypotenuse.

Sticks of lengths 3, 4, and 5 make a right triangle because the square of 3 is 9, and the square of 4 is 16, and 9 and 16 add up to 25, which is the square of 5. Also, as Pythagoras and his buddies figured out, 3, 4, and 5 are not the only set of integers that fit the formula. Another famous trio is 5, 12, and 13:

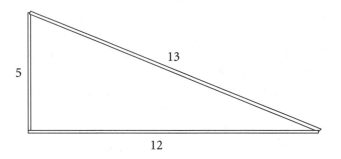

Sticks of those lengths make a right triangle because $5^2 + 12^2 = 13^2$.

To state the Pythagorean Theorem more algebraically (you remember algebra, don't you?), call the legs *a* and *b*, and call the hypotenuse *c*. Then:

The Pythagorean Theorem $a^2 + b^2 = c^2$

A set of positive integers *a*, *b*, and *c* that satisfies the Pythagorean relationship is called a *Pythagorean triple*. So no, Pythagoras never played for the Twins. The triples you'll encounter most frequently are the 3-4-5 and 5-12-13

○ᴧᴧᴧ○**MATH LAUGH**○ᴧᴧᴧ○

Q: What do you call a teapot of boiling water on top of Mount Everest?

A: A high-pot-in-use

shown above. But the list of them never stops.

Once you have identified a Pythagorean triple, you can multiply all three numbers by some common factor and make another triple. You can think of 6-8-10, 9-12-15, etc. as special cases of the 3-4-5 triple. And you can think of 10-24-26, 15-36-39, etc. as special cases of the 5-12-13 triple.

Here is the complete list of Pythagorean triples *a*, *b*, and *c* in which *c* < 100:

3, 4, 5	15, 20, 25	25, 60, 65	40, 42, 58
5, 12, 13	15, 36, 39	27, 36, 45	40, 75, 85
6, 8, 10	16, 30, 34	28, 45, 53	42, 56, 70
7, 24, 25	16, 63, 65	30, 40, 50	45, 60, 75
8, 15, 17	18, 24, 30	30, 72, 78	48, 55, 73
9, 12, 15	18, 80, 82	32, 60, 68	48, 64, 80
9, 40, 41	20, 21, 29	33, 44, 55	51, 68, 85
10, 24, 26	20, 48, 52	33, 56, 65	54, 72, 90
11, 60, 61	21, 28, 35	35, 84, 91	57, 76, 95
12, 16, 20	21, 72, 75	36, 48, 60	60, 63, 87
12, 35, 37	24, 32, 40	36, 77, 85	65, 72, 97
13, 84, 85	24, 45, 51	39, 52, 65	
14, 48, 50	24, 70, 74	39, 80, 89	

In fact, most of the 50 triples listed above are multiples of the 3-4-5 and 5-12-13 triples. If you remove those and the other multiples, you get the following list of the first 16 *primitive Pythagorean triples*—that is, triples with no common factors:

3, 4, 5	9, 40, 41	16, 63, 65	36, 77, 85
5, 12, 13	11, 60, 61	20, 21, 29	39, 80, 89
7, 24, 25	12, 35, 37	28, 45, 53	48, 55, 73
8, 15, 17	13, 84, 85	33, 56, 65	65, 72, 97

As you might expect, primitive Pythagorean triples have attracted a lot of scrutiny over the centuries. Here are some intriguing characteristics math heads have uncovered:

1. c is always odd.
2. Either $c - a$ or $c - b$ is a perfect square.
3. Either $a + c$ or $b + c$ is a perfect square.
4. Either a or b is a multiple of 3.
5. Either a or b is a multiple of 4.
6. Either a or b or $a + b$ or $b - a$ is a multiple of 7.

Test these on any of the Pythagorean triples listed above. The last one, 65-72-97, for example:

1. 97 is odd.
2. $97 - 72 = 25$, a perfect square.
3. $72 + 97 = 169$, a perfect square.
4. 72 is a multiple of 3.
5. 72 is a multiple of 4.
6. $72 - 65 = 7$, a multiple of 7.

They all fit—every time!

◦ᴡᴡ◦ POWER SURGE ◦ᴡᴡ◦

It's really amazing that there are so many integer triples that fit the Pythagorean relationship $a^2 + b^2 = c^2$. Amazing because there are absolutely *no* integer triples that fit any of the following relationships:

$$a^3 + b^3 = c^3$$

$$a^4 + b^4 = c^4$$

$$a^5 + b^5 = c^5$$

$$a^6 + b^6 = c^6$$

In fact, there are no integer solutions for a, b, and c to the equation $a^n + b^n = c^n$ for *any* integer value of n greater than 2. In fact, there aren't even any *rational* solutions! This is the substance of *Fermat's Last Theorem*.

One day, way back when, 17th-century French math-head extraordinaire Pierre Fermat scribbled in the margin of a math book: "It is impossible to separate a cube into two cubes, a fourth power into two fourth powers, or generally any power above the second into two powers of the same degree. I have discovered a truly marvelous proof which this margin is too narrow to contain."

Though he was obviously feeling like hot stuff that day, Fermat unfortunately died without ever explaining his "marvelous proof." For more than three centuries math heads tried to prove Fermat's Last Theorem.

Amazingly, it took until the 1990s to do it. The brilliant math head who did it: Andrew Wiles.

THE PROOF IS IN THE PYTHAGOREAN PUNCH

Pythagoras and his cronies didn't make up the Pythagorean relationship; they just discovered it. And they weren't even able to *prove* it—and they didn't even really care (those reckless Pythagoreans!) To them, numbers were magical, and the Pythagorean relationship was a mystery to be marveled at, not explained.

It was our old buddy Euclid who proved the relationship.

Euclid starts his proof by showing, in the figure below, that the two triangles highlighted are congruent. (Side-Angle-Side.) Can you see that the triangle with the thick gray lines has half the area of the shaded square, and that the triangle with the thick black lines has half the area of the shaded part of the big square? (Same base and same height in each case.) So the two shaded areas are equal.

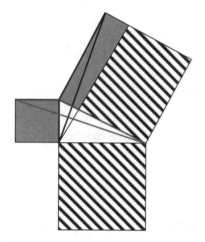

By similar reasoning you can show that the two striped areas are also equal. Therefore, the big square has the same area as the two smaller squares together. A square on the hypotenuse is equal to the sum of the squares on the legs. The theorem is proved. Did you follow that?

─ᐱᐱᐯᐱ° **SPARK** °ᐱᐱᐯᐱ─

Geometry heads have always been into the Pythagorean theorem. Over the years they have devised hundreds of different ways to prove it. There's even a proof discovered and published in 1876 by a member of the House of Representatives, James A. Garfield, who would later become the 20th president of the United States.

Garfield published his proof in the *New England Journal of Education*. He wrote that he came upon the idea while "in some mathematical amusements and discussions" with other members of Congress. Excuse me, Prez: isn't "mathematical amusements" a contradiction in terms?

Special Rights

So far we've just been looking at right triangles with all integer sides. In fact, these Pythagorean triples are special cases. If you were to pick a couple of integers at random to be the two legs of a right triangle, it's way more likely that the hypotenuse will not be an integer; the hypotenuse would be an irrational number. It was the Pythagorean Theorem that first led Greek math heads to the concepts of square roots and irrational numbers. What if you took a 1-by-1 square and divided it diagonally? You'd get two congruent right isosceles triangles.

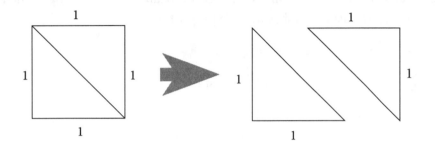

In each of these triangles, the legs are both 1. What's the hypotenuse?

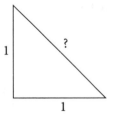

Well, with two sides of a right triangle and the Pythagorean theorem, you can always find the third side. Plug $a = 1$ and $b = 1$ into the formula, and solve for c:

$$c^2 = a^2 + b^2$$
$$c^2 = 1^2 + 1^2$$
$$c^2 = 2$$

Your next step is to take the square root of both sides. If this were a pure algebra problem, you'd get $c = \pm \sqrt{2}$. But this is a geometry problem (that's

good, it means it's easier), so you can forget the negative square root. The length of the hypotenuse is $\sqrt{2}$.

All right isosceles triangles are similar, and so they all exhibit the same side proportions. By the definition of isosceles, the two legs are equal. And, according to the Pythagorean Theorem, the hypotenuse is equal to one leg times $\sqrt{2}$. Now that you've used the Pythagorean Theorem once to find the hypotenuse of a right isosceles triangle, you never need to use it again. Don't you feel lucky? From now on, as soon as you realize you're looking at such a triangle, you'll just remember the side proportions:

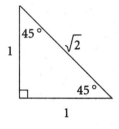

Question: The hypotenuse of a right isosceles triangle is 6. What is the length of one of the legs?

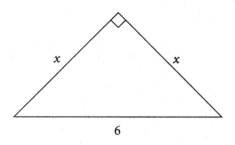

Solution: The ratio of leg to hypotenuse for all right isosceles triangles is $1:\sqrt{2}$, so you can set up a proportion:

$$\frac{x}{6} = \frac{1}{\sqrt{2}}$$

$$x\sqrt{2} = 6$$

$$x = \frac{6}{\sqrt{2}}$$

To rationalize the denominator, multiply the top and bottom by $\sqrt{2}$:

$$\frac{6}{\sqrt{2}} \times \frac{\sqrt{2}}{\sqrt{2}} = \frac{6\sqrt{2}}{2} = 3\sqrt{2}$$

Each leg is $3\sqrt{2}$.

~WW~ **CONNECTION** ~WW~

Read about rationalizing the denominator in chapter 8.

The isosceles right triangle comes up with such frequency, it has taken on a somewhat catchier name, the *45°-45°-90° triangle*—after the measures of its interior angles.

The 45°-45°-90° triangle has a famous cousin, also named for its interior angles—the *30°-60°-90° triangle*. That's what you get when you take an equilateral triangle and split it down the middle like this:

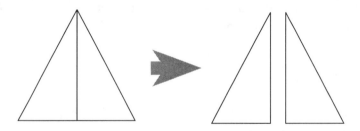

In each of the right triangles that result from the split, the short leg is half of what was one side of the original equilateral triangle, so you can say it's now half the hypotenuse. Call the short leg 1 and the hypotenuse 2, and you can use the Pythagorean Theorem to solve for the long leg:

$$a^2 + b^2 = c^2$$
$$1^2 + b^2 = 2^2$$
$$b^2 = 4 - 1$$
$$b^2 = 3$$
$$b = \sqrt{3}$$

Now you've used the Pythagorean Theorem once on a 30°-60°-90° triangle, and you'll never have to again. Just remember the side proportions:

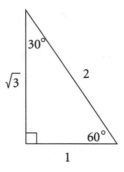

Using the Pythagorean Theorem

The Pythagorean Theorem is the source of lots of geometry formulas, such as that for the area of a regular hexagon. What we're trying to say here, is that you gotta know it! Anyway, if you think you have it down already, try cranking your math power up another notch for this chapter's Do the Math problem.

DO THE MATH

Use the Pythagorean Theorem to derive the formula for area of a regular hexagon in terms of the length of one of its sides s.

Solution: Connect opposite vertices like this:

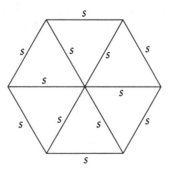

You have divided the hexagon into six equilateral triangles with sides that each have length s. The area of the hexagon will be 6 times the area of one equilateral triangle. To find the area of one triangle in terms of s, drop an alti-

The triangle has been split into two *30°-60°-90° triangles*, and so the short legs are both $\frac{s}{2}$, and the altitude is $\frac{s\sqrt{3}}{2}$.

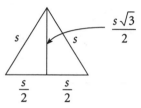

So the area of one equilateral triangle is $\frac{1}{2}$(base × height) $= \frac{1}{2}\left(s \times \frac{s\sqrt{3}}{2}\right) = \frac{s^2\sqrt{3}}{4}$. The area of the hexagon is 6 times that, or $6 \times \frac{s^2\sqrt{3}}{4} = \frac{3s\sqrt{3}}{2}$.

Area of equilateral triangle $= \frac{(\text{side})^2\sqrt{3}}{4}$

Area of regular hexagon $= \frac{3(\text{side})^2\sqrt{3}}{2}$

And we're giving you the extra formula absolutely free of charge!

🐭 *Plug In*

Now we've whizzed you through the basic maneuvers patented by those crazy Pythagoreans. Let's see if you can do some for yourself!

1. In △*ABC* in Figure 1, ∠*B* is a right angle. If *AB* = 1 and *BC* = 2, how long is *AC* ?

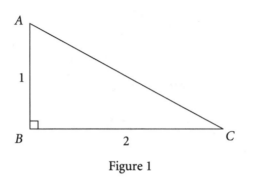

Figure 1

2. In Figure 2, *AC* is perpendicular to *BD*, the measure of ∠D is 30°, and the measure of ∠B is 45°. If *AD* = 6, how long is *AB* ?

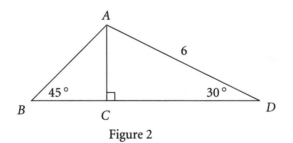

Figure 2

3. In Figure 3, what is the area of quadrilateral *ABCD* ?

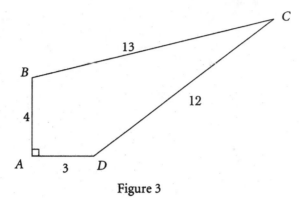

Figure 3

4. In Figure 4, if the area of square *ABCD* is 5, what is the area of square *BEFD* ?

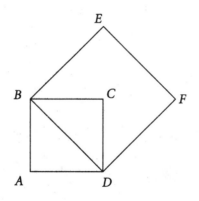

Figure 4

5. In Figure 5, if *ABCDEF* is a regular hexagon, what is the length of *AE* if
    AB = 4?

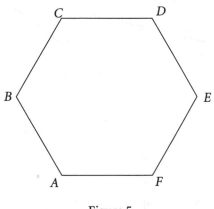

Figure 5

CHAPTER SEVENTEEN

Circles: There's No Getting Around Them

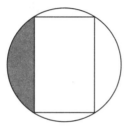

⌐√⋀⋀⋁∘ DO THE MATH ∘⋀⋁⋀√⌐

In the figure to the left, a rectangle is inscribed in a circle. If the radius of the circle is 1 and the length of one of the shorter sides of the rectangle is 1, what is the area of the shaded region? (See the solution near the end of this chapter.)

It would be great if geometric circles were as easy to grasp as a shiny new quarter; unfortunately, things don't always make sense on paper the same way they do in your hand (and you can't use a geometric circle to make a phone call). Lucky for you, we put together this little chapter, all about circles, so you won't feel so mystified by them. You'll even learn how to put a square peg in a round hole.

THE CIRCLE GAME

Circles don't come in as many varieties as triangles do. In fact, all circles are similar—they're all the same shape (like you didn't know). The only difference among them is size, so you don't

⌐√⋀⋀⋁∘ POWER LINE ∘⋀⋁⋀√⌐

Albert Einstein, who fancied himself as a violinist, was rehearsing a Haydn string quartet. When he failed for the fourth time to get his entry in the second movement, the cellist looked up and said, "The problem with you, Albert, is that you simply can't count."

have to learn to recognize types or remember names. All you have to know about circles is how to find four aspects of them: the *circumference*, the *area*, the *length of an arc*, and the *area of a sector*. If you want, you can think of it as just memorizing four formulas, but you'll do better if you have some idea of where the arc and sector formulas come from and how they are related to the circumference and area formulas.

Will the Circle Be Unbroken

Circumference is a measurement of length. You could think of it as the perimeter: It's the total distance around the circle. If the radius of the circle is *r*:

Circumference = $2\pi r$

Since the diameter is twice the radius, you can easily express the formula in terms of the diameter *d*:

Circumference = πd

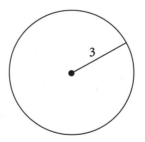

In the circle above, the radius is 3, and so the circumference is $2\pi(3) = 6\pi$.

Raiders of the Lost Arc

An *arc* is a piece of the circumference. If *n* is the degree measure of the arc's central angle, then the formula is:

Length of an Arc = $\left(\dfrac{n}{360}\right)(2\pi r)$

In the figure below, the radius is 5 and the measure of the central angle is 72°.

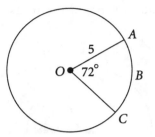

The arc length is $\frac{72}{360}$ or $\frac{1}{5}$ of the circumference:

$$\left(\frac{72}{360}\right)(2\pi)(5) = \left(\frac{1}{5}\right)(10\pi) = 2\pi$$

In Your General Area

The *area* of a circle is usually found using this formula in terms of the radius r :

Area of a Circle $= \pi r^2$

The area of the circle below is $\pi(4)^2 = 16\pi$:

The Private Sector

A *sector* is a piece of the area of a circle. If n is the degree measure of the sector's central angle, then the area formula is:

Area of a Sector $= \left(\frac{n}{360}\right)(\pi r^2)$

In the figure below, the radius is 6 and the measure of the sector's central angle is 30°:

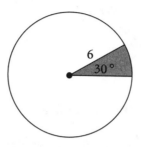

The sector has $\dfrac{30}{360}$ or $\dfrac{1}{12}$ of the area of the circle:

$$\left(\frac{30}{360}\right)(\pi)\left(6^2\right) = \left(\frac{1}{12}\right)(36\pi) = 3\pi$$

Fitting a Square Peg in a Round Hole

Some of the most challenging plane geometry questions are those that combine circles with other figures, like this chapter's Do the Math question. To get through it, you'll need to combine stuff you learned in this chapter and in the last one. Let's give it a whirl:

DO THE MATH

In the figure below, a rectangle is inscribed in a circle. If the radius of the circle is 1 and the length of one of the shorter sides of the rectangle is 1, what is the area of the shaded region?

⌁ᴡᴡᴠ POWER SURGE ᴠᴡᴡ⌁

Here's a hot tip to help you when you're stumped by your math homework. Check out the website, *Ask Doctor Math*! You can email the doctor with current questions, or search their archives for answers from math experts across the globe. The address for turning up the volume on your math power is: http://forum.swarthmore.edu/dr.math

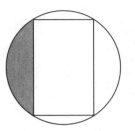

Once again, the key here is to add to the figure. And in this case, as is so often the case when there's a circle, what you should add is radii. The equilateral triangles tell you that the central angles are 60° and 120°.

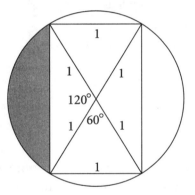

The shaded region is what's left of the 120° sector after you subtract the triangle on the left with the 120° angle. To find the area of the shaded region, you want the find the areas of the sector and triangle, and then subtract. The sector is exactly one-third of the circle (because 120° is one-third of 360°), and so:

$$\text{Area of sector} = \frac{1}{3}\pi r^2 = \frac{1}{3}\pi(1)^2 = \frac{\pi}{3}$$

You can divide the triangle into two 30°-60°-90° triangles:

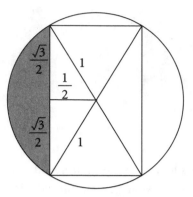

The area of each 30°-60°-90° triangle is $\frac{1}{2}\left(\frac{1}{2}\right)\left(\frac{\sqrt{3}}{2}\right) = \frac{\sqrt{3}}{8}$, so the area of

the triangle with the 120° vertex is twice that, or $\frac{\sqrt{3}}{4}$. The shaded area, then,

is $\frac{\pi}{3} - \frac{\sqrt{3}}{4}$.

🔌 Plug In

Now that we've *rounded* out your math education with a chapter on circles, how about trying some of our review problems for the chapter.

1. In the circle centered at O in Figure 1, the measure of $\angle AOB$ is 40°. If OA = 9, what is the length of minor arc AB?

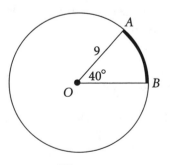

Figure 1

2. In Figure 2, *ABCD* is a square and *AB* is a diameter of the circle centered at *O*. If *AD* = 10, what is the area of the shaded region?

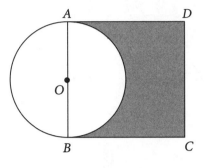

Figure 2

3. In Figure 3, if triangle *ABC* is an isosceles triangle of perimeter 20, what is the area of the circle with center *O* ?

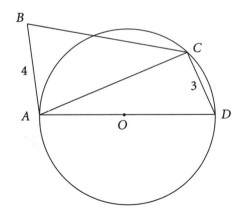

Figure 3

4. In Figure 4, the area of the circle centered at *O* is 25π, and *AC* is perpendicular to *OB*. If *AC* = 8, what is the length of *BD* ?

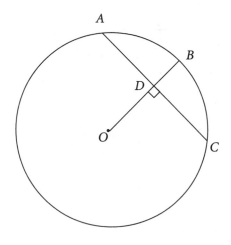

Figure 4

5. In Figure 5, *AB* is tangent to the circle at *A*. If the circumference of the circle is 12π, and if *OB* = 12, what is the area of the shaded region?

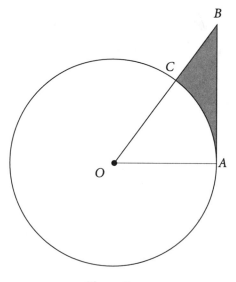

Figure 5

○ Solids: Put on Your 3-D Glasses

ON SOLID GROUND

Now that you've gotten acquainted with the art appreciation class that is Geometry, let's talk about sculpture. In other words, we're moving from two dimensions to three, into the realm of length, width, and depth. Think of this chapter as the one where we show you how to pump up the *volume*—literally! And if you've ever thought of architecture, or any other 3-D design profession, as a career option, this is the chapter for you!

> ∿∿**DO THE MATH**∿∿
>
> A right circular cone and a sphere have equal volumes. If the radius of the base of the cone is $2x$ and the radius of the sphere is $3x$, what is the height of the cone in terms of x ? (See the solution near the end of this chapter.)

The Rectangular Solid

The granddaddy of all solids is the *rectangular solid*. That's the official geometric term for a box, which has six rectangular *faces*, twelve *edges* that meet at right angles, and eight *vertices*:

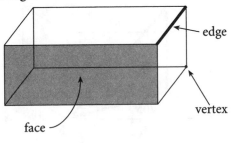

edge

vertex

face

The *surface area* of a rectangular solid is simply the sum of the areas of the faces. That's what the formula "Surface Area = $2lw + 2lh + 2wh$" says. If the length is l, the width is w, and the height is h, then two rectangular faces have area lw, two have area lh, and two have area wh. The total surface area is the sum of those three pairs of areas.

Surface Area = $2lw + 2lh + 2wh$

Instead of just finding the surface area, you may sometimes be asked to find the distance between opposite vertices of a rectangular solid. It's like boring diagonally through the middle of a solid, from one corner to the opposite.

Question: In the rectangular solid below, what is the distance from vertex A to vertex B?

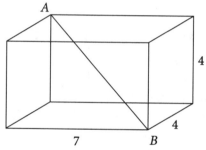

Solution: One way to find this distance is to apply our old pal, the Pythagorean theorem, twice. First plug the dimensions of the base into the Pythagorean Theorem to find the diagonal of the base:

$$\text{Diagonal of base} = \sqrt{4^2 + 7^2} = \sqrt{16 + 49} = \sqrt{65}$$

Notice that the base diagonal combines with an edge and with the segment AB you're looking for to form a right triangle:

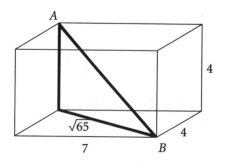

So you can plug the base diagonal and the height into the Pythagorean Theorem to find AB:

$$AB = \sqrt{(\sqrt{65})^2 + 4^2} = \sqrt{65 + 16} = \sqrt{81} = 9$$

Another way to find this distance is to use the formula, which you could say is just the Pythagorean Theorem taken to another dimension. If the length is l, the width is w, and the height is h, the formula is:

Distance $= \sqrt{l^2 + w^2 + h^2}$

It's All The Same: Uniform Solids

A rectangular solid is one type of *uniform solid*. A uniform solid is what you get when you take a plane figure and move it, without tilting it, through space. Here are some uniform solids:

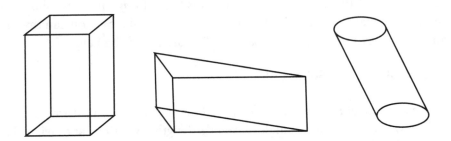

The way these solids are drawn, the top and bottom faces are parallel and congruent. These faces are called the *bases*. You can think of each of these solids as the result of dragging the base through space for a certain distance. The perpendicular distance through which the base slides is called the *height*:

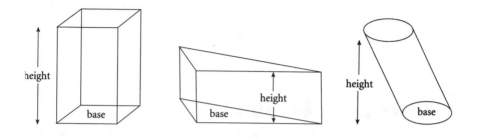

In every one of the above cases—and this is true of *any* uniform solid—the volume is equal to the area of the base times the height. So, you can say this for any uniform solid, given the area of the base *B* and the height *h*.

Volume of Uniform Solid = Bh

- *Volume of Rectangular Solid:* A rectangular solid is a uniform solid whose base is a rectangle. Given the length *l*, width *w*, and height *h*, the area of the base is *lw*, and so the volume formula is:

Volume of Rectangular Solid = lwh

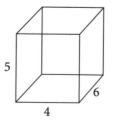

The volume of a 4-by-5-by-6 box is $4 \times 5 \times 6 = 120$

- *Volume of Cube*: A cube is a rectangular solid with length, width, and height all equal. If e is the length of an edge of a cube, the volume formula is:

Volume of Cube $= e^3$

The volume of this cube is $2^3 = 8$.

- *Volume of Cylinder*: A *cylinder* is a uniform solid whose base is a circle. Given base radius r and height h, the area of the base is πr^2, and so the volume formula is:

Volume of Cylinder $= \pi r^2 h$

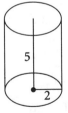

In the cylinder above, $r = 2$, $h = 5$, so:

$$\text{Volume} = \pi(2^2)(5) = 20\pi$$

The following example gives you the volume of a uniform solid and asks for the surface area:

Question: In the figure below, the bases of the right uniform solid are triangles with sides of length 3, 4, and 5. If the volume of the solid is 30, what is the total surface area?

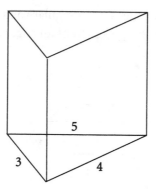

Solution: The surface area is the sum of the areas of the faces. To find the areas of the faces, you need to figure out what kinds of polygons they are so that you'll know what formulas to use. Start with the bases, which are said to be "triangles with sides of length 3, 4, and 5." If these side lengths don't ring a bell in your head, then you'd better go back to chapter 16 and bone up on your Pythagorean triples.

Each base is a 3-4-5 triangle, which means that each base is a right triangle, so you can use the legs as the base and height to find the area:

- Area of Right Triangle $= \frac{1}{2}(\text{leg}_1)(\text{leg}_2) = \frac{1}{2}(3)(4) = 6$

That's the area of each of the bases. The other three faces are rectangles. To find their areas, you need first to find out the height of the solid. If the area of the base is 6, and the volume is 30, then:

○ᴡᴡ○**CONNECTION**○ᴡᴡ○

Chapter 16: Pythagorean triples. (Hint, it's not a play in baseball).

$$\text{Volume} = Bh$$
$$30 = 6h$$
$$h = 5$$

So the areas of the three rectangular faces are $3 \times 5 = 15$, $4 \times 5 = 20$, and $5 \times 5 = 25$. The total surface area, then, is $6 + 6 + 15 + 20 + 25 = 72$.

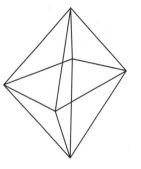
Seeing Things 1: Visualizing Rotating Polygons

You might be thinking that solid geometry questions are a real pain because of all these formulas we're throwing at you. But once you get used to them, they're pretty routine and dependable (if a bit dull). It's the special cases that can be the most challenging, since there's no quick fix formula for you to bust out. Those are the solid geometry problems that require you to *visualize*. For example:

Question: If the rectangle below is rotated 360° about side BC, what is the volume of the resulting solid?

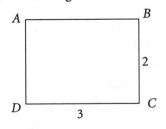

Solution: Can you picture in your mind what the resulting solid looks like. Since it can be almost impossible to sketch 3D geometry, you're probably better off if you can just "see" it in your head. It'll look something like this:

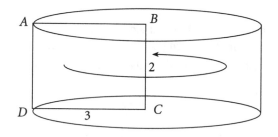

It's a cylinder with base radius 3 and height 2. So now all you have to do is plug $r = 3$ and $h = 2$ into the formula:

Volume of Cylinder $= \pi r^2 h = \pi(3^2)(2) = 18\pi$

Applying the formula was easy once you knew what to apply it to. It's getting an accurate picture of the cylinder and figuring out what's r and what's h that takes some getting used to.

Seeing Things 2: Let Me Count the Ways

Many questions that ask you to see things are really asking you to find a maximum or to count possibilities.

Question: The maximum possible number of identical rectangular blocks are placed inside a rectangular carton. The rectangular blocks each have dimensions length = 7 centimeters by width = 5 centemeters by height = 4 centimeters. The rectangular carton has

⌁⫶⫶⫶○POWER SURGE○⫶⫶⫶⌁

Suppose you're an architect, and you're designing an apartment complex for a big building developer. She wants to get the most rental bang for her buck, so she asks you how many 500-square-foot apartments you can fit into a ten-story building on a 5,000-square-foot lot. Better bone up on this section, because you're gonna need this information to figure that out.

KAPLAN

inside dismensions length = 16 centimeters, by width = 15 centimeters, by height = 14 centimeters. What is the total surface area, in square centimters, of the rectangular blocks that are inside the regular carton?

Solution: Notice that each of the dimensions of a rectangular block is a factor of a different one of the inside dimensions of the carton. Specifically, 7 is a factor of 14, 5 is a factor of 15, and 4 is a factor of 16. So you can place the blocks in the carton by placing the dimension 7 centimeters of the blocks along the dimension 14 centimeters of the carton, the dimension 5 centimeters of the blocks along the dimension 15 centimeters of the carton, and the dimension 4 centimeters of the blocks along the dimension 16 centimeters of the carton. By placing the blocks in the carton in this way, you will completely fill up the rectangular carton. The number of times you can place the dimension 7 centimeters of a block along the dimension 14 centimeters of the carton is $\frac{14}{7}$, or 2. The number of times you can place the dimension 5 centimeters of a block along the dimension 15 centimeters of the carton is $\frac{15}{5}$, or 3. The number of times you can place the dimension 4 centimeters of a block along the dimension 16 centimeters of the carton is $\frac{16}{4}$, or 4. So you will completely fill the volume of the carton with $2 \times 3 \times 4 = 6 \times 4 = 24$ rectangular blocks. Thus, the maximum number of rectangular blocks that can be placed in the carton is 24.

Now all that remains to be done is to find the surface area of one rectangular block and to multiply that by 24. The formula for the surface area S of a rectangular solid having a length l, a width w, and a height h is:

$S = 2lw + 2lh + 2wh$

Here, each rectangular block has dimensions, in centimeters, of $l = 7$, $w = 5$, and $h = 4$. So the surface area of one rectangular block, in square centimeters, is:

$$2 \times 7 \times 5 + 2 \times 7 \times 4 + 2 \times 5 \times 4 = 70 + 56 + 40 = 166.$$

Since there are 24 blocks in the carton, the total surface area of these 24 blocks, in square centimeters, is $24 \times 166 = 3{,}984$.

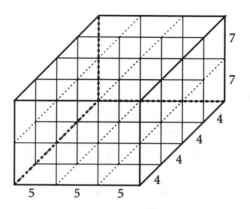

More Solid Footing

There are a few other solids formulas you're going to need. These are not derived by purely Euclidean and algebraic means. They come from applying the methods of—*cringe!*—calculus to the formulas you've already seen. Lucky for all of us, calculus is beyond the scope of this book, and so we won't get into that mess yet.

There's one general class of solids you can think of as variations on the uniform solids. These are the solids that have a plane figure—either a polygon or a circle—at one end and a point at the other. You can call these *tapered solids*. The plane figure at one end is the *base*, and the point at the other end is the *vertex*. If the base is a polygon, the lateral faces will all be triangles, and the solid is a *pyramid*:

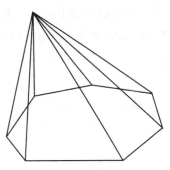

If the base is a circle, then the solid is a *cone*:

The formula for all tapered solids is the same. If B is the area of the base, and h is the perpendicular distance from the base to the vertex, then:

Volume $= \frac{1}{3}Bh$

For example, in the figure below, $h = 3$ and, the base is a square of area 16:

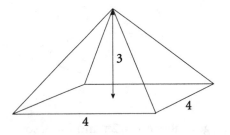

The volume of the pyramid is $\frac{1}{3}(16)(3) = 16$.

You can give a more specific formula for the cone by plugging πr^2 in for B.

- *Volume of Cone:* Given base radius r and height h,

Volume of Cone $= \frac{1}{3}\pi r^2 h$

For example, in the figure below, $r = 3$, and $h = 6$:

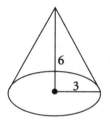

Therefore, the volume is $\frac{1}{3}\pi(3^2)(6) = 18\pi$

Here are a few more formulas you might like to know:

- *Lateral Area of Cone:* Given base circumference c and slant height l,

Lateral Area of Cone $= \frac{1}{2}cl$

The lateral area of a cone is the area of the part that extends from the vertex to the circular base. It does not include the circular base.

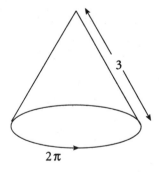

For example, in the figure above, $c = 2\pi$ and $l = 3$, so:

Lateral Area $= \frac{1}{2}(2\pi)(3) = 3\pi$

- *Surface Area of Sphere:* Given radius *r*:

Surface Area of Sphere = $4\pi r^2$

For example, if the radius of a sphere is 2, then:

Surface Area = $4\pi(2^2) = 16\pi$

- *Volume of Sphere:* Given radius *r*:

Volume of Sphere = $\frac{4}{3}\pi r^3$

For example, if the radius of a sphere is 2, then:

Volume = $\frac{4}{3}\pi(2)^3 = \frac{32\pi}{3}$

With these formulas in your arsenal, you're ready to attack this chapter's Do the Math extravaganza.

DO THE MATH

A right circular cone and a sphere have equal volumes. If the radius of the base of the cone is 2*x* and the radius of the sphere is 3*x*, what is the height of the cone in terms of *x*?

Solution: This is no mere matter of plugging values into a formula and cranking out the answer. This question is more algebraic than that and takes a little thought. (But you get extra credit for thinking.) It's really a word problem. It describes in words a mathematical situation (in this case, geometric) that can be translated into algebra. The pivot in this situation is that the cone and sphere have equal volumes. You're looking for the height h in terms of *x*, and fortunately you can express both volumes in terms of those two variables. Be careful. Both formulas include r, but they're not the same *r*'s: in the case of the cone, *r* = 2*x*; but in the case of the sphere, *r* = 3*x*:

$$\text{Volume of cone} = \frac{1}{3}\pi r^2 h = \frac{1}{3}\pi(2x)^2 h = \frac{4}{3}\pi x^2 h$$

$$\text{Volume of sphere} = \frac{4}{3}\pi r^3 = \frac{4}{3}\pi(3x)^3 = 36\pi x^3$$

Now set these expressions for the two volumes equal to each other and solve for h:

$$\frac{4}{3}\pi x^2 h = 36\pi x^3$$

$$\pi x^2 h = \frac{3}{4}\left(36\pi x^3\right)$$

$$\pi x^2 h = 27\pi x^3$$

$$h = \frac{27\pi x^3}{\pi x^2} = 27x$$

The answer is $27x$.

Now that we've made you a real geometry head, you're ready to do the review questions for this chapter. (Answers are at the back of the book.)

Plug In

1. In Figure 1, the radius of the base of the right circular cone is 3. If the volume of the cone is 12π, what is the lateral area of the cone?

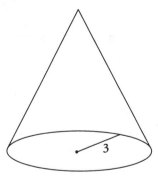

Figure 1

2. A cube with edge of length 4 is divided into 8 identical cubes. How

much greater is the combined surface area of the 8 smaller cubes than the surface area of the original cube?

3. In Figure 2, *d* is the distance from vertex *A* to vertex *B*. What is the volume of the cube in terms of *d*?

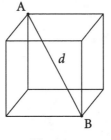

Figure 2

4. When a right triangle of area 3 is rotated 360° about its shorter leg, the solid that results has a volume of 30. What is the volume of the solid that results when the same right triangle is rotated about its longer leg?

5. The prism in Figure 3 is composed of a square base of area 12 and four equilateral triangles. What is the volume of the prism?

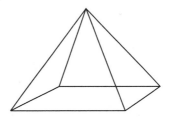

Figure 3

Plug-In Solutions

CHAPTER 1

1. To add two negatives, add the number parts (42 + 40 = 82) and then attach a minus sign. The answer is **–82**.

2. Subtracting a positive is the same as adding a negative. The sum of –25 and –25 is **–50**.

3. To multiply a series of signed numbers, multiply the number parts, and then attach a minus sign if there were originally an *odd* number of factors. The product of the number parts here is $1 \times 2 \times 3 \times 4 = 24$. The number of minus signs is *four*, which is even, so the product is positive, and the answer is **24**.

4. When you divide numbers with opposite signs—whether it's negative divided by positive or positive divided by negative—the result is negative. So 48 divided by –6 is the same as –48 divided by 6, which is **–8**.

5. The rational numbers between 0 and 1 can be paired off systematically with the rational numbers between 0 and 2. Each number in the first range will be paired with twice that number in the second range. Because there is a one-to-one correspondence between the members of the two sets, you can say that the sets are the **same size**.

CHAPTER 2

1. You can rule out 699 quickly—it's clearly a multiple of 3. You can rule out even numbers, of course, so the next number to consider is 697. Try dividing primes into 697, and you'll find that 17 goes in 41 times—so 697 is *not* prime. You can rule out 696 (even), 695 (multiple of 5), and 694 (even) quickly. The next smaller number, 693, is a multiple of 3. Skip the even 692, and the next number to think about is 691. Keep trying all the primes up to the square root of 691 (which is about 26.3) and you won't find any factors. The answer is **691**.

2. The prime factorization of 105 is $3 \times 5 \times 7$. The prime factorization of 255 is $3 \times 5 \times 17$. The overlap is $3 \times 5 = $ **15**.

3. The prime factorization of 45 is $3 \times 3 \times 5$. The prime factorization of 63 is $3 \times 3 \times 7$. The combination of these factorizations, leaving out the unnecessary extra 3's, is $3 \times 3 \times 5 \times 7 = $ **315**.

4. What you're looking for is 12 more than the least common multiple of 13 and 14. Because 13 and 14 are consecutive integers, you know they're relative primes and that their least common multiple is simply their product: $13 \times 14 = 182$, and 12 more than that is 182 1 12 = **194**.

5. The proper factors of 56 are: 1, 2, 4, 7, 8, 14, and 28. The sum of those factors is $1 + 2 + 4 + 7 + 8 + 14 + 28 = 64$, which is greater than 56, and so 56 is **abundant**.

CHAPTER 3

1. Before you can divide, you need to turn the mixed number into an improper fraction:

$$3\frac{3}{5} = \frac{3 \times 5 + 3}{5} = \frac{18}{5}$$

Now, to divide by $\frac{9}{10}$, multiply by the reciprocal $\frac{10}{9}$:

$$\frac{18}{5} \div \frac{9}{10} = \frac{18}{5} \times \frac{10}{9}$$

You can save yourself some work by canceling a common factor of 9 from 18 on top and 9 on the bottom, as well as a common factor of 5 from 10 on top and 5 on the bottom:

$$\frac{18}{5} \times \frac{10}{9} = \frac{2}{1} \times \frac{2}{1} = \textbf{4}$$

2. To make the fractions easy to compare, multiply the top and bottom of the first by 2:

$$\frac{9}{25} = \frac{9 \times 2}{25 \times 2} = \frac{18}{50}$$

Now you're comparing $\frac{18}{50}$ and $\frac{18}{51}$. When two positive fractions have the same numerator, the greater fraction is the one with the *smaller denominator*—and so the answer is $\frac{18}{50}$, or $\frac{9}{25}$.

3. First change both fractions to decimals: $\frac{1}{50} = \frac{2}{100} = .02$, and $\frac{1}{1,000} = .001$. The sum, then, is $.02 + .001 = \textbf{.021}$.

4. The fraction $\frac{3}{70}$ written in decimal form is $.04\overline{28571}$ or $0.0428571428571428571\ldots$

   After the 0 in the tenths place, the pattern 428571 repeats. So we want the 299th digit in the repeating pattern $428571428571428571\ldots$.. Now 299 divided by 6 is 49 with a remainder of 5. Thus, to arrive at the 299th digit of the repeating pattern $428571428571428571\ldots$ we must go through 49 complete sets of 428571 and then the first 5 digits of 428571. The fifth digit in 428571 is a 7, so the 299th digit in the repeating pattern $428571428571428571\ldots$ is a 7. Thus, the 300th digit in the decimal $0.428571428571428571\ldots$ is a 7.

5. Multiply the decimal by $\frac{100}{100}$ to move the repeating sequence right up against the decimal point:

$$.12\overline{3} = \frac{12.\overline{3}}{100}$$

Now $.\overline{3}w$ is equal to $\frac{1}{3}$, so $12.\overline{3}$ is equal to $12\frac{1}{3}$, or $\frac{37}{3}$. Now you can say that $\frac{12.\overline{3}}{100}$ is equal to $\frac{37}{3}$ divided by 100, or $\boldsymbol{\frac{37}{300}}$.

CHAPTER 4

1. Multiply .084 by 125, and you get **10.5.**

2. If 450 is a certain percent of 3, then that percent is equal to 450 divided by 3, which is 150. The first number is 150 times the second, and 150 is $150 \times 100\%$, or **15,000%.**

3. The amount of increase is 10 cents. The original whole was 5 cents. The amount of increase is twice as big as the original whole, so the percent increase is **200%.**

4. If something goes up 5%, it's like being multiplied by 1.05. To figure out what this number was *before* a 5% increase, *divide* by 1.05:
$$59,346 \div 1.05 = \mathbf{56,520}$$

5. If the population increases 50 percent in 50 years, then 50 years ago it was $\dfrac{100\%}{150\%} = \dfrac{2}{3}$ what it is now. Two-thirds of 810,000 is 540,000—so that was the population in 1900. Fifty years before that (1850) it was $\dfrac{2}{3}$ of 540,000, or 360,000. Continue this way and here's what you get:

1950	810,000
1900	540,000
1850	360,000
1800	240,000
1750	160,000

The answer is **1750.**

CHAPTER 5

1. To end up with a five-test mean score of 86, Lily needs to have five scores that add up to $5 \times 86 = 430$. The four scores she has so far add up to $82 + 82 + 76 + 92 = 332$. She needs another $430 - 332 = \mathbf{98}$ to reach her goal.

2. If the class mean is 90, and there are $12 + 18 = 30$ students in the class, then the 30 scores add up to $90 \times 30 = 2,700$. The boys' scores add up to

a total of $87 \times 12 = 1,044$. That leaves $2,700 - 1,044 = 1,656$ for the sum of the girls' scores. There are 18 girls, so the mean of the girls' scores is $1,656 \div 18 = \textbf{92}$.

3. If the mean of 32 numbers is 66, then the 32 numbers add up to $32 \times 66 = 2,112$. When the numbers 95 and 97 are removed, the total drops to $2,112 - 95 - 97 = 1,920$. Now there are only 30 numbers, so the mean is $1,920 \div 30 = \textbf{64}$.

4. Figure out how many there are and what their mean is. The first multiple of 3 between 400 and 500 is 402, and the last is 498. The mean is easy—it's $\dfrac{402 + 498}{2} = 450$. It's a little harder to figure out how many there are. Think of the multiples of 3 from 402 through 498 as 3×134 through 3×166. The number of integers from 134 through 166 is $166 - 134 + 1 = 33$. So, there are 33 numbers, and their mean is 450, so their sum is $33 \times 450 = \textbf{14,850}$.

5. The median is defined as the middle term, except that if there are an even number of terms, the median is halfway between the two middle terms. If the median is not one of the terms, then it must be the case that **there are an even number of terms.**

CHAPTER 6

1. Here the parts add up to the whole—everyone is either American or non-American—and so 1 out of $4 + 1$ people, or $\frac{1}{5}$ of the people in the group, are non-American. The answer is $\frac{1}{5}$.

2. The thing about people is that they come only in integer amounts. If the ratio of males to females is 5 to 4, then you know that the number of males is a multiple of 5, that the number of females is a multiple of 4, and that the number of people in the room is a multiple of $5 + 4 = 9$. Similarly, the number 21 and older is a multiple of 4, the number under 21 is a multiple of 3, and the number of people in the room is a multiple of $4 + 3 = 7$. If the number of people in the room is a multiple of both 9 and 7, and also less than 100, then the only possibility is $9 \times 7 = 63$.

3. Set up a proportion. One-quarter inch is to one mile as $1\frac{5}{8}$ inches is to x miles:

$$\frac{\frac{1}{4}}{1} = \frac{1\frac{5}{8}}{x}$$

$$\frac{1}{4}x = 1\frac{5}{8}$$

$$\frac{1}{4}x = \frac{13}{8}$$

$$x = \frac{13}{8} \times \frac{4}{1} = \frac{13}{2} = 6\frac{1}{2}$$

4. Set up a proportion: .01 km is to 1 second as x km is to 1 hour. Re-express 1 hour as $60 \times 60 = 3,600$ seconds:

$$\frac{.01 \text{ km}}{1 \text{ sec}} = \frac{x \text{ km}}{1 \text{ hour}}$$

$$\frac{.01 \text{ km}}{1 \text{ sec}} = \frac{x \text{ km}}{3,600 \text{ sec}}$$

$$x = .01 \times 3,600 = \mathbf{36}$$

5. It's possible because **nothing is said about actual numbers of at bats.** Here's one way it could happen: Both players play every game and have good batting averages in the first half of the season, but Jones's .300 is slightly better than Lopez's .290. In the first game of the second half, Jones goes 2 for 5, but breaks his leg in the ninth inning and is out for the rest of the season. Jones's average for the second half is .400, but that's based on so few at bats that it raises his season average to only about .302. Meanwhile, Lopez plays every game in the second half and bats .320, bringing his season average up to .305.

	1st half	2nd half	whole season
Jones	$\frac{60}{200} = .300$	$\frac{2}{5} = .400$	$\frac{62}{205} \approx .302$
Lopez	$\frac{58}{200} = .290$	$\frac{64}{200} = .320$	$\frac{122}{400} = .305$

So Jones had a higher batting average in the first and in the second half, but Lopez had a higher batting average for the season as a whole. Surprising, isn't it?

CHAPTER 7

1. The word OHIO has 4 letters, of which one pair is indistinguishable. So the number of permutations is $\frac{4!}{2!}$ = **12**.

2. The number of circular permutations of 6 objects is $(6-1)! = 5! =$ **120**.

3. When you're seating five people in six chairs, you can think of the emptiness you're putting in one chair as a distinct item. Think of it as five people and a nothing—that's still 6 distinct items to arrange in a row, so the number of permutations is 6! = **720**.

4. If it's a fair coin, previous events will have no effect on future probabilities. On the sixth toss, heads and tails are **equally likely**.

5. There are four combinations that add up to 10: 1 and 9; 2 and 8; 3 and 7; 4 and 6. There are also four combinations that add up to 13: 3 and 10; 4 and 9; 5 and 8; 6 and 7. Thus totals of 10 and 13 are **equally likely**.

CHAPTER 8

1. First express 81 as 3^4:

$$81^{12} = \left(3^4\right)^{12}$$

To raise a power to an exponent, multiply the exponents:

$$\left(3^4\right)^{12} = 3^{4 \times 12} = \mathbf{3^{48}}$$

2. When you add three identical things, the result is 3 times one of them, so:

$$3^7 + 3^7 + 3^7 = 3 \times 3^7 = 3^8$$

You can reexpress 3^8 as $\left(3^2\right)^4$, which is the same as $\mathbf{9^4}$.

3. Don't jump to the conclusion that something to the tenth will be greater than the same thing to the ninth. Raising a number to a higher exponent does not necessarily make it larger. If you raise a number between 0 and

1 to a higher exponent, it gets *smaller*. Here the base is less than 1—just barely—and so the greater exponent will make for the smaller result. The larger number is **(.999999999)⁹**.

4. Think of this as the product of two powers of 100:

$$\sqrt[3]{100} \times \sqrt[6]{100} = 100^{\frac{1}{3}} \times 100^{\frac{1}{6}}$$

$$= 100^{\left(\frac{1}{3} + \frac{1}{6}\right)} = 100^{\frac{1}{2}}$$

$$= \sqrt{100} = \mathbf{10}$$

5. Re-express both as powers of 888:

$$\sqrt[6]{888^2 \times 888^3} = \sqrt[6]{888^5} = 888^{\frac{5}{6}}$$

and:

$$\sqrt[7]{(888^2)^3} = \sqrt[7]{888^6} = 888^{\frac{6}{7}}$$

Because the base (888) is greater than one, the expression with the greater exponent will be greater: $\frac{6}{7}$ is greater than $\frac{5}{6}$, and so the larger expression is the second one, $\sqrt[7]{(888^2)^3}$.

CHAPTER 9

1. Use FOIL:

$$(2x + 1) \times (3x + 2)$$
$$= (2x \times 3x) + (2x \times 2) + (1 \times 3x) + (1 \times 2)$$
$$= 6x^2 + 4x + 3x + 2$$
$$= \mathbf{6x^2 + 7x + 2}$$

2. Use FOIL:

$$(x^2 - 4) \times (x + 2)$$
$$= (x^2 \times x) + (x^2 \times 2) + (-4 \times x) + (-4 \times 2)$$
$$= \mathbf{x^3 + 2x^2 - 4x - 8}$$

3. Use FOIL:

$$(x + 5)(x - 5)$$
$$= x \cdot x + (-5x) + 5x - 25$$
$$= \mathbf{x^2 - 25}$$

4. Use FOIL:

$$(x + 3)(x + 3)$$
$$= x \cdot x + 3x + 3x + 9$$
$$= \mathbf{x^2 + 6x + 9}$$

5. Use FOIL:

$$(x - 3)(x - 3)$$
$$= x \cdot x - 3x - 3x + 9$$
$$= \mathbf{x^2 - 6x + 9}$$

CHAPTER 10

1. It's the square of a binomial:
$$4x^2 + 12x + 9 = (2x + 3)^2$$

2. First factor out the common monomial factor of 4:
$$4x^2 + 8x + 4 = 4(x^2 + 2x + 1)$$

   What's left inside the parentheses is the square of $x + 1$, so the completely factored form is:
$$4(x + 1)^2$$

3. **Not factorable.**

4. Factor out the common monomial factor of 4:
$$4x^3 - 12x^2 + 12x - 4 = 4(x^3 - 3x^2 + 3x - 1)$$

   What's left inside the parentheses is the cube of $x - 1$, so the completely factored form is:
$$4(x + 1)^3$$

5. Factor the numerator and the denominator. The numerator is relatively easy—it's the cube of $2x + 3$. The denominator takes some thought—not to mention trial and error—but you can bet that $2x + 3$ will be a factor. (If it's not then there's no way to simplify.) As it turns out, the factored form of the denominator is $(2x + 3)(2x - 3)^2$, and the whole fraction factors and simplifies like this:

$$\frac{8x^3 + 36x^2 + 54x + 27}{8x^3 - 12x^2 - 18x + 27} = \frac{(2x + 3)^3}{(2x + 3)(2x - 3)^2}$$

$$= \frac{(2x + 3)^2}{(2x - 3)^2}$$

CHAPTER 11

1. Start by cubing both sides:

$$\sqrt[3]{8x + 6} = -3$$
$$(\sqrt[3]{8x + 6})^3 = (-3)^3$$
$$8x + 6 = -27$$
$$8x = -27 - 6$$
$$8x = -33$$
$$x = -\frac{33}{8}$$

2. Don't cross-multiply without thinking. Notice that each side is a fraction with a numerator of 19. For the two sides to be equal, you can just set the denominators equal:

$$5x + 17 = 31$$
$$5x = 31 - 17$$
$$5x = 14$$
$$x = \frac{14}{5}$$

3. Express both sides as powers of 2:

$$8^x = 16^{x-1}$$
$$(2^3)^x = (2^4)^{x-1}$$
$$2^{3x} = 2^{4x-4}$$

Now that the bases are the same, you can say the exponents are equal:

$$3x = 4x - 4$$
$$3x - 4x = -4$$
$$-x = -4$$
$$x = 4$$

 293

4. Use the CeRTiFieD method:

$$a = \frac{b + x}{c + x}$$

$$a(c + x) = b + x$$

$$ac + ax = b + x$$

$$ax - x = b - ac$$

$$x = \frac{b - ac}{a - 1}$$

5. Use the CeRTiFieD method:

$$2(x - 1) = (2 - x)\sqrt{2}$$

$$2x - 2 = 2\sqrt{2} - x\sqrt{2}$$

$$2x + x\sqrt{2} = 2\sqrt{2} + 2$$

$$(2 + \sqrt{2})x = 2\sqrt{2} + 2$$

$$x = \frac{2\sqrt{2} + 2}{2 + \sqrt{2}}$$

To rationalize the denominator, multiply the top and bottom by $2 - \sqrt{2}$:

$$x = \frac{2\sqrt{2} + 2}{2 + \sqrt{2}}$$

$$= \left(\frac{2\sqrt{2} + 2}{2 + \sqrt{2}}\right)\left(\frac{2 - \sqrt{2}}{2 - \sqrt{2}}\right)$$

$$= \frac{4\sqrt{2} - 4 + 4 - 2\sqrt{2}}{4 - 2}$$

$$= \frac{2\sqrt{2}}{2}$$

$$= \sqrt{2}$$

CHAPTER 12

1. If you add the equations as presented, the y terms will drop out:

$$\begin{aligned} ax - by &= 1 \\ \underline{2ax + by} &= \underline{8} \\ 3ax &= 9 \end{aligned}$$

$$x = \frac{9}{3a} = \frac{3}{a}$$

Now take that expression for x and plug it into one of the original equations to solve for y:

$$\begin{aligned} ax - by &= 1 \\ a\left(\frac{3}{a}\right) - by &= 1 \\ 3 - by &= 1 \\ -by &= -2 \\ y &= \frac{2}{b} \end{aligned}$$

And so the answer is $x = \dfrac{3}{a}$ and $y = \dfrac{2}{b}$.

2. Multiply the second equation by -1 and you'll get just what you want when you add the two equations:

$$\begin{aligned} 2x - 3y &= 6 \\ \underline{-x + 4y} &= \underline{-4} \\ x + y &= 2 \end{aligned}$$

3. When the absolute value of an expression is less than 5, then the expression without the absolute value signs is less than 5 and greater than -5:

$$|x + 4| < 5$$
$$-5 < x + 4 < 5$$
$$-9 < x < 1$$

4. Put the equation into standard $ax^2 + bx + c = 0$ form:

$$x^2 + 2x = 1$$
$$x^2 + 2x - 1 = 0$$

Now plug $a = 1$, $b = 2$, and $c = -1$ into the quadratic formula:

$$x = \frac{-b \pm \sqrt{b^2 - 4ac}}{2a}$$

$$= \frac{-2 \pm \sqrt{2^2 - 4(1)(-1)}}{2(1)}$$

$$= \frac{-2 \pm \sqrt{8}}{2} = \frac{-2 \pm 2\sqrt{2}}{2} = -1 \pm \sqrt{2}$$

5. Square both sides—and watch out for an extraneous solution!

$$\sqrt{x + 9} = x + 7$$

$$\left(\sqrt{x + 9}\right)^2 = \left(x + 7\right)^2$$

$$x + 9 = x^2 + 14x + 49$$

$$x^2 + 13x + 40 = 0$$

$$(x + 5)(x + 8) = 0$$

$$x = -5 \text{ OR } -8$$

Try those possibilities back in the original equation and you'll find that −5 works but that −8 does not work. And so the only solution is $x = -5$.

KAPLAN

CHAPTER 13

1. You're looking for the largest of five consecutive integers, so call it n and call the other four $n-1$, $n-2$, $n-3$, and $n-4$. The sum of these is 5 times the middle number:

$$\text{Sum} = 5 \times (n-2) = 5n - 10$$

That's 6 times the smallest number—in other words, $5n - 10$ is equal to 6 times $n - 4$:

$$5n - 10 = 6(n-4)$$
$$5n - 10 = 6n - 24$$
$$-10 + 24 = 6n - 5n$$
$$n = \textbf{14}$$

2. This is a variation on the Two-Trains Scenario. Population A is heading towards B at the rate of 120 persons per year. And B is headed in the opposite direction at a rate of 80 persons per year. They will meet when they erase the difference of $6,800 - 4,200 = 2,600$:

$$120x + 80x = 2,600$$
$$200x = 2,600$$
$$x = \frac{2,600}{200} = 13$$

The populations will meet in **13 years**.

3. Let x be the number of 25-cent papers and let y be the number of 40-cent papers. The total number is 100, so $x + y = 100$. That's one equation. To construct the second equation, note that 25 cents times x plus 40 cents times y should add up to 28 dollars:

$$.25x = .40y = 28$$

This is a good candidate for the substitution method. You're only asked for x, so you can use the first equation to express y in terms of x, plug the result into the second equation, and then just solve for x. The first equation becomes $y = 100 - x$. Plug that into the second equation and solve:

$$.25x + .40(100 - x) = 28$$
$$.25x + 40 - .40x = 28$$
$$.25x - .40x = 28 - 40$$
$$-.15x = -12$$
$$x = \frac{-12}{-.15} = \frac{1200}{15} = 80$$

4. The basic set up, crudely put, is:

$$\frac{1}{\text{John}} + \frac{1}{\text{Peter}} = \frac{1}{\text{together}}$$

Since you want the answer in minutes, put John's time and Peter's time in terms of minutes:

$$\frac{1}{120 \text{ minutes}} + \frac{1}{80 \text{ minutes}} = \frac{1}{x \text{ minutes}}$$
$$\frac{1}{120} + \frac{1}{80} = \frac{1}{x}$$
$$\frac{1}{x} = \frac{2}{240} + \frac{3}{240}$$
$$\frac{1}{x} = \frac{5}{240} = \frac{1}{48}$$
$$x = 48$$

5. Be careful. When Charles gives Darla x dollars, both amounts change. Charles's amount goes down by x, and Darla's amount goes up by x. So the difference between their amounts goes down by $2x$. The difference is now y; it used to be $2x$ more than that, so it was $y + 2x$.

CHAPTER 15

1. Translate into Algebra. You're looking for the largest angle, so call that x. It's 10 degrees more than the middle-sized angle, so call the middle-sized angle $x - 10$. And it's twice the smallest angle, so call the smallest angle $\frac{x}{2}$. The three angles add up to 180°, so the equation is:

$$x + (x - 10) + \frac{x}{2} = 180$$

To solve, first clear the denominator and remove the parentheses:

$$2 \times \left[x + (x - 10) + \frac{x}{2} \right] = 180 \times 2$$

$$2x + 2(x - 10) + x = 360$$

$$2x + 2x - 20 + x = 360$$

$$5x = 360 + 20$$

$$x = \frac{380}{5} = \mathbf{76}$$

2. Because the two angle measures provided add up to 180°, they tell you that BE and CD are parallel. And that, in turn, tells you that $\triangle ABE$ is similar to $\triangle ACD$—because they have the same three angles. Because it's given that $AB = BC$, you know that AC is twice AB and that corresponding sides are in a ratio of 2:1. Each side of the larger triangle is twice the length of the corresponding side of the smaller triangle. That doesn't mean, however, that the ratio of the *areas* is also 2:1. In fact, the area ratio is the *square* of the side ratio, and the larger triangle has *four times* the area of the smaller triangle, and so the answer is **4x**.

3. The only information that's in the question and not in the figure is that QS and PT are parallel and that the area of $\triangle QRS$ is x. That QS and PT are parallel tells you that triangles PRT and QRS are similar—they have the same angles. Because the triangles are similar, the sides are proportional. Because the ratio of PR to QR is $\frac{5}{2}$, the ratio of any pair of corresponding sides will also be $\frac{5}{2}$. But that's not the ratio of the areas. Remember

that the area ratio between similar figures is the square of the side ratio. Here the side ratio is $\frac{5}{2}$, so the area ratio is $\left(\frac{5}{2}\right)^2 = \frac{25}{4}$. If the area of the small triangle is x, then the area of the large one is $\frac{25x}{4}$.

4. The angle marked 130° is an exterior angle and is equal to the sum of the remote interior angles marked $x°$ and $(x - 10)°$:

$$x + (x - 10) = 130$$
$$2x - 10 = 130$$
$$2x = 140$$
$$x = \mathbf{70}$$

5. Mark up the figure. The squares are identical, so $AD = DG$ and triangle ADG is isosceles. That makes the measure of $\angle DGA$ 75 degrees, and the measure of $\angle ADG$ is therefore $180 - 75 - 75 = 30$ degrees. Now you know every angle in the figure:

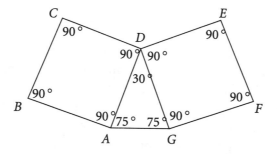

The measure of $\angle ADE$ is $30 + 90 = \mathbf{120\ degrees}$.

CHAPTER 16

1. The Pythagorean theorem says: $(\text{leg}_1)^2 + (\text{leg}_2)^2 = (\text{hypotenuse})^2$. Here the legs have lengths of 1 and 2, so plug them into the formula:

$$1^2 + 2^2 = (\text{hypotenuse})^2$$
$$1 + 4 = x^2$$
$$x^2 = 5$$
$$x = \sqrt{5}$$

2. The indicated angles tell you that $\triangle ABC$ is a 45-45-90 triangle and that $\triangle ACD$ is a 30-60-90 triangle. AD is the hypotenuse and AC is the shorter leg of the 30-60-90 triangle, so $AC = \frac{1}{2}(AD) = 3$. AC is also a leg of the 45-45-90, and AB, the side you're looking for, is the hypotenuse. Therefore, $AB = (AC)\sqrt{2} = 3\sqrt{2}$.

3. Add to the figure. Diagonal BD will divide the quadrilateral into two familiar triangles:

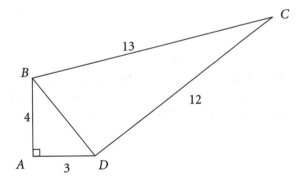

ABD is a right triangle with legs 3 and 4, so $BD = 5$, and therefore BCD is a 5-12-13 triangle. The area of the 3-4-5 triangle is $\frac{1}{2}(\text{leg}_1)(\text{leg}_2) = \frac{1}{2}(3)(4) = 6$, and the area of the 5-12-13 triangle is $\frac{1}{2}(\text{leg}_1)(\text{leg}_2) = \frac{1}{2}(5)(12) = 30$. The quadrilateral's area, then, is $6 + 30 = \mathbf{36}$.

 301

4. The area of the smaller square is 5, so each side is $\sqrt{5}$. Diagonal *BD* divides the square into 45-45-90 triangles, so the hypotenuse *BD* equals one of the legs times $\sqrt{2}$:

$$BD = (\sqrt{5})(\sqrt{2}) = \sqrt{10}$$

Now that you know that one side of the big square is $\sqrt{10}$, you know that the area of the big square is $(\sqrt{10})^2 = 10$.

5. Mark up the figure. Draw in not only the segment *AE* you're looking for, but also the perpendicular that makes the two right triangles as shown:

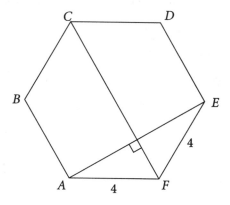

Each of the interior angles of a regular hexagon measures 120°, and these two right triangles split one of those 120° angles. That means the two right triangles are in fact 30°-60°-90° triangles:

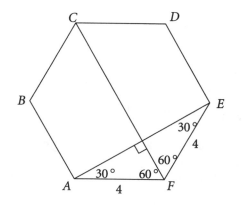

The hypotenuse of each 30°-60°-90° is 4, so the short legs are each 2, and the long legs are each $2\sqrt{3}$. Segment AE is composed of two legs of $2\sqrt{3}$, so $AE = 4\sqrt{3}$.

CHAPTER 17

1. The central angle of minor arc AB is 40°, which is $\frac{1}{9}$ of the whole circle's 360°. The length of minor arc AB, then, is $\frac{1}{9}$ of the whole circle's circumference.

$$C = 2\pi r = 2\pi(9) = 18\pi$$

$$\frac{1}{9}C = \frac{1}{9}(18\pi) = 2\pi$$

2. The shaded region is equal to the area of the square minus the area of the semicircle. The area of the square is $10 \times 10 = 100$. The radius of the circle is half of 10, or 5, so the area of the whole circle is $\pi(5)2 = 25\pi$, and the area of the semicircle is $\frac{25\pi}{2}$. The square minus the semicircle, then, is: $100 - \frac{25\pi}{2}$.

3. The perimeter of triangle ABC is 20. One side is given as 4, so the other two sides add up to 16. The three sides cannot be 4, 4, and 12, because that violates the Triangle Inequality Theorem. The sides must be 4, 8, and 8:

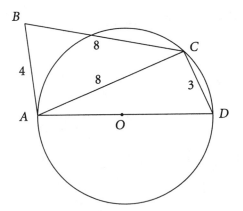

You know that triangle *ACD* is a right triangle because side *AD* is a diameter and *C* is a point on the circle. The legs of right triangle *ACD* are 8 and 3, so the hypotenuse $AD = \sqrt{8^2 + 3^2} = \sqrt{73}$. The radius is half that, or $\dfrac{\sqrt{73}}{2}$. Plug $r = \dfrac{\sqrt{73}}{2}$ into the circle area formula:

$$\text{Area of Circle} = \pi r^2 = \pi\left(\frac{\sqrt{73}}{2}\right)^2 = \frac{73\pi}{4}$$

4. This is a tough one. It's not easy to see how to get *BD* from the given information. You can use the area—25π—to figure out the radius, and then you'd know the length of *OB*:

$$\text{Area} = \pi r^2$$
$$25\pi = \pi r^2$$
$$25 = r^2$$
$$r = 5$$

So you know *OB* = 5, but what about *BD*? If you knew *OD*, you could subtract that from *OB* to get what you want. But do you know *OD*? This is the place where most people get stuck.

The inspiration that will lead to a solution is that you can take advantage of the right angle at *D*. Look what happens when you take a pencil and physically add *OA* and *OC* to the figure:

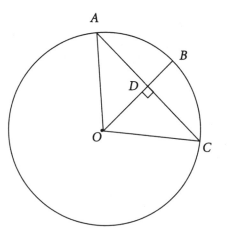

$\triangle OAD$ and $\triangle OCD$ are right triangles. And when we write in the lengths, we discover some special right triangles:

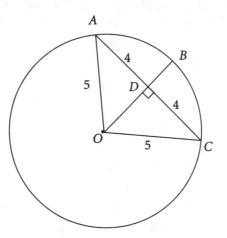

Now it's apparent that $OD = 3$. Since $OB = 5$, BD is $5 - 3 = $ **2**.

5. Think of the shaded region as:

    (the area of $\triangle AOB$) − (the area of sector AOC)

With that in mind, you know you need to figure out the area of the triangle and the area of the sector.

First, the triangle. You are explicitly given $OB = 12$. You are also given that AB is tangent to the circle at A, which tells you that OA is a radius and that $\angle OAB$ is a right angle. So if you can figure out the radius of the circle, you'll have two sides of a right triangle, which will enable you to figure out the third side, and then figure out the area.

You can get the radius from the given circumference. Plug what you know into the formula and solve for r:

$$\text{Circumference} = 2\pi r$$
$$12\pi = 2\pi r$$
$$r = \frac{12\pi}{2\pi} = 6$$

$OA = 6$. Aha! So it turns out that $\triangle AOB$ is no ordinary right triangle. Since one leg—6—is exactly half the hypotenuse—12—you're looking at a 30°-60°-90° triangle. By applying the well-known side ratios (1:$\sqrt{3}$:2) for a 30°-60°-90° triangle, you determine that $AB = 6\sqrt{3}$. Now you can plug the lengths of the legs in for the base and altitude in the formula for the area of a triangle:

$$\text{Area} = \frac{1}{2}bh$$

$$= \frac{1}{2}\left(6\sqrt{3}\right)\left(6\right)$$

$$= 18\sqrt{3}$$

Next, the area of the sector. Fortunately, while working on the triangle, you figured out the two things you need to get the area of the sector: the radius of the circle (6) and the measure of the central angle (60°). The radius tells you that the area of the whole circle (πr^2) is 36π. And the central angle tells you that the area of the sector is $\frac{60}{360}$ or $\frac{1}{6}$ of the area of the circle. $\frac{1}{6}$ of 36π is 6π. So the area of the shaded region is **18$\sqrt{3}$ – 6π.**

CHAPTER 18

1. The formula for the lateral surface area of a cone is in terms of c = base circumference and l = slant height. You can use the given base radius to get the base circumference:

$$c = 2\pi r = 2\pi(3) = 6\pi$$

The slant height you can think of as the hypotenuse of a right triangle whose legs are the base radius and height of the cone.

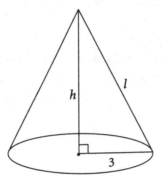

To get l, first you need to find h :

$$\text{Volumn of Cone} = \frac{1}{3}\pi r^2 h$$

$$12\pi = \frac{1}{3}\pi(3^2)h$$

$$12\pi = 3\pi h$$

$$h = \frac{12\pi}{3\pi} = 4$$

Now you can see that the triangle is a 3-4-5 and that $l = 5$. Now plug $c = 6\pi$ and $l = 5$ into the lateral area formula:

$$\text{Lateral Area} = \frac{1}{2}cl = \frac{1}{2}(6\pi)(5) = \mathbf{15\pi}$$

2. When a cube of edge length 4 is divided into 8 identical smaller cubes, the edge of each of the smaller cubes is 2:

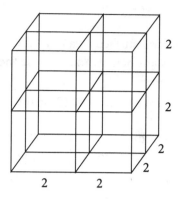

The surface area of the original cube is $6 \times 4 \times 4 = 96$. The surface area of one of the smaller cubes is $6 \times 2 \times 2 = 24$. There are eight small cubes, so their combined surface area is $8 \times 24 = 192$. The difference is $192 - 96 = \mathbf{96}$.

3. Use the formula for the distance between opposite vertices:

$$d = \sqrt{l^2 + w^2 + h^2}$$

Here what you have is a cube, so the length, width, and height are all the same—call them each x:

$$d = \sqrt{x^2 + x^2 + x^2} = \sqrt{3x^2} = x\sqrt{3}$$

$$x = \frac{d}{\sqrt{3}}$$

Now you have the length of an edge in terms of d. Cube that and you have the volume in terms of d:

$$\text{Volume} = (\text{edge})^3$$

$$= x^3$$

$$= \left(\frac{d}{\sqrt{3}}\right)^3$$

$$= \frac{d^3}{3\sqrt{3}}$$

$$= \frac{d^3}{3\sqrt{3}} \cdot \frac{\sqrt{3}}{\sqrt{3}}$$

$$= \frac{d^3\sqrt{3}}{9}$$

4. When you rotate a right triangle about a leg, you get a cone:

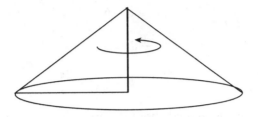

One leg becomes the base radius and the other becomes the height of the cone. Call the long leg a and the short leg b and plug them into the cone volume formula:

$$\text{Volume of Cone} = \frac{1}{3}\pi r^2 h = \frac{1}{3}\pi a^2 b$$

It's also given that the area of the right triangle is 3, so:

$$\text{Area of Right Triangle} = \frac{1}{2}(\text{leg}_1)(\text{leg}_2)$$

$$3 = \frac{1}{2}ab$$

$$ab = 6$$

Plug $ab = 6$ into the expression for the volume of the cone and you can solve for a:

$$\frac{1}{3}\pi a^2 b = 30$$

$$\frac{1}{3}\pi a(ab) = 30$$

$$\frac{1}{3}\pi a(6) = 30$$

$$2\pi a = 30$$

$$a = \frac{15}{\pi}$$

Then you can plug $a = \dfrac{15}{\pi}$ into the equation $ab = 6$ to solve for b:

$$ab = 6$$

$$\left(\frac{15}{\pi}\right)b = 6$$

$$b = \frac{6\pi}{15} = \frac{2\pi}{5}$$

When the triangle is rotated about its longer leg, a becomes the height and b becomes the base radius, so:

$$\frac{1}{3}\pi r^2 h = \frac{1}{3}\pi b^2 a$$

$$= \frac{1}{3}\pi\left(\frac{2\pi}{5}\right)^2\left(\frac{15}{\pi}\right)$$

$$= \frac{60\pi^3}{75\pi}$$

$$= \frac{4\pi^2}{5}$$

5. To find the volume of a prism, you need the area of the base, which is given here as 12, and you need the height, which here you have to figure out. Imagine a triangle that includes the height and one of the lateral edges:

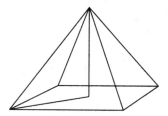

This triangle is a right triangle. The hypotenuse is the same as a side of one of the equilateral triangles, which is the same as a side of the square, which is the square root of 12, or $2\sqrt{3}$:

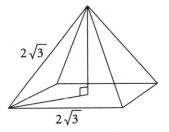

One of the legs of this right triangle is half of a diagonal of the square base—that is, half of $(2\sqrt{3})(\sqrt{2})$, which is $(\sqrt{3})(\sqrt{2})$, or $\sqrt{6}$:

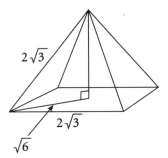

Now you can use the Pythagorean Theorem to find the height:

$$(\sqrt{6})^2 + h^2 = (2\sqrt{3})^2$$
$$6 + h^2 = 12$$
$$h^2 = 6$$
$$h = \sqrt{6}$$

Finally you have what you need to get use the volume formula:

$$\text{Volume} = \frac{1}{3}Bh = \frac{1}{3}(12)\sqrt{6} = 4\sqrt{6}$$

Glossary

The number in parentheses refers to the chapter in which the term is introduced and discussed.

abundant number (2) positive integer less than the sum of its proper factors

acute angle (14) angle measuring less than 90°

acute triangle (15) triangle with three acute angles

adding-equations method (12) solving simultaneous equations by adding equations

algebraic expression (9) one or more algebraic terms connected with plus and minus signs

altitude (15) perpendicular line segment from the base to the top

angle (14) two line segments coming together at a point called the vertex

arc (17) portion of the circumference of a circle

area (15) measure, in square units, of the size of a region in a plane

average rate (6) total A divided by total B

axiom (14) precept, statement accepted as true

base (15) side of a triangle chosen to be used in the area formula. (18) closed figure at one end of a uniform or tapered solid.

base angles (15) angles opposite the equal sides in an isosceles triangle

binomial (9) polynomial that is the sum of two terms

bisector (15) line or line segment that divides an angle in half or divides a line segment in half

canceling (3) eliminating common factors from the top and bottom

circle (17) set of points in a plane at a particular distance from a central point

circular permutation (7) distinguishable arrangement of items in a circle

circumference (17) linear distance around a circle

closed (1) A set of numbers is said to be "closed" under an operation if performing that operation on members of that set always produces a result that is also a member of that set.

coefficient (8) number in front of a radical

coefficient (9) number part at the beginning of an algebraic term

combinations (7) subgroupings with no regard to order

common denominator (3) number that can be used as the denominator for two or more fractions so that they can be added or subtracted

common fraction (3) number in the form $\frac{A}{B}$

common monomial factor (10) monomial that can be factored out of every term in a polynomial

common multiple (2) multiple shared by two integers

common notions (14) Euclid's nongeometric axioms

complete-the-square method (12) procedure for solving quadratic equations that entails turning one side of the equation into the square of a binomial and then taking the square root of both sides

complex number (12) number in the form $a + bi$ in which a and b are real numbers and i is the square root of -1

cone (18) solid with a circle at one end and a single point at the other

congruent (14) same size and same shape; having the same side lengths and the same angle measures

conjecture (2) generalization that is apparently true but has not been proved

convex polygon (14) polygon with interior angles all less than 180°

countably infinite (1) in a one-to-one correspondence with the set of positive integers

counting numbers (1) {1, 2, 3, 4, 5,...}, also called "natural numbers" and "positive integers"

cube (18) rectangular solid with six square faces

cube of a binomial (10) factorable polynomial form:

$$a^3 + 3a^2b + 3ab^2 + b^3 = (a + b)^3$$
$$a^3 - 3a^2b + 3ab^2 - b^3 = (a - b)^3$$

cube root (8) number which raised to an exponent of 3 equals the number in question

cylinder (18) solid with two circular ends connected by "straight" sides

decagon (15) ten-sided polygon

deficient number (2) positive integer greater than the sum of its proper factors

denominator (3) the number on bottom in a fraction

deviation (5) a term minus the mean. Terms greater than the mean have positive deviations; terms less than the mean have negative deviations.

difference of cubes (10) factorable polynomial form:

$$a^3 - b^3 = (a - b)(a^2 + ab + b^2)$$

difference of squares (10) factorable polynomial form:

$$a^2 - b^2 = (a - b)(a + b)$$

distributing (9) multiplying a quantity written outside a set of parentheses by each quantity on the inside

edge (18) line segment formed by the intersection of two faces

equilateral triangle (15) triangle with three equal sides

 315

Euclid's Famous Fifth Postulate (14) the least elemental of Euclid's postulates—and the first one questioned. It reads: If a line segment connecting two straight lines makes two interior angles on the same side that add up to less than two right angles, then the two straight lines will intersect somewhere on that side.

Euler's Law (18) relationship of number of faces F, vertices V, and edges E in any polyhedron:

$$V + F = E + 2$$

evaluate (9) plug in a number and determine the value of an algebraic expression

exponent (8) small, raised number written to the right of a variable or number, indicating the number of times that variable or number is to be used as a factor

exterior angle (15) angle formed by extending a side of a polygon

extraneous solution (11) false solution that sometimes results when you raise both sides of an equation to an even power

face (18) polygon formed by edges of a solid

factor (2) positive integer that divides into a given integer with no remainder

factorial (7) product of consecutive integers from 1 up to and including the integer in question

factoring (10) re-expressing a polynomial as the product of simpler expressions

factoring method (12) procedure for solving quadratic equations that entails factoring one side and then setting each factor separately equal to 0

Fermat's Last Theorem (16) proposition that there are no rational solutions for a, b, and c to the equation $a^n + b^n = c^n$ for any integer value of n greater than 2—finally proved in the 1990s

FOIL (9) mnemonic for the procedure you follow in multiplying binomials—stands for: First, Outer, Inner, Last

45°-45°-90° triangle (16) isosceles right triangle, with sides in the ratio 1:1: $\sqrt{2}$

Fundamental Counting Principle (7) basic notion that, if there are m ways one event can happen and n ways a second event can happen, then there are $m \times n$ ways for the two events to happen

Goldbach's Conjecture (2) that every even integer greater than 2 can be expressed as the sum of two primes

Golden Rectangle (15) rectangle with length-to-width ratio equal to ϕ (phi)

golden ratio (12) ratio equal to ϕ (phi)

greatest common factor (2) greatest integer that is a factor of both numbers under consideration

height (15) perpendicular distance from the base to the top

heptagon (15) seven-sided polygon

hexagon (15) six-sided polygon

hypotenuse (15) the side opposite the right angle in a right triangle

imaginary numbers (12) number of the form ai, where a is a real number and $i = \sqrt{-1}$

improper fraction (3) fraction with a numerator that's greater than the denominator

inconsistent equations (12) ostensibly simultaneous equations that cannot be satisfied by the same solutions

indirect proof (14) proof by showing that negation leads to contradiction

integers (1) whole numbers, including 0 and negatives

interior angle (15) angle inside a polygon formed by two adjacent sides

irrational numbers (1) real numbers that cannot be expressed as the ratio of integers

isosceles triangle (15) triangle with two equal sides

least common multiple (LCM) (2) smallest integer that is a multiple of both given integers

leg (15) one of the sides that form the right angle in a right triangle

like terms (9) algebraic terms in which the elements other than the coefficients are alike

lowest common denominator (3) least common multiple of the denominators in question—used in adding and subtracting fractions

mean (5) sum of the terms divided by the number of terms

median (5) the middle term—or, if there are an even number of terms, the number halfway between the two middle terms

mixed number (3) noninteger greater than 1 written with a whole number part and a fractional part

mode (5) the term that appears with greatest frequency

monomial (9) algebraic expression that has one term

multiple (2) integer that a given integer will divide into with no remainder

natural numbers (1) {1, 2, 3, 4, 5,...}, also called "counting numbers" and "positive integers"

negative (1) less than zero

nonagon (15) nine-sided polygon

numerator (3) the number on top in a fraction

obtuse triangle (15) triangle with an obtuse angle

octagon (15) eight-sided polygon

odd (2) integer that is not a multiple of 2

one-to-one correspondence (1) ability to pair off every member of one set with a unique member of another set

parallelogram (15) quadrilateral with two pairs of parallel sides

Pascal's Triangle (9) triangular arrangement of integers that are the coefficients in the binomial expansion

pentagon (15) five-sided polygon

percent (4) one hundredth

percent decrease (4) amount of decrease expressed as a percent of the original amount

percent increase (4) amount of increase expressed as a percent of the original amount

perfect number (2) positive integer equal to the sum of its proper factors

perimeter (15) sum of the lengths of the sides of a polygon

permutation (7) ordered arrangement of objects

phi (12) the Greek letter φ, which represents the irrational number $\dfrac{1+\sqrt{5}}{2}$, which is the golden ratio and is approximately equal to 1.618

Playfair's Axiom (14) logical equivalent to Euclid's Fifth Postulate. It says: Given a line and a point not on that line, there exists in the plane determined by that point and line exactly one line that includes the given point and is parallel to the given line.

polygon (15) closed figure with any number of straight sides

polyhedron (18) solid whose faces are all polygons

polynomial (9) algebraic expression that is the sum of more than one term

positive (1) greater than zero

postulates (14) Euclid's geometric axioms

power (8) product obtained by multiplying a quantity by itself one or more times

prime factorization (2) integer expressed as the product of prime numbers

prime number (2) integer greater than 1 that has no integer factors other than 1 and itself

principal root (8) For even roots, the principal root is the nonnegative real root. For odd roots, the principal root is the one real root.

probability (7) likelihood of a particular event, expressed as the ratio of the number of "favorable" outcomes to the total number of possible outcomes

product (1) result of multiplication

proportion (6) expression of the equality of ratios

proposition (14) statement proven true based on accepted axioms and previous propositions

pyramid (18) solid with a polygon at one end and a point at the other end

Pythagorean Theorem (15) relationship of the legs and hypotenuse of any right triangle: the sum of the squares of the legs is equal to the square of the hypotenuse

Pythagorean triple (16) trio of positive integers that fits the Pythagorean relationship $a^2 + b^2 = c^2$

quadratic equation (12) equation that can be expressed in the form $ax^2 + bx + c = 0$

quadratic formula (12) formula $x = \dfrac{-b \pm \sqrt{b^2 - 4ac}}{2a}$, which produces the solutions to an equation in the form $ax^2 + bx + c = 0$

quadrilateral (15) four-sided polygon

quotient (1) result of division

radical (8) symbol $\sqrt{}$, which by itself represents the positive square root, and with a little number written in—as in $\sqrt[3]{2}$—represents a higher root

rate (6) ratio of quantities measured in different units

ratio (6) fraction that expresses the relative sizes of two quantities

rational number (1) number that can be expressed as the ratio of integers

rationalizing the denominator (8) re-expressing a fraction so that it does not have a radical in the denominator

real numbers (1) numbers that have a location on the number line

reciprocals (3) pair of numbers whose product is 1

rectangle (15) quadrilateral with four right angles

rectangular solid (18) solid with six rectangular faces

regular polygon (15) a polygon with all equal sides and all equal angles

relative primes (2) integers with no common factors greater than 1

remainder (2) integer amount left over after division

repeating decimal (3) decimal with a digit or cluster of digits that repeats indefinitely

rhombus (15) quadrilateral with four equal sides

right triangle (15) triangle with a right angle

scalene triangle (15) triangle with no equal sides

sector (17) region bounded by two radii and an arc

Side-Angle-Side Theorem (SAS) (14) method of proving congruence of triangles—really a postulate

Sieve of Eratosthenes (2) method for identifying prime numbers

similar (15) same shape; having the same angle measures

simplify (3) express a fraction in lowest terms by factoring out and canceling any common factors

simultaneous equations (12) two or more equations in which each variable represents the same quantity in one equation as in another

solid (18) three-dimensional figure

solve (11) isolate the given variable

sphere (18) set of all points in space a particular distance from a central point

square (15) quadrilateral with four right angles and four equal sides

square of a binomial (10) factorable polynomial form:

$$a^2 + 2ab + b^2 = (a + b)^2$$
$$a^2 - 2ab + b^2 = (a - b)^2$$

square root (8) number which squared yields the given quantity

substitution method (12) procedure for solving simultaneous equations that entails using one equation to express one variable in terms of the other, and then plugging the expression you get into the other equation

sum of cubes (10) factorable polynomial form:

$$a^3 + b^3 = (a + b)(a^2 - ab + b^2)$$

surface area (18) sum of the areas of the surfaces of a solid

tapered solid (18) solid with a plane figure at one end and a point at the other end

term (5) one of the quantities under consideration when determining the mean, median, or mode

term (9) part of an algebraic expression that either stands by itself or is connected to other terms with plus and minus signs

theorem (14) statement proven true based on accepted axioms and previous theorems, also called "proposition"

30°-60°-90° triangle (16) right triangle with sides in the ratio $1:\sqrt{3}:2$

trapezium (15) (*Amer.*) quadrilateral with no parallel sides; (*Brit.*) quadrilateral with one pair of parallel sides

trapezoid (15) (*Amer.*) quadrilateral with one pair of parallel sides; (*Brit.*) quadrilateral with no parallel sides

triangle (15) three-sided polygon

trinomial (10) polynomial that is the sum of three terms

Twin Primes Conjecture (2) that there are infinitely many twin primes

twin primes (2) pair of prime numbers that differ by 2

uncountably infinite (1) too many to be in a one-to-one correspondence with the set of positive integers

uniform solid (18) solid with a pair of opposite faces that are congruent and parallel

variable (9) letter representing an unknown or unspecified quantity

vertex (18) point of intersection, such as a corner of a rectangular solid or a polygon

vertex angle (15) angle opposite the unequal side in an isosceles triangle

volume (18) measure of the amount of room contained in a solid